Eighth Edition

Steps to Small Business Start-Up

**Everything You Need to Know to Turn
Your Idea into a Successful Business**

Linda Pinson

published by

OM..IM

**Out of Your Mind...
and Into the Marketplace™**

Author: Linda J. Pinson

Assistant Publisher: Ndaba Mdhlongwa

Editor: Julie Filppi

Interior and cover design: Linda Pinson

Cover Photo: The cover photo is used by permission and copyrighted by the photographer, Nolte Lourens (©Nolte Lourens. Image from BigStockPhotos.com).

Published by: OUT OF YOUR MIND…AND INTO THE MARKETPLACE™
13381 White Sand Drive
Tustin, CA 92780-4565

714-544-0248 (Information)
800-419-1513 (Orders)
www.business-plan.com

Printed in the United States of America

Pinson, Linda.
        Steps to small business start-up: everything you need to know to turn your idea into a successful small business / Linda Pinson – 8th ed.

        p.   cm.
        Includes index.
        ISBN-13: 978-0944205-59-4
        ISBN-10: 0-944205-59-3
        1.   New business enterprises—United States. 2. Small business—United States. 3. Success in Business—United States. I. Title
        HD62.5.P565 2014
        658.1'11—dc22

About the Author

Linda Pinson is an award-winning author, business planning expert, speaker, consultant, and nationally recognized business educator with a specialty in financial management and small business curriculum development. The author of seven popular entrepreneurial books, she has also developed and published the bestselling business plan software program, Automate Your Business Plan. Linda's books are widely used as curriculum in colleges and universities. They have been translated into several foreign languages including Spanish, Chinese, and Italian.

Linda served for seven years on the Small Business Financial Development Corporation Executive Board of Directors and for nine years on its Loan Committee. She also served for several years on the Tri County SBDC Board of Directors and as a member of the Entrepreneurial Advisory Committee at California State University at Fullerton. Her dedication to the small business community has been recognized through awards from the U.S. Small Business Administration, the National Association of Women Business Owners, and the State of California. Linda served as a delegate and tax issue chair at the White House Conference on Small Business.

Linda resides in Tustin, California with her husband Ray. She is an avid golfer (one hole-in-one) and bowler, paints watercolors, and loves to fish. Linda and Ray have two sons, two daughter-in-laws, two grandsons, and one granddaughter (all great, of course).

Dedication

I dedicate this book to my husband, Ray Pinson. For fifty-one years, he has supported and encouraged me in everything that I wanted to do. He has been not only my husband, but my best friend throughout all of these years. I cannot even imagine life without him by my side.

I also dedicate this book to my mother, Sue Pearce Area. She has been gone for fifteen years, but I will always remember that she believed in me when I wrote and published the 1st edition of this book in 1987. She was a single working woman who had to watch her pennies carefully, but she never blinked an eye when she loaned me the money to go to print. She had more confidence in my success than I did.

Acknowledgments

During the writing and revision of this edition of my business start-up book, it has been my good fortune to have the help of many talented and generous individuals.

- **Ndaba Mdhlongwa,** my assistant publisher and the owner of Business Plan Solutions in Dallas, Texas (www.businessplanprofessionals.com) worked with me during the writing and editing of new chapters for the book. Ndaba has worked with me for fifteen years on various other book and software tasks, including the development of a great Instructor's Manual for this edition of *Steps to Small Business Start-Up and the other two books in our Small Business Advisor Series—Anatomy of a Business Plan and Keeping the Books.*

- **Julie Filppi**, my able assistant works by my side on revisions of our books and software (in addition to all of her other daily tasks). Among other things, she catches typos and other errors that might have slipped through the cracks.

- **Mary Rowles and Richard Williams,** from IPG in Chicago, have both made themselves accessible to review covers and answer any and all of our questions regarding production and distribution of this and our other books. They are truly experts in the publishing industry and I thank them from the bottom of my heart.

Thank you, Ndaba, Julie, Mary, Richard, and the rest of you. This is not only a better book because of you. Without you, this new edition would not exist. I thank you— and I know that my readers would also thank you personally if they had the chance.

Thank You, Educators!

Over the past 27 years, we have received great support and encouragement from the many universities, colleges, entrepreneurial schools, and technical institutes that have adopted our business books and business plan software as required course material for their classes. With each semester (or term) that passes, we are always happy to receive new inquiries and orders from dedicated educators throughout the United States.

One of our ongoing objectives has been to continually provide you with up-to-date resources that will spur students to success in their business ventures. We are pleased to let you know that we have new 2014 editions of our three most popular books (and eBooks) and also our business plan software. Each of the books has an up-to-date instructor's manual (free for you) with lesson plans for each chapter, extensive presentation slides and printable handouts, and two basic tests with answer keys. The books can be adopted individually or as a series package.

Once again, we are happy to offer you the latest materials and information for teaching your entrepreneurship courses. We hope that, through the continued utilization of our books and software, you can help your students and clients to launch their businesses, familiarize themselves with small business accounting and tax issues, develop a marketing plan, and put it altogether by writing a winning business plan that will serve as a lifetime guide for their companies.

  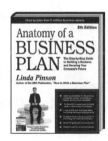 

Thank You to All of Our Educators!

We would like to take this time and space to extend a special thank you to each and every one of you – and to wish you and your students continued success. You are highly valued and it is an honor to serve you.

Table of Contents

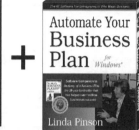

Preface

Thank you for choosing *Steps to Small Business Start-Up* as the tool to help you start your new business or to use as a textbook in your entrepreneurial classes. I hope that it will prove to be of great help to you.

It has often been said that, "You can run your business by the seat of your pants—but you will probably end up with torn pants." One of the principal reasons for business failure is the lack of proper planning. In today's world, both small and large businesses have come to understand that they need to take the time to evaluate their business potential and map a plan for the future. Start-up is where the planning and implementation begins.

It is the goal of this book to give a clear, concise, and easy-to-understand process to follow during business start-up. I have been working with business owners for many years and most of them have the same problem—they are experts in their industries, but are novices when it comes to knowing how to start and operate a business.

I, on the other hand, am not an expert in most industries, but I can provide you with what I hope are the necessary guidelines to follow in order to get a business organized, legalized, and operating. I would suggest that you start by reading through the entire book to get an overall picture of what you will be doing. Then you can go back to the beginning and work your way through the start-up process.

Who is this book for?
This business start-up book has been written for new business owners and for small business entrepreneurship program managers and instructors.

- **If you are a new business owner**, you can use it as a home-study course, moving along at a pace that will meet your own goals. Each chapter will take you through a particular task and provide you with instructions, examples, and references.

- **If you are a program manager or instructor**, you can adopt *Steps to Small Business Start-Up* as a classroom text. I will be happy to provide a free Instructor's Manual that has lesson plans and student activities for each chapter, numerous presentation slides, and even a couple of tests. To get the instructor's manual, please give me a call at 714-544-0248 or email me at LPinson@aol.com

Thank you again for choosing *Steps to Small Business Start-Up* to help you accomplish your goals. I appreciate your confidence in the book and wish you success in your new venture.

Linda Pinson

It's Time to Be Your Own Boss

You have decided that you would like to be a business owner. You want to quit working at that "nine to five" job that doesn't seem to pay well or to bring any excitement to your life. Instead, it sounds like a great idea to take the leap into entrepreneurship and be your own boss.

Why Do You Want to Own a Business?

Business ownership is often looked upon as a means of creating wealth and achieving personal freedom. Some of the most common reasons why you might choose to go into your own business are:

✓ *To build a business for yourself instead of for someone else*

✓ *To pursue a passion (e.g. "I've always wanted to own a restaurant.")*

✓ *To be your own boss and master of your own time*

✓ *To make a living doing what you really enjoy doing (woodworking, photography, writing, childcare, etc.)*

✓ *To capitalize on an invention*

✓ *To replace income from the loss of a job*

✓ *To create net worth (long-term capital appreciation)*

Are You Ready to Make the Transition?

When you are contemplating business ownership, it tends to be exhilarating. However, it is common to experience uncertainty as well. Am I willing to invest the time it takes to start and run a business? Can I deal with the emotions that come with running a business? Will enough people use my services or buy my products? Will I make enough money to sustain the business and my desired lifestyle? Am I mentally prepared to give up my current salary and accept the financial uncertainties that come with running my own business? Will I be able to support my family?

In order to be successful in your new business you have to be fully committed to your vision. Instead of working eight hours a day, most new business owners work sixteen hours a day with very few days off for leisure activities. You will indeed be your own boss and the master of your time – but, that does not mean that you will be free. I have always thought that I am the toughest boss that I ever worked for.

Think about it and make sure that the timing is right to make your move from employee to business owner. Review possible threats that are likely to arise and determine how you will mitigate them. Determine what your strengths are and how you will use them to get your business up and running and on the road to profitability.

To complete your reality check, ask yourself the all-important question, *"Am I ready to accept the responsibilities of business ownership?"* If the answer is "yes," then it is time for you to move forward in a logical way to decide on a business and to get it off the ground and running smoothly.

Match Your Skills and Interests to Your Business

Skills are the things that you are good at. Interests are the things that you like to do. When you are considering the type of business you want to start, it is generally best to find one that utilizes your skills **and** that captures your interest. If you are good at something, but don't like doing it, you will soon find yourself wishing that you were doing something else. Likewise, if you are interested in what you are pursuing, but you are not good at it, you are not likely to stick with it for long.

After you have identified your various skills and interests, you can then begin to identify potential businesses that satisfy both requirements. This is where the true entrepreneur can use imaginative processing to come up with creative ideas for new and unique businesses.

Examples:

- You know lots about flowers and plants, but you do not like to be outdoors. Don't go into the landscaping business. However, you might think about providing and maintaining indoor plants for restaurants, professional offices, real estate brokerages, and other commercial businesses.

- You like working with pre-school children (interest) and you are trained as an elementary school teacher (skill). You might consider opening a day care center that specializes in learning activities and also offers after school care and tutoring.

- You have always wanted to open a clothing store. However, you hate being indoors. Most likely, you will probably always resent being stuck inside. Think about starting some kind of a kiosk clothing business in an outdoor mall or specialize in clothing sold at outdoor sports events, such as car rallies or surfing competitions.

 Skills & Interests Business Matching Worksheet
To help you think your way through the above process, you will find a worksheet at the end of this chapter (page 6).

Look at Your Financial Situation

One of the most glaring problems that I often see with potential business owners is their failure to plan properly for the financial transition from employee to business owner. Cash flow problems can lead to unpaid bills, continuous calls from debtors, and emotional stress. Consider your financial situation before starting your business.

- **Consider your personal financial situation.** If you plan to quit your current job and devote all of your energies to your new business, it is a great idea to set aside enough money to pay your living expenses for at least six months. If you have a spouse and/or other family members that work, can you live on their earnings?

  New businesses frequently are not very profitable in the early stages. Prior planning can provide you with a much-needed cushion in case you cannot take any money out of your business for a period of time.

- **Think about start-up costs.** If you are starting a new business from scratch, do you have the money you have to spend in order to get the business up and running? Think about whether you will have to rent an office, buy furniture, buy equipment, advertise, pay for permits, hire a lawyer, or a number of other initial things that require spending money before you make money. Fitness centers and restaurants are examples of businesses that are required to expend significant amounts of money before they open their doors.

- **Look realistically at initial sales potential of the business.** The opportunities for initial earnings vary greatly from business to business. For instance many service companies can be profitable from the very beginning.

  If you open a consulting business and have your office in your home, your earnings are limited only by your ability to attract and service clients. Likewise, a landscape or yard maintenance business can earn early profits if it has the right equipment, skilled labor, and customers. On the other hand, most product businesses, cannot earn income until the products are developed or purchased, advertised, and sold.

- **If you need a funding, be aware of lender requirements.** Get rid of the idea that business capital is easy to get. It is a common misconception that the U.S. Small Business Administration (SBA) and other government entities are waiting in the wings to dish out free money to entrepreneurs with great ideas. Nothing could be further from the truth. What is commonly referred to as an "SBA Loan" is really a loan from a traditional lending institution (bank), but guaranteed up to a certain percentage by the SBA to reduce the bank's risk factor.

  In addition to asking for a solid business plan, the bank will require that you have a high credit rating (FICO score), cash to invest in the business, and personal assets (equity) that can be captured in case you default on the loan.

 Note: See Chapter 14 for more information on financing your business.

Find a Mentor

Before you go into business, it would be great to align yourself with someone with experience in your industry and experience in business management. Working with a mentor can prepare you for the travels that lie ahead in your business journey by sharing knowledge and expertise. The relationship with your mentor will help prepare you for success and protect you from failure.

If you are one of the fortunate few, you will have a close friend or business associate who has the necessary skills and would be willing to advise you. If not, business mentors can generally be found through your local chamber of commerce and various business organizations.

Provided below are some resources:

- **Service Corps Of Retired Executives (SCORE)** – A national organization sponsored by the Small Business Administration (SBA) of volunteer business executives who provide free counseling, workshops and seminars to prospective and existing small business people. Local SCORE chapters consist of retired professionals who are available to give free business advice. (www.score.org)

- **Small Business Development Centers (SBDCs)** – Sponsored by the SBA in partnership with state and local governments, the educational community and the private sector. They provide assistance, counseling and training to prospective and existing business people.

- **Small Business Institutes (SBIs)** – Organized through the SBA on more than 500 college campuses around the nation. The institutes provide counseling by students and faculty to small business clients.

- **Chambers of Commerce** – Local branches of your chamber of commerce can be a great resource for mentors. An example is the Greater Dallas Hispanic Chamber of Commerce. (www.gdhcc.com)

- **MicroMentors** – MicroMentors help entrepreneurs grow their businesses through mentoring relationships with experienced business professionals. (www.micromentor.org)

Tech Tip

Search for Information about Business Mentors

You can also find useful information and articles on the Internet regarding business mentoring. Here are some web addresses that you might want to look at.

- www.sba.gov/content/find-business-mentor
- www.score.micromentor.org/resources/resource-center
- www.smallbiztrends.com/2014/02/what-to-expect-from-a-business-mentor.html
- www.inc.com/guides/growth/24509.html
- www.entrepreneur.com/article/45254
- www.peermentoring.com

What's Next?

In this chapter, you were encouraged to evaluate your own readiness to make the transition from employee to business owner. By now, you should also better understand how to evaluate business opportunities that match your skills and interests as well as your personal financial situation.

Chapter 2 will focus on the choices you will have as to whether you want to start a new business, buy an existing business, or purchase a franchise. You will also find some information to think about if you are toying with the idea of starting a nonprofit business or you are wondering how to capitalize on a new product or invention.

Skills & Interests Business Matching Worksheet

Skills (what I am good at)	Interests (what I like to do)	Business Possibilities (business ideas that match skills & interests)

Think About
Ways to Start a Business

Y ou have decided that entrepreneurship is for you and are ready to start a business. The next decision you will have to make is what kind of a business you will start. There are many routes that can be taken toward owning a business. For instance, you can:

- ✓ *Start your own business*
- ✓ *Buy an existing business*
- ✓ *Buy a franchise*
- ✓ *Invent a product and take it to market*
- ✓ *Become a social entrepreneur*

Start Your Own Business

Having decided to become a business owner, you now need to determine what business you will start. To help you in your decision making, ask yourself these questions. What kind of things do I like to do? Can my hobby or interests be turned into a commercially viable venture? Is there a need in the marketplace that I can fill? The last question will also help you determine if there is a niche in the marketplace that your new business will fit into.

Before embarking on your venture, do some research to determine who your competitors will be. Look at their strengths and weaknesses. Then think about how your business will be different and whether or not you can reasonably expect to gain that all important competitive edge in your industry and specifically within your target market.

If you are thinking of starting a business, there are several questions that you should ask yourself. The table below will guide you through some of those things.

Things to Consider as you Start Your Business	
Issue	**Questions to Ask**
About Me	What are my strengths? What skills do I have? What are my hobbies? Can any of these attributes be turned into a business venture?
Legal Structure of Business	What is the best legal structure for my business? Do I need (or want) a business partner? What skills and strengths does the potential business partner have? Will the partner have investment capital?
Location	Where will my business be located? Can I operate my business from home? Will I buy or lease a facility? How much space will I need to operate my business?
Money	How much money do I have to put into the business? Where will the rest of the money I need come from? Is my credit in good standing in case I need a bank loan? Are there specific financial programs that will help me start my business?
Customers	Who are my customers? How will I find my customers?
Advertising	How will I let people know my business exists? Where will I advertise my business? How much will it cost for advertising? Can I afford to hire an advertising professional or agency?

Buy an Existing Business

If you decide to buy an existing business, the first thing you will want to do is determine the type of business you want to own. This decision will be based on your skills, qualifications, interests, and overall abilities. In making this decision, find a business that will give you the opportunity to use your skills effectively.

How Do You Find a Business to Buy?

When you have decided on the type of business that you are best suited for, the next step is to search for a business. There are several considerations you will have to keep in mind as you look for a business to buy. These include location and how much you can afford to spend (budget). Now that you have an idea about where you want to look for a business and how much you have to spend, you can start looking.

- The Internet is a great place for you to start looking. You can simply start by going to any search engine and typing "businesses for sale" in the search box. Be more specific by putting your location. For example, if you are looking for a business in Phoenix, Arizona, type "businesses for sale in Phoenix, Arizona."

  Conducting the search on your own may prove to be time consuming and may not yield the best results. If so, you might want to use a business broker. You may be responsible for some business broker expenses. Doing your own search on the Internet will be free.

- Business brokers help people buy or sell a business and have the resources to help you reach your goals. You can tell them the type of business you would like to buy and they can search within their database to see if one is available. If not, they can search for one that meets your criteria, saving you the time. Business brokers typically charge the seller a percentage of the final sale price, payable at the close of the deal. Be sure to ask a broker up front if there are any fees or expenses you will be responsible for as the buyer and perform due diligence before selecting a business broker. Get references and check to see if he or she is a member of a local or national business broker association.

- Another free resource is your local newspaper. The Business Opportunities section will feature advertisements with businesses for sale. The Sunday paper has a larger listing in that section. You can also use the newspaper and the Internet to place ads stating the specific type of business you wish to purchase.

- You can also search for a business to buy by attending various networking events and using word of mouth as a starting point. Start by attending local civic and business organization meetings as well as events sponsored by your local Chamber of Commerce. There are also industry specific organizations or associations that you can visit. Networking with people that are in a specific industry will enable you to learn more about available opportunities.

Due Diligence Required

Regardless of the route you choose to take in your search, there are some key things you will need to do once you have found a business you are interested in buying. The first is doing comprehensive due diligence. A business may appear to be successful and show a profit. However, that does not mean it has no problems. You will want to find out everything about the business including what is owned, borrowed, leased, and owed. You do not want to get into a situation that leaves you with a stack of bills, unpaid vendors, rent due, and other outstanding debt.

The second thing you will want to know is the value of the business. You will have to conduct a detailed financial analysis and valuation to determine the appropriate price to pay. As part of your analysis, you will review profit and loss statements, balance sheets, key assets, contingent and actual liabilities, and cash flow statements.

With your due diligence and financial analysis complete, you are ready to move forward with the acquisition of the business.

Buy a Franchise

Buying a franchise is one of the most popular ways to start a business. By acquiring a franchise, you open yourself up to the possibility of selling products and/or services that have instant name recognition. You will also benefit from the training you will receive at the beginning as well as the ongoing support to help you become successful. Like any business venture, there are costs associated with purchasing a franchise. You may pay some or all of the following fees to the franchise: initial franchise fee, ongoing royalty payments, and advertising fees. Other start up costs will include rent, build-out, equipment, inventory, licenses, and insurance.

There are two common ways for participating in a franchise program.

- The classic method is to buy a new franchise. This means you will have to find a location and do the build out yourself. This is a start-up situation and you dive into the new business as an owner/operator. Many successful entrepreneurs have built multi-unit empires this way. Newer franchises usually provide this route for business ownership. During the process, you will have the assistance of the franchisor.

- The other way is to buy an existing franchise. Several types of franchises are available in various industries. To find a franchise of your choice, you can attend franchise trade shows with the goal of visiting exhibitors in an industry that has a strong appeal to you. While listening to the presentations given by the exhibitors, be sure to get answers to some of the following questions. How long has the franchisor been around? How many franchise units exist in your local area and where are they located? What is the initial franchise fee and are there additional start-up costs? Are there ongoing royalty payments and if so, how much are they? What assistance is provided at the beginning and on a continuing basis? What controls are imposed by the franchisor?

Before You Buy a Franchise

Before buying a franchise, there are several things to consider including the amount of money you have to invest, your skills and abilities, and the goals you have set for yourself. The table on the next page will guide you through some of the things you need to consider in order to make a sound decision.

Things to Consider When Selecting a Franchise	
Issue	**Questions to Ask**
Investment	How much do I have to invest? Will I need financing? Will I purchase the franchise by myself or with others (partners)?
Skills & Knowledge	What industry experience is required by the franchisor? What skills do I have that can be applied to this franchise? What specialized knowledge do I have?
Goals	Am I interested in getting into a particular industry? Am I interested in retail sales or providing a service? Do I want to operate the business myself or hire a manager? Will the income from the franchise be adequate if it is my only source of income – or does the franchise need only to serve as a source of supplemental income? Am I interested in owning just one franchise unit or several?

Caution! Read the Franchise Offering Carefully!

Franchise offers are written to convince prospective buyers that they should sign on the dotted line and send in their franchise fees as soon as possible. Proceed with caution. It is not always true that, "He who hesitates is lost." I periodically read franchise offers for clients and have discovered that they range from very simple to very complicated. The common denominator is that by law the franchisor is required to disclose somewhere in the document certain pieces of information that will allow you to form a fairly accurate picture of the viability of the franchise opportunity.

It is important that you read between the lines. Don't just look at revenue projections. Chart out all of the possible financial requirements that may be imposed on you by the franchisor during the opening and operating of the franchise – royalties, advertising, training, insurance, etc. If you are not careful, you can find yourself caught in a contract full of legal obligations that eat heavily into your profits.

Finally, be sure that there is a sufficient demand for the products or service in your geographic location. What works in one part of the country may not be feasible in another, either financially or otherwise. Talk to current franchisees to see how things are working out for them and what level of support they are receiving from the franchisor.

> ## *Tech Tip*
>
> ### Use the Internet to Research Franchises
>
> You can also use the following resources on the Internet to find a franchise:
>
> - www.franchise.org
>
> - www.franchise.com
>
> - www.franchisetimes.com
>
> - www.entrepreneur.com/franchise

Invent a Product

- Many great businesses have been developed from new product ideas. You may have a new business concept or a new product you feel would be viable in the marketplace. Be aware that the process of taking a new idea product onto the marketplace can be lengthy and in some cases difficult.

- In his book, *Successful Inventing,* Norman Parrish (inventor, author, and mentor) states that product development and business planning must be a concurrent process. "In order to have the financial support necessary to accomplish all of the tasks required to take an idea from its conceptual state through all of the subsequent stages, the inventor should have a realistic business plan and understand the nature of cash flow and how to manage it."

- The first step in launching your product is to determine its feasibility. This will let you know whether your new product is viable and help you determine the potential of it becoming a commercial success. Determining feasibility is a very important step and we suggest you take it seriously. You will need to make an informed decision as to whether to proceed with your business idea before you invest a lot of time and money only to find out it has no commercial value.

- If you have determined that your product has commercial viability, you will then want to check to make sure there are no similar products on the market. More importantly, there are no products that have intellectual property you may infringe upon as this could result in lawsuits against you. To do this, go to the United States Patent and Trademark Office (USPTO) website (www.uspto.gov) to conduct a patent search.

- Now that you have determined that your product has commercial viability and know that there are no similar products out there with intellectual property protection, you are now ready to move to the next step: protecting your product. You will want to protect your product with a patent(s) or related intellectual property rights. You can do this step on your own by going to the USPTO website. You can also use the services of a patent attorney. While costly, consulting with a patent attorney or patent agent at an early stage will provide you with the best solution for protecting your product as well as your business.

- Once the product has been protected, you will need to develop a working prototype of your invention. You can do this by buying the various components that make up your invention and assemble them yourself. Alternatively, you can work with a manufacturer in your area to build the prototype. At this stage you will have to decide whether you want to license your invention to a company that will manufacture and market the product or start a business of your own. In making your decision, consider the costs associated with starting your own business.

Become a Social Entrepreneur
(Commonly a Nonprofit)

You can start a business by becoming a social entrepreneur. A social entrepreneur recognizes a social problem and uses entrepreneurial skills and traits to start a business that will address the social problem and make a significant change. Success for the social entrepreneur is measured by the impact they have on society as opposed to financial measures.

Your vehicle as a social entrepreneur will most likely be a nonprofit organization. Social entrepreneurship is becoming so popular that a growing number of colleges and universities are establishing programs focused on educating and training social entrepreneurs.

Creating a nonprofit organization is like creating a for-profit business. Just as you would do when creating a for-profit company, you will need to do some extensive planning before you start filing incorporation papers and applying for your tax exemption from the Internal Revenue Services. Running a nonprofit organization will take more than just compassion. Much like starting a for-profit entity, you will have to conduct research and ask yourself several questions. What nonprofit am I interested in starting? What products and/or services will be offered through my organization?

What needs will my organization fulfill in the community? Who currently provides similar services in the community (competition)? What competitive advantages do I have over existing nonprofit organizations? What will I do to create demand for my organization and sustain operations?

As you would need to start a for-profit business, you will need start-up finances. The capital will enable you meet your start up expenses as well as help you to obtain professional services such as legal and accounting. You will want to seek legal assistance to incorporate into a nonprofit entity. The professional you use will also help you draft a set of corporate bylaws, which will serve as the procedure that the Board of Directors, and possibly the members of the corporation, will utilize to make decisions on behalf of the corporation. Once you have drafted bylaws, you will hold an organizational meeting to formally create the nonprofit corporation. At this meeting the bylaws should be adopted, the Board of Directors should be elected, and all other relevant business should be conducted.

Before developing your nonprofit organization, ask yourself the following questions. Do I have the necessary skills and experience to operate a nonprofit organization? What managerial and financial resources do I have access to? Who will make up my Board of Directors? Where will I locate my organization? What position will I hold in the organization and how will I be compensated? The answers to these questions will help you create an operational plan that will serve as a blueprint for running a successful nonprofit organization.

Tech Tip

Examples of Social Entrepreneurs

Below are examples of successful social entrepreneurs:

- Margarita Quihuis, Hispanic-Net
  www.hispanic-net.org

- Muhammad Yunus, Grameen Bank
  www.grameen-info.org

- Margaret Sanger, Planned Parenthood Federation of America
  www.plannedparenthood.org

- Vikram Akula, SKS Microfinance
  www.sksindia.com

- John Muir, The Sierra Club
  www.sierraclub.org

Start Branding Your Business:
Name, Logo, Business Card, Letterhead

Branding defines and focuses a company's image. Branding is one of the most important concepts in today's business world.

Strong brands today are reinforced through a mix of advertising online and offline, public relations strategies, sales incentives, and customer service efforts. Consumer reaction defines the branding in the long run.

Where do you begin?

When your company is in the start-up phase, you can begin the branding process by properly packaging your company's image to be visually recognizable.

In this chapter, we will guide you through the following processes:

✓ *Naming your company to its best advantage*

✓ *Developing an effective logo for your company*

✓ *Designing your first business cards*

✓ *Creating letterhead and envelopes*

Name Your Company!

Choosing your business name will be one of the most important decisions you will make when you are starting your company. It is the first opportunity you have to package – or brand – your company for everyone with whom your business will be dealing.

Whenever your company name is heard or viewed in written form, it will be the defining factor as to how your company is initially perceived (branded) in the mind of your target audience. If your company manages to stay in business for the next twenty years, the name you chose will still be with you unless you changed it somewhere along the way.

Many times a prospective business owner is in a hurry and picks a company name that seems to be appropriate at the time, only to find out later on that it has become a nemesis. That actually happened in my own case.

> My company name, established in 1986, has the name **OUT OF YOUR MIND...AND INTO THE MARKETPLACE™**. I taught entrepreneurial classes to inventors and called the class by the same name. I was soon selling a self-help book, also by the same name. Then I needed a business name to obtain a business license, repay sales tax to the SBE, and to file income tax returns. Why not use the same name? And that's just what I did. That was fine at the time, but eventually, I became a publisher of business books and business plan software. I began dealing with large companies, universities and colleges, and other major clients and venders. It has now been twenty-eight years since I named my company. Others say what a neat name it is.

> As for me, I have regretted it for every reason, but one – it is memorable. It does not reflect what I do (publishing business books and developing business plan software), it is not a very serious sounding name, and it sometimes embarrasses me to say it in front of certain audiences with whom I have had no previous business relationship. However, after twenty-eight years, I would be hard-put to change the name and to get the information out to my expanded marketplace. I have learned to smile and accept that it is my business name and will be until the business dies. However, I have had to combat it by having a dignified logo, earned credibility, and incredible customer service.

How Do You Choose a Name for Your Business?

There are several questions you can ask yourself when you are considering the name for your business. Some of them might be as follows:

- **Are you buying a franchise?** If so, chances are that the business will already be named. In that case, your problem is solved for you. If not, the franchisor will guide you as to what names will be acceptable to them.

- **Are you buying an existing business?** You will have to decide if you want to keep the current name of the company or rename it. Ask yourself if the current name suits your vision of the business and if it is important to keep it the same in order to best serve previous customers. If the answer is "no", you will have to decide on a new name. If so, apply the following questions to the renaming of the business.

- **Is your name descriptive of the business?** It is important that your business name conveys an image of your products and/or services. The name should not be long and cumbersome. Your target market needs to perceive that yours is the company that can solve its problems and fill its needs.

- **If your business expands, will the name still be appropriate?** The name you choose should not be restrictive. It should be general enough that it will still encompass the essence of the company after several years' growth and expansion.

- **How well will your name combine with your logo?** Can the name be abbreviated and be utilized as an acronym? Can you incorporate it into your logo to further brand your company? I have used **OM..IM** with my logo (a fanned book). It looks great, but when you say it out loud, it doesn't have much of a ring to it.

- **Should you consider using your domain name as your business name?** Many companies who operate solely on the Internet choose to use their domain names as their business names. Examples are "buy.com" and "Amazon.com". If the company has brand identity, using its domain name provides customers with instant recall of both name and location on the net.

- **Where will your name fall in alphabetical listings?** It has long been a habit on most occasions to place lists of names in alphabetical order. This holds true for telephone books, internet listings, membership directories, etc. People also tend to choose the first name that they perceive as appropriate to what they are looking for. If it will work for you, you might just as well choose a name beginning with "A" as one that begins with "Z".

- **Will your name work internationally?** Sometimes, a company name does not translate well in other languages. "Osco" was the name of a well-known drugstore in the U.S. The name did not have a pleasant meaning in Spanish. The name was changed to maintain the large Hispanic customer base.

- **What is your legal structure?** Depending on the legal structure you have chosen (and the form of that legal structure), your name may have to reflect that choice. For instance, corporation names generally end with "Inc." Law firm partnerships often have the designation "LLP".

- **Would your business be best served by using your own name?** Many service providers (and/or product sellers) already have name identity and credibility. In that case, it might be best to use your own name, either by itself or in conjunction with words that describe your business. Some examples might be:

  - Naming a law firm "Martin and Chen, LLP"

  - Incorporating a tax firm under the name, "Slack Tax, Inc."

  - Naming a company "John Chavez Professional Diving School"

Develop a List of Business Names

After taking all of the previous questions into consideration, it is best to formulate a list of possible names for your business and then make your decision.

- **Enlist other people to help you come up with names.** Sharing your ideas with other people who understand the nature of your business and the market that you are targeting can be interesting. They can often come up with names that you have not thought of.

- **After you make your list, sort the names according to priority.** Then go back and look at the questions on the previous page to see if the selected names meet most of the criteria for choosing an effective business name.

- **Resort your list of names and establish their final priority.** You will now have the most desirable candidates for your business name.

If the Name is Available, Register It

The final links in the process of naming your business are to: 1. find out if the name(s) on your list are available for use. – and - 2. file your DBA or your Certificate of Incorporation.

- **If you are a sole proprietor or a partnership,** you should check with the county in which your business will be located. All businesses operating under a fictitious name are required to submit a Fictitious Name Statement to register their DBA (Doing Business As) business name. The county will have a record of all DBAs that have been filed and are current.

  If a business has already registered the name that you were planning to use, you cannot use the same name. Go to the second name on your list and check that out – and so on – until you arrive at the name that is both appropriate and available.

  The next step is to go ahead and file your DBA to gain ownership of your business name. Be aware that you will have to name a location for your business in the process. (For more information, see Chapter 9, "Register Your Fictitious Business Name (File a DBA)".

- **If your business is a corporation,** you will need to check out the availability of your corporate name at the state level. Generally there will be an office under the jurisdiction of the Secretary of State that is responsible for the registration of businesses incorporated within the state, registration of out-of-state corporations qualified to do business within the state, and names registered or reserved by other corporations.

  If the name you have selected is available, you can use it when you file your certificate of incorporation. A charter will not be issued until the state determines that the name is available, the certificate has been executed, and there has been no violation of state law.

Develop Your Company's Logo

After you have decided on your company name and established its ownership through registration with the county and/or your state, the next step is to design your logo – the graphic image that you will use identify your business and distinguish it from the competition.

Your logo should be chosen before your business is launched on the market. It will become increasingly important as your business matures. The right logo will help promote your business in the market and will aid in attracting potential customers. Two examples of logos that have become well-known over the years are McDonalds' golden arches and Nike's single swoosh.

Your logo should create a long-lasting impression on your customers and evoke feelings of trust and reliability. Just this morning, a plumbing company's van passed me on the freeway. The first thing I noticed was the company logo. It was a graphic of a plumber cheerfully scrambling to fix his customer's problem. It wasn't the name that attracted me. It was the logo!

Designing Your Logo

A logo design should be eye catching and simple. The most important logo features are the shape of the design and the balance of the colors used.

Simplicity is the key to an effective logo. It should not have overwhelming colors and details. If you use lettering, it should be in a simple and easy-to-read font type. Remember that your logo should attract and make a positive impact on your customers.

Some options to consider for designing your logo might be as follows:

- **You can hire a graphic designer.** If you decide to use a professional to design your logo, it would be a good idea to ask to see samples of other logos developed for previous customers. In the beginning, it will be necessary for you to work together to decide on the components (shape, color, lettering) of the logo. The designer needs to know what your business is all about and what message you wish to convey to your customers. You will most likely be provided with four or five design ideas to choose from. As the design progresses, you will continue to proof changes until the logo has been refined to your satisfaction.

- **You may choose to design your own logo.** This could work very well, especially if you or one of your friends has artistic talent and a working knowledge of graphics software such as CorelDraw or Adobe Illustrator. This would give you unlimited creative freedom.

- **You can opt to use logo design software.** The best logo programs have a friendly user interface and will help you to generate logos using predefined designs combined with color and other choices. The disadvantage of using logo software is that your logo may end up being similar to those of other businesses.

Tech Tip

Free Logo Designs

If you are on a really tight budget, free logo designs may be a great option. There are many logo design companies on the Internet that offer free logo designs. They are absolutely free of cost and come with no extra hidden charges.

Free logo designs are easy to get, simple designs that can convey your business' message in the simplest terms. They come in nearly every color and all that is required of you is adding your company name. With literally hundreds of logo designs to choose from, getting a free logo design is ideal for those who cannot afford to spend much when starting a business.

Note: Since they are free, you can have no modifications made to them other than adding your company name. Any modifications you wish to make with free logo designs require extra charges.

Design Your Business Cards

Business cards are the one marketing tool used by every business, large or small. They give your business credibility and provide your customers and your associates with a reminder of what your business is about and that you are the person who will be their point of contact.

Your business card will incorporate the name of your company and your logo, utilizing the basic design and colors that you have chosen. In addition, your business cards should have the following information:

- Key information about your products and services
- Your name and position with the company
- Company address
- Telephone number
- Fax number
- Website address
- Email address

In the beginning, I would suggest that you do not print too many business cards unless you are sure that all of the information will stay the same. If you have a computer, you can buy business card stock from you local office supply store and use your jet ink printer for your first cards. When you are ready for higher quality cards, you can use a printer and make selections regarding paper quality, type of printing, colors, size, etc.

Create Letterhead and Envelopes

The last of the basics needed for initially branding your company is to design and print your letterhead and envelopes. It is important when you communicate by mail for your company to project professionalism. Even the smallest business will be well-served by having simple, well-designed stationery.

This is a fairly simple task. It generally utilizes your logo and your company name. In addition, both the letterhead and envelope will have the company's contact information including:

- Company address
- Telephone number
- Fax number
- Website address
- Email address

 Note: *If your company is a corporation, the letterhead may contain additional information, such as corporate officers, board members, etc. Generally these are in small print on the left side of the letterhead.*

As with business cards, I would suggest that you do not print letterhead and envelopes in large quantities unless you are sure that all of the information will stay the same. You can buy good quality paper and business envelopes (in whatever color and texture you choose) from your local office supply store. Lay out your letterhead and envelopes in your word processor or a graphics program. Your jet ink printer will provide for your needs without a heavy front-end investment.

Later on, if you decide that you want higher quality letterhead and envelopes in a larger quantity, you can use a printer. The key is deciding which choice will serve your company better in terms of budget, timing, and quality.

Summary

The purpose of this chapter has been to lead you through some of the key tasks that will begin the branding process for your company – your name, your logo, your business cards, and your letterhead and envelopes.

In the marketing chapter (Chapter 17), you will develop your marketing strategy and see how everything you do in this chapter will contribute to defining and focusing your company's image and successfully selling your products and/or services into the marketplace.

CHAPTER

4

Learn About Proprietary Rights:

Copyrights, Trademarks, and Patents

Copyright, Trademark, and Patent are three of the most often confused terms in U.S. government. All three protect your rights to own, use, and potentially make money from things you create.

This chapter is meant to give you basic information – not legal advice – and to guide you to some resources where you can learn more about proprietary rights that you may need to secure for your business.

In the following pages, you will learn the basics about copyrights, trademarks, and patents.

> ✓ *What are they?*
>
> ✓ *Which one(s) do you need?*
>
> ✓ *How do you get them?*

Copyrights

What is a Copyright?

Copyright is a form of protection provided by the laws of the United States to the authors of "original works of authorship," including literary, dramatic, musical, artistic, and certain other intellectual works.

Copyright protection is available to both published and unpublished works. Section 106 of the 1976 Copyright Act generally gives the owner of copyright the exclusive right to do and to authorize others to do the following:

- To reproduce the work in copies or phonorecords;

- To prepare derivative works based upon the work;

- To distribute copies or phonorecords of the work to the public by sale or other transfer of ownership, or by rental, lease, or lending;

- To perform the work publicly, in the case of literary, musical, dramatic, and choreographic works, pantomimes, and motion pictures and other audiovisual works;

- To display the work publicly, in the case of literary, musical, dramatic, and choreographic works, pantomimes, and pictorial, graphic, or sculptural works, including the individual images of a motion picture or other audiovisual work; and

- In the case of sound recordings, to perform the work publicly by means of a digital audio transmission.

Who Needs a Copyright?

Persons or organizations creating "original works of authorship" including literary, dramatic, musical, architectural, cartographic, choreographic, pantomimic, pictorial, graphic, sculptural, and audiovisual displays usually register copyrights. Authors, artists, song writers and creators of computer programs typically register copyrights. Businesses often copyright their logos and other artwork that is representative of their companies.

 Important Note: There is no need to "apply" for a copyright. A copyright is automatically considered to be granted to the author or creator of the work as soon as it is finished and considered "fixed" in a copy or recording. While there is no need to apply for copyrights, there are definite advantages to registering them through the Copyright Office. Primarily, registering a copyright establishes a legally enforceable public record of the creator's copyright claim.

What a Copyright Does

The word "copyright" literally means the right to copy. According to the U.S. Copyright Office, "The owner of copyright has the exclusive right to reproduce, distribute, and, in the case of certain works, publicly perform or display the work; to prepare derivative works; or to license others to engage in the same acts under specific terms and conditions." For example, the author of a book will typically sell all or part of his or her copyrights to a publisher who actually prints and markets the book to the public.

What Can and Cannot be Copyrighted?

The U.S. Copyright Office defines the following broad categories of works for which copyrights can be registered:

- literary works
- musical works, including any accompanying words
- dramatic works, including any accompanying music
- pantomimes and choreographic work
- pictorial, graphic, and sculptural works
- motion pictures and other audiovisual works
- sound recordings
- architectural works

Computer program copyrights are typically registered as "literary works." Architectural plans and maps are registered as "pictorial, graphic, and sculptural works."

Things that cannot be copyrighted include any inventions, ideas, procedures, processes, slogans, principles, or discoveries.

Notice of Copyright

The required use of a copyright notice (1976 Copyright Act) was eliminated when the United States adhered to the Berne Convention, effective March 1, 1989. Because prior law did contain such a requirement, however, the use of notice is still relevant to the copyright status of older works.

Use of the notice may be important because it informs the public that the work is protected by copyright, identifies the copyright owner, and shows the year of first publication. The use of the copyright notice is the responsibility of the copyright owner and does not require advance permission from, or registration with, the Copyright Office.

Form of Notice for Visually Perceptible Copies: The notice for visually perceptible copies should contain all the following three elements:

1. The symbol © (the letter C in a circle), or the word "Copyright," or the abbreviation "Copr."; and

2. The year of first publication of the work.

3. The name of the owner of copyright in the work, or an abbreviation by which the name can be recognized, or a generally known alternative designation of the owner.

Example: © 2014 John Doe

The "C in a circle" notice is used only on "visually perceptible copies." Certain kinds of works—for example, musical, dramatic, and literary works—may be fixed not in "copies" but by means of sound in an audio recording. Since audio recordings such as audio tapes and phonograph disks are "phonorecords" and not "copies," the "C in a circle" notice is not used to indicate protection of the underlying musical, dramatic, or literary work that is recorded.

Tech Tip

How to Register a Copyright

The U.S. Copyright Office website (www.copyright.gov) has everything you need to understand and to register your copyright. The process of registering a copyright differs considerably depending on the type of work created.

- **U.S. Copyright Information, Circulars, Factsheets**
  Available as PDF files, these publications provide basic information about registration, fees, compulsory licenses, and other aspects of the copyright process.
  www.copyright.gov/pubs.html

- **U.S. Copyright Forms**
  Copyrights can be registered with paper forms ($65) by download and mailed in. Certain copyrights can be registered with (eCO) Electronic Copyright Office for $35. A different form is required for each category of creative work. Be sure to read the instructions for filling out and submitting the forms.
  www.copyright.gov/forms/

- **U.S. Copyright Law**
  Go here to research topics relating copyright law. You can download individual sections or a complete version of the U.S. Copyright Law in PDF format.
  www.copyright.gov/title17/

- **Frequently Asked Questions**
  Answers to questions commonly received by the Copyright Office.
  www.copyright.gov/help/faq/

Trademarks

What is a Trademark or Service Mark?

According to the U.S. Patent and Trademark office:

- **A trademark** is a word, phrase, symbol or design, or a combination of words, phrases, symbols or designs, that identifies and distinguishes the source of the goods of one party from those of others.

- **A service mark** is the same as a trademark, except that it identifies and distinguishes the source of a service rather than a product.

Registering a trademark is not required by law. However, most businesses choose to do so. Registering a mark with the federal government establishes legal public notice of the registrant's claim of ownership of the mark. In addition, registration establishes the registrant's exclusive legal right to use the mark throughout the United States.

Is Registration of Your Mark Required?

Registering a trademark is not required by law. However, most businesses choose to do so. You can establish rights in a mark based on legitimate use of the mark. However, owning a federal trademark registration on the Principal Register provides several advantages, e.g.,

- constructive notice to the public of the registrant's claim of ownership of the mark;

- a legal presumption of the registrant's ownership of the mark and the registrant's exclusive right to use the mark nationwide on or in connection with the goods and/or services listed in the registration;

- the ability to bring an action concerning the mark in federal court;

- the use of the U.S. registration as a basis to obtain registration in foreign countries; and

- the ability to file the U.S. registration with the U.S. Customs Service to prevent importation of infringing foreign goods.

Using the Trademark Symbols: TM, SM and ®

Any time you claim rights in a mark, you may use the "TM" (trademark) or "SM" (service mark) designation to alert the public to your claim, regardless of whether you have filed an application with the USPTO. However, you may use the federal registration symbol "®" **only** after the USPTO actually *registers a mark*, and **not** while an application is pending. Also, you may use the registration symbol with the mark only on or in connection with the goods and/or services listed in the federal trademark registration.

Research and Register Your Trademark or Service Mark

The first thing to do is make sure nobody else has already registered a similar trade or service mark. One way to do this is by using TESS - the Trademark Electronic Search System. Updated daily, TESS now contains more than 3 million pending, registered and dead federal trademarks.

Tech Tip

Learn More and Register Online

To learn more details about trademarks and service marks and how to file an online application, you can access the United States Patent and Trademark Office website. Go to the USPTO *"Basic Facts about Trademarks"* web page at: www.uspto.gov/web/offices/tac/doc/basic/

Hand Deliver or Mail an Application

While the Patent and Trademark Office prefers online filing, you can file an application by hand or regular mail. The only way you can get a paper copy of the trademark application form is by calling USPTO's automated telephone line, at (703) 308-9000 or (800) 786-9199. Paper trademark applications should be mailed to:

Commissioner for Trademarks
Box-New App-Fee
2900 Crystal Drive
Arlington, VA 22202-3513

For More Information

While it is greatly preferred that you file electronically using TESS, you may either mail or hand deliver a paper application to the USPTO. You can call the USPTO's automated telephone line at (800) 786-9199 to obtain a printed form. *You may not submit an application by facsimile.*

The mailing address to file a new application is:

Commissioner for Trademarks
P.O. Box 1451
Alexandria, VA 22313-1451

Applications delivered by hand or courier should be taken to:

Trademark Assistance Center
James Madison Building - East Wing
Concourse Level, 600 Dulany Street
Alexandria, VA

Patents

What is a Patent?

A patent for an invention is the grant of a property right to the inventor, issued by the United States Patent and Trademark Office. Generally, the term of a new patent is 20 years from the date on which the application for the patent was filed in the United States or, in special cases, from the date an earlier related application was filed, subject to the payment of maintenance fees. U.S. patent grants are effective only within the United States, U.S. territories, and U.S. possessions. Under certain circumstances, patent term extensions or adjustments may be available.

The right conferred by the patent grant is "the right to exclude others from making, using, offering for sale, or selling" the invention in the United States or "importing" the invention into the United States. What is granted is not the right to make, use, offer for sale, sell or import, but the right to exclude others from making, using, offering for sale, selling or importing the invention. Once a patent is issued, the patentee must enforce the patent without aid of the USPTO.

Utility, Design, and Plant Patents

There are three types of patents:

- **Utility** patents may be granted to anyone who invents or discovers any new and useful process, machine, article of manufacture, or composition of matter, or any new and useful improvement thereof. Inventors of the proverbial "better mousetrap," seek utility patents.

- **Design** patents may be granted to anyone who invents a new, original, and ornamental design for an article of manufacture. For example, if you design an ornamental telephone that in no way improves or changes the basic function of the telephone, you might seek a design patent.

- **Plant** patents may be granted to anyone who invents or discovers and asexually reproduces any distinct and new variety of plant.

Do You Need a Patent?

For several years, I gave business planning seminars at the Invention Convention in Pasadena, CA. The first thing an inventor worried about was how to keep the invention a secret until a patent was obtained. Since this process takes up to two year (or more) to accomplish, there was a problem – getting the invention to market. Mike Rounds, who taught marketing for inventors, maintained that the decision as to whether or not to go after a patent should be determined according to whether the product was "timeless" or "timely". In other words, if it was a hot product that needed to be marketed quickly, "skip the patent, produce the product, and jump on the market before someone else does." If it was a timeless invention (like the paper clip) that would have staying power, take the time to apply for a patent and protect your rights.

Applying for a Patent

Understanding about and applying for a patent can be a very daunting experience. In all probability, you will require help from a Patent Agent or Patent Attorney to guide you through the process.

Tech Tip

Learn More about Patents Online

The best way to learn more about the patenting process is to pay a visit to the U.S. Patent and Trademark Office "General Information Concerning Patents" web page. You can access it at: www.uspto.gov/patents/resources

At this site, you will find links to patent laws, patent searches, listings of U.S. PTO registered patent attorneys and agents, independent inventor resources, applications, drawing specifications, fees, etc.

For More Information

All business with the United States Patent and Trademark Office (USPTO or Office) should be transacted in writing. Be sure to include your full return address, including zip code. All correspondence relating to patent matters should be addressed to:

Commissioner for Patents
P.O. Box 1450
Alexandria, VA 22313-1450

The principal location of the USPTO is:

U.S. Patent and Trademark Office
600 Dulany Street
Alexandria, Virginia

Questions of a general nature only can be answered by Patent Assistance Center telephone service. Telephone numbers are: Toll Free - 800-PTO-9199 (800-786-9199) or 703-308-HELP (703-308-4357).

Decide on
Your Business Location

Where will your business be located? Fifty years ago, almost every business was operated out of a commercial location. Skip forward to today's world of technology and the scenario is very different.

In the first chapter of this book, you were encouraged to think about your own skills and interests and make a decision as to what kind of business you would like to go into. You also had to decide on whether you would start a new business, buy an existing business, or purchase a franchise. Once that decision has been made, it is time for you to choose a location (or base of operation) for your business.

How Do You Choose a Location?

Establishing your location is no longer a matter of checking for available commercial property and renting (or buying) the most suitable site. It is now a process of looking closely at your business and its particular needs for dealing most effectively with its customers.

A good way to begin the decision making process, is to look at the type of business that you are planning to operate and how the location will support the needs of your target markets. In other words, how will your location affect your efforts to reach your customers?

Retailers

If you are planning to open a "brick-and-mortar" retail store, you need to be accessible to your customers. The question you should ask yourself is, "What locations are available that are frequented by consumers who are likely to buy my particular products?" The type of retail business you are in will definitely drive your decision.

If you are opening a grocery store specializing in Latino foods, you should consider locating in an area with a predominantly Hispanic population. If you are selling music CDs, you will probably need to locate in a shopping mall or strip center that has adequate parking as well as foot traffic.

On the other hand, if you are opening a sandwich shop to service students taking night classes, it would obviously be best to see if you can actually locate in an area in the school and adjacent to the classrooms.

- **If you are buying an existing retail business:** The business will already have a location. Before you buy, you should determine if the present location is a plus or minus for the business.

  If you are not also buying the facility, you will have to negotiate a lease agreement with the landlord. Be sure that you understand the terms of the agreement before you enter into it. How much is the rent? How long will it be in effect? Is it renewable? Who pays the expenses (leasehold improvements, maintenance, utilities, insurance, etc.)? Generally, it is best to have an attorney look over your lease agreement so that any issues can be resolved ahead of time.

- **If you are starting a new retail business:** Putting your business in the right location might be the single most important thing you do. No matter how good your products are, you will not sell them unless you can get the customers through the door.

  Assess your situation. Make a list of your location requirements – population density, traffic patterns, access, zoning and permits, affordability, etc. Then you can search for available properties that will meet those needs. You can probably do a property search via the Internet. Alternately, there are business brokers who specialize in finding available property and helping you to negotiate a lease agreement. You can also check with the Chamber of Commerce in the area in which you wish to locate.

- **If you are buying a retail franchise:** You should have already evaluated the franchise in terms of the concept and product. Now it is time to look for a location. It should be visible to the flow of traffic and have easy access for your customers' convenience. The franchisor will control the area where you operate and will most likely help you to decide on and negotiate the location.

Wholesalers and Manufacturers

Wholesalers and manufacturers sell their products in bulk (at a discount) to retailers who in turn sell those products to their customers. Therefore, location would not be driven by the consumer market. Following are some of the questions that you would most likely ask yourself before making your decision.

- How much square footage will my business require?
- What are the choices available that will work for my business?
- What are the costs per square foot of available locations?
- Can my products easily be distributed from this location?
- If I am manufacturing my products, is the location zoned for this purpose?
- Will I be able to get all of the permits I need to operate legally?

Service Businesses

Due to the nature of service businesses, there are several alternatives regarding location. The location may be the place where the service takes place or it may be used solely for administrative purposes – or it may be a combination of both.

- **The location is used to service the customer.** Many service businesses are wholly dependent on being able to service their customers at their locations. Examples of these businesses would be medical offices, beauty salons, shoe and jewelry repair shops, dry cleaners, day care facilities, and professional (legal and accounting) practices. Although some of these service businesses could legally operate from a home location, they might choose a commercial location to be perceived as more credible and high-end by their clients.

  In cases such as these, your considerations will be much the same as those of a retail business. Your location should be easily accessible to the customer, especially if your business is dependent on consistently attracting new customers.

- **The location is used for administrative purposes only.** These service businesses do not meet with their customers at their location. The office is used solely to do administrative work such as bookkeeping and arranging appointments to service the customers. Typically, this might be the case if you have a landscaping, house cleaning, plumbing, painting, or other type of maintenance or repair service. It would also apply if you have a mobile service business, such as screen repair, pool cleaning, or food catering.

  If your location is not used to meet with your customers, it would be best to consider a low-cost location that will adequately service your business and that will not require extensive travel time to and from work.

  Small service businesses can often benefit by having their administrative offices at home. However, cities and counties do have some restrictions regarding licensing of home-based businesses. Also, if you want to utilize deductions for a home office, you will have to abide by IRS rulings. (See Chapter 6, Home-Based Business: Is It Right for You?).

The Virtual Location

With the advent and subsequent advances in technology, another type of business location has emerged – the virtual location. Millions of product and service businesses now exist entirely on the Internet. There are no limits to the ways that they operate.

- Retailers who choose not to setup brick and mortar (physical) locations, put their products up on their websites and use online marketing strategies to reach and sell to their target markets via shopping carts.

- Affiliates set up websites and sell other people's products without ever handling the merchandise. They merely advertise the product, take the order, and use the manufacturer for fulfillment.

- Virtual service professionals utilize company websites and email databases to simultaneously market their services and keep clients abreast of the latest industry information. Then they service their customers via electronic communications, sometimes never physically meeting face-to-face.

The interesting feature of the virtual location is that the consumer seldom knows (or cares) what is behind the scenes in the operation. The only thing that matters is that the product or service fills his needs in terms of quality and timing.

The opportunities are as limitless as the imagination in the minds of today's entrepreneurs. I have seen thousands of part-time employees contracted out for construction jobs, heavy equipment moved across the country, giant auctions taking place, cars sold, betting taking place, and every other unimaginable type of trade pursued – all arranged and taking place from virtual offices in homes. Now, with smart phones and other portable communication devices, businesses can communicate with customers and venders from literally any location that is within range of wireless connectivity.

Making the Final Decision

I think you can now see that choosing your location requires that you consider the nature of your business, who your customers are and how you will reach them, and how your choice will affect your bottom line (profitability).

Some businesses require commercial locations and others are appropriately operated in out-of-the way locations or as home-based businesses. Some will find their best option to be a physical location enhanced by an online presence. Others will operate 100% online.

If your business grows or changes, you can always re-evaluate your location needs. The important thing is to make the best choice you can for your initial location needs. That will help you to get your company off the ground and headed in the right direction.

 Note: You will find a Location Analysis Worksheet for your own use in Appendix II, Blank Forms and Worksheets, page 183.

Home-Based Business:
Is it Right for You?

One of the fastest growing markets in the United States is the home-based business. More than half of all U.S. businesses are based out of an owner's home. Apple Computer, Mary Kay Cosmetics, Hershey's, and Ford Motor Company are well-known corporations that started out as home-based businesses. 69% of U. S. entrepreneurs start their businesses at home (*Small Business Trends,* Feb. 19, 2014). More than half of U.S. entrepreneurs continue to operate their businesses from home long after those businesses are up and running. According to the U.S. Small Business Administration, there are an estimated 18.3 million home-based businesses in the United States (more than 53% of all small businesses).

Home-based businesses span a wide range of occupations and industries. One multi-state study conducted by a team of university-based researchers found that the top five occupations were marketing/sales (24%), contracting (15%), mechanical/transportation (13%), services (12%), and professional/technical (12%). Other studies yield varying results, but they all indicate that home businesses represent a wide range of occupations and industries.

The continuing trend toward home-based business has occurred for several reasons. According to a study entitled *Homepreneurs: A Vital Economic Force*, "Running a business from home has never been easier – technologically, at least. Fax services, the Internet, and smart phones have seen to that. So not surprisingly, a new study revealed that homepreneurs are becoming *an underlying long-term trend* that has been facilitated by the recession." Job insecurities and layoffs have forced white-collar workers to pile out of corporations. Many of these displaced middle-management people have taken their skills home and translated them into viable businesses run from their home offices. The home-based business trend has also been impacted by economic considerations such as eliminating rent and utilizing other home-office deductions. As an additional bonus, having a home-based business has allowed parents to stay home with their families and addressed elder care and parental leave without added costs.

What This Chapter Is About. Home-based businesses can be very successful. They can also turn into disasters or, at the very least, unproductive semi-attempts at dabbling at business. In order to help you get off to a good start, we have devoted this chapter to some of the most important considerations that will contribute to the success of your home-based business.

How Does a Home-Based Business Differ from Other Businesses?

With the exception of the location, a home-based business is the same as any other business. All other issues including the need for a strong marketing plan and sufficient funding apply. The determining factor that favors operating out of your home will be that marketing your business will not be adversely affected by the physical location of your business.

Advantages	Disadvantages
Lower Overhead	Feeling Isolated
Work Flexibility	Need for Self-Discipline

Do You Qualify for a Home-Office Deduction?

To qualify for a home office deduction for the business use of your home, you must use that portion of your home *exclusively* and *regularly* for your trade or business and it must be your *principal place of business*.

1. **Exclusive Use.** To qualify under the exclusive use test, you must use a specific area of your home *only* for your trade or business. The area used for business can be a room or other separately identifiable space. The space does not need to be marked off by a permanent partition. You do not meet the requirements of the exclusive use test if you use the area in question both for business and for personal purposes. Exceptions apply if you use part of your home for the storage of inventory or product samples, or you use part of your home as a dare-care facility.

2. **Regular Use.** To qualify under the regular use test, you must use a specific area of your home for business on a continuing basis. You do not meet the test if your business use of the area is only occasional or incidental, even if you do not use that area for any other purpose.

3. **Trade or Business Use.** To qualify under the trade or business use test, you must use part of your home in connection with a trade or business. If you use your home for a profit-seeking activity that is not a trade or business, you cannot take a deduction for its business use.

4. **Principal Place of Business.** You can have more than one business location, including your home, for a single trade or business. To qualify to deduct the expenses for the business use of your home, your home must be your principal place of business for that trade or business.

   Your home office will qualify as your principal place of business for deducting expenses for its use if:

   - You use it exclusively and regularly for administrative or management activities of your trade or business—and

- You have no other fixed location where you conduct substantial administrative or management activities of your trade or business. Some of these activities are:
    - Billing customers, clients or patients.
    - Keeping books and records.
    - Ordering supplies.
    - Setting up appointments.
    - Forwarding orders or writing reports.

The following administrative or management activities performed at other locations *will not disqualify* your home office as your principal place of business.

- You have others conduct your administrative or management activities at locations other than your home. (For example, another company does your billing from its place of business.)

- You conduct administrative or management activities at places that are not fixed locations of your business, such as in a car or a hotel room.

- You occasionally conduct minimal administrative or management activities at a fixed location outside your home.

- You conduct substantial non-administrative or non-management business activities at a fixed location outside your home. (For example, you meet with or provide services to customers, clients, or patients at a fixed location of the business outside your home.)

- You have suitable space to conduct administrative or management activities outside your home, but choose to use your home office for those activities instead.

Other Tests. The rules for *"principal place of business"* will not affect the other tests you must meet to claim the expenses for the business use of your home. You still must use the business part of your home both **exclusively** and **regularly** for your trade or business. If you are an employee, the business use of your home must be for *the convenience of your employer.* In addition your deduction may be limited if gross income from the business use of your home is less than total business expenses.

5. **Place to Meet Patients, Clients, or Customers.** If you meet or deal with patients, clients, or customers in your home in the normal course of your business, even though you also carry on business at another location, you can deduct your expenses for the part of your home used exclusively and regularly for business if you meet the following tests.

- You physically meet with patients, clients or customers on your premises. The part of your home that you use exclusively and regularly for theses meetings does not have to be your principal place of business.

- Their use of your home is substantial and integral to the conduct of your business.

  Note: *Using your home for occasional meetings and telephone calls will not qualify you for a home-office deduction.*

6. **Separate Structure.** You can deduct expenses (subject to the deduction limit) for a separate free-standing structure, such as a studio, garage, or barn, if you use it exclusively and regularly for your business. The structure does not have to be your principal place of business or a place where you meet patients, clients, or customers.

 To Help You

"Can You Deduct Business Use of Your Home Expenses?" Flowchart
Use the flowchart on page 45 to help you to determine if you will qualify for a home office deduction.

IRS Form 8829: Expenses for Business Use of Your Home
For your convenience, you can see a filled-in example of the IRS form that is used to report deductions for business use of your home on page 46.

Calculating Your Deduction

After you determine that you meet the tests that qualify you for a home office deduction, you can figure how much you can deduct. You will need to figure the percentage of your home used for business and the limit on the deduction.

Business Percentage

To determine the deduction for the business use of your home, you have to compare the size of the part of your home that you use for business to your whole house and find the percentage that is being used for business.

The following are two commonly used methods for figuring the percentage.

- Divide the area (length multiplied by the width) used for business by the total area of your home.

- If the rooms in your home are all about the same size, you can divide the number of rooms used for business by the total number of rooms in your home.

For example, *if your home measures 2,000 square feet and you are using 500 square feet for your home office, you will be able to deduct 25 percent of expenses such as rent, mortgage, interest, depreciation, taxes, insurance, utilities, repairs, etc. There are also other issues to be considered pertaining to the legalities of deductions. You will have to spend some time familiarizing yourself with them.*

Part-Year Use

You cannot deduct expenses for the business use of your home incurred during any part of the year you did not use your home for business purposes. Consider only your expenses for the business use portion of the year.

Deduction Limit

If gross income from the business use of your home equals or exceeds your total business expenses (including depreciation), you can deduct all of your business expenses related to the use of your home. If gross income from the business use of your home is less than your total business expenses, your deduction of otherwise nondeductible expenses, such as insurance, utilities, and depreciation, allocable to the business is limited. (See IRS Pub. 587 for thorough explanation)

Deducting Expenses

If you qualify to deduct expenses for the business use of your home, you will also have to divide the expenses of operating your home between personal and business use.

Types of Expenses

The part of your home operating expense you can use to figure your deduction depends on both of the following:

- Whether the expense is direct, indirect, or unrelated.
- The percentage of your home used for business.

Descriptions and examples of direct, indirect, and unrelated expenses are:

Direct (expenses only for business part of your home): painting or repairs only in the area used for business. These expenses are deductible in full (subject to the deduction limit). The exception is that they may be only partially deductible in a daycare facility.

Indirect (expenses for keeping up and running your entire home): insurance, utilities, and general repairs. Deductibility is based on the percentage of your home used for business.

Unrelated (expenses only for the parts of your home not used for business): lawn care or painting a room not used for business. These expenses are not related to your business and are not deductible.

Examples of Expenses

Certain expenses are deductible whether or not you use your home for business. If you claim business use of the home expenses, use the business percentage of these expenses to figure your total business use of the home deduction. These expenses include the following:

- Real estate taxes
- Deductible mortgage interest
- Casualty loss

Other expenses are deductible only if you use your home for business. You can use the business percentage of these expenses to figure your total business use of the home deduction. These expenses generally include (but are not limited to) the following:

- Depreciation (see rulings)
- Insurance
- Rent
- Repairs
- Security system
- Utilities and Services

Tech Tip

Download and Print
IRS Pub. 587: Business Use of Your Home

The Internal Revenue Service has a 31-page publication that will give you more comprehensive information on issues pertaining to business use of your home. It addresses such things as: qualifying for a deduction, figuring deductions, deducting expenses, depreciating your home, day-care facilities, sale or exchange of your home, business furniture and equipment, recordkeeping, etc. It also contains worksheets that will help you figure your own deduction.

Publication 587, *Business Use of Your Home (Including Use by Day-Care Providers)* can be downloaded via the Internet from: www.irs.gov and select Forms and Publications.

Increasing Your Chances for Success

If you are going to operate out of your home, there are several things you can do to ensure that you will be more successful. Home offices have long been under scrutiny by many who wish to question their credibility. In the following pages, we will discuss some of the issues that may make the difference between success and failure.

Organize Your Work Space

Setting aside your work space is not only an IRS requirement, but a necessary element of any business. It is important to understand that a home-based business is the same as a business in a commercial location with the exception of some special tax considerations. That's exactly the way you should treat it.

Organize your work space in an efficient manner and eliminate non-work items so that you will not be tempted to mix the two during working hours. If you are operating a lawn mower repair shop out of your garage, don't use it to house your cars, bicycles, freezer and old clothes. If you have an office in your family room, get rid of the TV, pool table, exercise machine and ironing board. When a customer steps through the door into your office, it should feel like a business.

Take Care of Legal Responsibilities

A home business has the same legal requirements as any other business. You will still need a business license, DBA, seller's permit, etc. You should never mix your business finances with your personal finances. An effective recordkeeping system will have to be set up and you will need to find an accounting professional who can help you to maximize your tax benefits and prepare your final tax return. You will need a separate bank account and a business telephone. You will need business insurance tailored to your products and services.

In other words, pretend that you have just opened business in a commercial location and do the same things that you would do there to get your business underway.

Set Business Hours

It will be very important for you to establish regular business hours. Credibility is hard to come by, but especially if you work out of your home. Your customers will take you more seriously if they see that you are operating on a schedule. If you are not available when they call, you will soon find that they will be looking elsewhere for the same service or product.

When you are required to be away from your business during normal working hours, be sure that you have provided for a way to take a message and return your customer's call. Invest in a good answering machine and leave a new message telling when you will be back in your office and assuring the customer that you will return the call promptly.

I knew one business owner who continually left the message, "I am away from my office right now and will return in two hours." The problem was that the caller never knew what time the message was left or when the two hours would be up. A better message would have been, "I have an appointment with a client and will be back in my office at 2 p.m." Also be sure to ask for a name and phone number and offer to return the call.

Protect Your Work Hours

Inform your family and friends that you are serious about your business and will need to work without interruption. For some reason, a home-based business is usually perceived as being a place where visitors are welcome to show up and stay for a friendly visit. They would never think of popping into a corporate office for a cup of coffee, but surely you would welcome a break in your working hours!

Unfortunately, this is one of the most serious problems encountered in home-based businesses and one that is difficult to solve. It not only applies to family and friends, but to some of your customers who are anxious to establish a friendly relationship. I have used every trick in the book to get rid of unwanted visitors without offending them. I have resorted to proclaiming nonexistent appointments, walking visitors slowly out the door, and any other means within my imagination. When all else fails, tell the truth and it might just work.

Protect Your Free Hours

In addition to protecting your business hours, you will also have to decide what days and hours you wish to be closed and promise yourself that you will use them for non-business pursuits. In fact, guard that free time with your life.

Be sure to inform your customers in regard to your working hours. If they want to come during your off hours, tell them nicely but firmly that you are closed. Most will respect you and return during your regular business hours.

At the end of your working day, turn on your answering machine and shut the door to your business. Plan for activities with your family or friends and try not to overwhelm them with your business problems. The idea is to have fun and give yourself a break. You will soon feel overwhelmed and tired of your business if you never have the opportunity to get away from it.

It would be naive to pretend that a business owner will never have to work extra hours to make the business prosper. Do what you need to do to run your business, but don't let it run you—and don't let it cause you to burn out your enthusiasm and create problems with the people you care about. Remember, owning your own business is supposed to be a plus in your life!

Be Self-Disciplined

Owning your own business requires a great deal of time and effort. I have heard potential business owners exclaim that they are going to quit working eight hours a day for a company and be free to set their own hours. It is true that you can decide on your hours. However, working for yourself will probably be equivalent to holding down two jobs, at least for the first three or four years until the business is functioning smoothly. For this reason, it will be necessary to develop a high degree of self-discipline.

Be willing to work long hours when it is necessary. If an extra effort is needed to get a job done, you will have to do it. Decide what needs to be done and stick to your goals. Don't fall into the trap of thinking that you are free. You may be your own boss, but you will work longer and harder than any employee.

Dress for Success

Just because you are working at home, don't use it as an excuse to be a slob. Every trade has an acceptable mode of dress that should be adhered to. A home business is the perfect target for a 24-hour a day onslaught by customers. They will call on the telephone and ring the doorbell seven days a week from dawn to dark—and that includes holidays. No one can see what you look like on the other end of the phone, but if you are going to answer the door, look like a business person. If your customer is going to have confidence in your products or services, he or she must first have confidence in you. You are your best advertisement.

Be Totally Credible

Home-based business has come to represent a large segment of today's workforce and a powerful force in the economy. In fact, due in a large part to modern technology, almost every kind of business imaginable is being run out of a home office somewhere. Unfortunately, those same home businesses are often regarded as "little hobbies." I was in home-based businesses long before I started teaching business classes and writing and publishing business books. It would probably be impossible to count the times that I was told what a wonderful hobby I had. I liked my business, but can assure you that my reasons for being in business were measured in dollars as well as fun.

The truth is that a home-based business owner will have to expend extra effort to prove credibility and attract customers. Many professional business organizations, including chambers of commerce, are forming focus groups to help overcome this stigma. Meanwhile, professionalism is the only weapon that can be effectively used to overcome misconceptions about the seriousness of this major economic force.

A Last Reminder

- Check zoning laws to be sure that you can legally operate your business out of your home.

- Be self-disciplined and don't allow distractions.

- Set fixed hours and an environment of professionalism.

- Have dedicated space for your business.

- Dress for work.

- Ensure that you have the technological support and furnishings without going overboard (business phone line and answering system, fax, computer system, copier, scanner, etc.).

- Make sure your business is compatible with your homeowner's policy; look at commercial coverage as an option.

- Keep efficient records.

- NEVER combine home and business accounts.

- Set up a network to avoid isolation.

- Have a good relationship with your neighbors and be sensitive to deliveries, customer parking, etc.

- Maintain a supportive family network.

IRS Warning!
Home-Based Business Tax Avoidance Schemes

The Internal Revenue Service has issued consumer alerts regarding home-based business schemes that purport to offer tax "relief." In reality they provide bad advice to unwary taxpayers that, if followed, results in improper tax avoidance.

Promoters of these schemes claim that individual taxpayers can deduct most, or all, of their personal expenses as business expenses by setting up a bogus home-based business. But the tax code firmly establishes that a clear business purpose and profit motive must exist in order to generate and claim allowable business expenses.

Some examples of personal expenses that are not deductible, but are commonly claimed business expenses in home-based business tax avoidance schemes include

- Deducting all or most of the cost and operation of a personal residence. For example, placing a calendar, desk, file cabinet, telephone, or other business-related item in each room does not increase the amount that can be deducted.

- Deducting a portion of the total house payment is not allowable if the business is not real.

- Paying children a salary for services, such as answering telephones, washing cars or other tasks and then deducting these costs as a business expense is not real.

- Deducting education expenses from the salary wrongfully paid to children as employees is not allowed

- Deducting excessive car and truck expenses when the vehicle has been used for both business and personal use is not allowed.

- Deducting personal furniture, home entertainment equipment, children's toys, etc. is not allowed.

- Deducting personal travel, meals, and entertainment under the guise that "everyone is a potential client" is not allowed.

Any tax scheme that claims a person can deduct what would normally be personal expenses should be considered highly suspect. Taxpayers who have questions on this subject or wish to report possible schemes can call 1-866-775-7474. They can also contact the IRS by sending an email to irs.tax.shelter.hotline@irs.gov.

Can You Deduct Business Use of Home Expenses?

source: IRS Publication 587, Business Use of Your Home

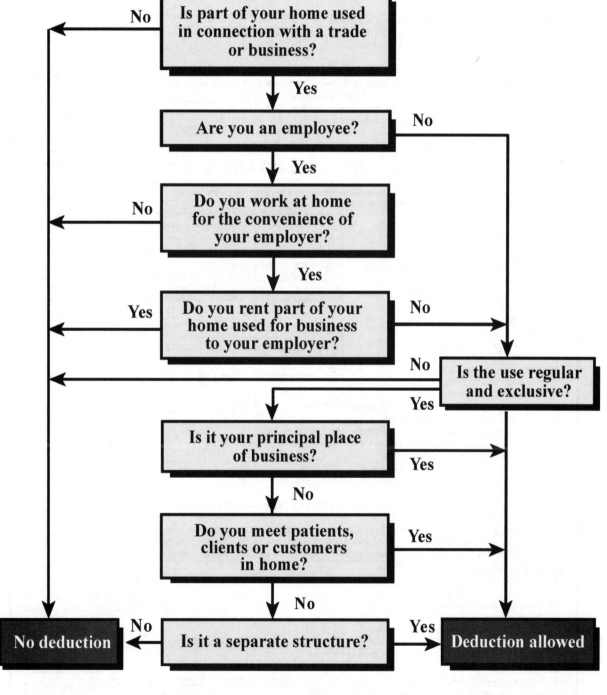

Note: Daycare and inventory storage are exceptions to the exclusive use test.

IRS Form 8829
Expenses for Business Use of Your Home

Form **8829**	**Expenses for Business Use of Your Home**	OMB No. 1545-0074
Department of the Treasury Internal Revenue Service (99)	▶ File only with Schedule C (Form 1040). Use a separate Form 8829 for each home you used for business during the year. ▶ Information about Form 8829 and its separate instructions is at *www.irs.gov/form8829*.	**2013** Attachment Sequence No. **176**

Name(s) of proprietor(s) | Your social security number

Part I — Part of Your Home Used for Business

1	Area used regularly and exclusively for business, regularly for daycare, or for storage of inventory or product samples (see instructions)	**1**
2	Total area of home	**2**
3	Divide line 1 by line 2. Enter the result as a percentage	**3** %
	For daycare facilities not used exclusively for business, go to line 4. All others go to line 7.	
4	Multiply days used for daycare during year by hours used per day	**4** hr.
5	Total hours available for use during the year (365 days x 24 hours) (see instructions)	**5** 8,760 hr.
6	Divide line 4 by line 5. Enter the result as a decimal amount	**6** .
7	Business percentage. For daycare facilities not used exclusively for business, multiply line 6 by line 3 (enter the result as a percentage). All others, enter the amount from line 3 ▶	**7** %

Part II — Figure Your Allowable Deduction

8	Enter the amount from Schedule C, line 29, **plus** any gain derived from the business use of your home and shown on Schedule D or Form 4797, minus any loss from the trade or business not derived from the business use of your home and shown on Schedule D or Form 4797. See instructions	**8**

See instructions for columns (a) and (b) before completing lines 9–21.

			(a) Direct expenses	(b) Indirect expenses	
9	Casualty losses (see instructions)	**9**			
10	Deductible mortgage interest (see instructions)	**10**			
11	Real estate taxes (see instructions)	**11**			
12	Add lines 9, 10, and 11	**12**			
13	Multiply line 12, column (b) by line 7			**13**	
14	Add line 12, column (a) and line 13				**14**
15	Subtract line 14 from line 8. If zero or less, enter -0-				**15**
16	Excess mortgage interest (see instructions)	**16**			
17	Insurance	**17**			
18	Rent	**18**			
19	Repairs and maintenance	**19**			
20	Utilities	**20**			
21	Other expenses (see instructions)	**21**			
22	Add lines 16 through 21	**22**			
23	Multiply line 22, column (b) by line 7			**23**	
24	Carryover of operating expenses from 2012 Form 8829, line 42			**24**	
25	Add line 22, column (a), line 23, and line 24				**25**
26	Allowable operating expenses. Enter the **smaller** of line 15 or line 25				**26**
27	Limit on excess casualty losses and depreciation. Subtract line 26 from line 15				**27**
28	Excess casualty losses (see instructions)			**28**	
29	Depreciation of your home from line 41 below			**29**	
30	Carryover of excess casualty losses and depreciation from 2012 Form 8829, line 43			**30**	
31	Add lines 28 through 30				**31**
32	Allowable excess casualty losses and depreciation. Enter the **smaller** of line 27 or line 31				**32**
33	Add lines 14, 26, and 32				**33**
34	Casualty loss portion, if any, from lines 14 and 32. Carry amount to **Form 4684** (see instructions)				**34**
35	**Allowable expenses for business use of your home.** Subtract line 34 from line 33. Enter here and on Schedule C, line 30. If your home was used for more than one business, see instructions ▶				**35**

Part III — Depreciation of Your Home

36	Enter the **smaller** of your home's adjusted basis or its fair market value (see instructions)	**36**
37	Value of land included on line 36	**37**
38	Basis of building. Subtract line 37 from line 36	**38**
39	Business basis of building. Multiply line 38 by line 7	**39**
40	Depreciation percentage (see instructions)	**40** %
41	Depreciation allowable (see instructions). Multiply line 39 by line 40. Enter here and on line 29 above	**41**

Part IV — Carryover of Unallowed Expenses to 2014

42	Operating expenses. Subtract line 26 from line 25. If less than zero, enter -0-	**42**
43	Excess casualty losses and depreciation. Subtract line 32 from line 31. If less than zero, enter -0-	**43**

For Paperwork Reduction Act Notice, see your tax return instructions.   Cat. No. 13232M   Form **8829** (2013)

Choose Your Legal Structure

When you start your business, it will be necessary for you to select its legal structure. This chapter will help you to understand and make your decision by introducing you to the definition, benefits, and risks of each of the following legal entities.

✓ *Sole Proprietor*

✓ *Partnership*

✓ *S Corporation*

✓ *Corporation*

✓ *Limited Liability Company (LLC)*

Will your business be a sole proprietorship, partnership, S corporation, corporation, or a limited liability company? Before you make that decision, you should ask yourself a few basic questions regarding the business and your own personal situation. Answering the questions on the next page will help you to make an intelligent decision.

- What type of business will you start?
- How small (or large) will the business be?
- How many owners will there be?
- Who will be making decisions for company?
- Where (geographically) will you be doing business?
- Will you need capital from a lender or investor?
- What are the liability risks of the business?
- What kind of personal assets do you have?
- Will you need to protect those assets from the business?

Do You Need Professional Help?

If your company will be anything other than a sole proprietorship, I would suggest that you at least consult with a professional (business attorney or business accountant) to help you choose and legally form your business entity. This can help you to avoid many problems in the future.

For instance, in today's world, many new entrepreneurs form partnerships with their friends and associates, but fail to clearly define the terms of the partnership. It is a well-recognized fact that a majority of partnerships do not work out for various reasons – lack of defined responsibilities, failure on partners to contribute equal effort, disagreement over expenditures, partners wishing to exit the business, etc. A well-executed partnership agreement will spell out contributions and responsibilities of the partners and provide for an equitable dissolution in the event that it is necessary.

Another example would be using a professional to help you choose between corporate structures. Many new companies decide for themselves that they will form a limited liability company (LLC), which is a state entity. The laws that govern this legal structure have great variations from one state to another. If your company intends to operate throughout the United States or internationally, it may be advisable to incorporate under national law. A professional can help you to make the correct choice.

Note. Although you can change the legal structure of your company at a later date, it is less expensive and less time consuming to make the right choice in the beginning. Also, keep in mind that moving from a sole proprietorship (or partnership) to a corporation is easier than moving backwards from a corporation to a more simple legal structure.

Understanding Legal Structures

The choice you make requires that you understand the definition of each type of legal structure, its benefits and risks, and how they would affect your business and your personal situation.

1. Sole Proprietor

You are a sole proprietor if you are self-employed and are the sole owner of an unincorporated business. You report your income, expenses, and net profit from your business or profession on a Schedule C and file it with your regular Form 1040 income tax return. There is no tax effect if you transfer money to or from your business. Sole proprietors pay estimated income and self-employment taxes to the IRS on a quarterly basis based on net earnings from the business.

 Benefits

- **It is the simplest form of legal structure.** Becoming a sole proprietor does not require a legal agreement. If you file a DBA (business name statement) and obtain a business license from your city or county government, you are generally considered to be a sole proprietor.

- **You are sole owner of the business.** As the sole owner, you make 100% of the profits of the business (or losses). You also have the power to make all decisions and accept all responsibilities regarding the business.

- **You are taxed as an individual.** The business itself does not pay taxes. The profits (losses) from a sole proprietorship are reported as earnings from a business on your personal tax return and are computed with other earnings and deductions at the appropriate rate.

- **There are fewer governing regulations.** Some legal structures must follow extensive government regulations during operation. If a sole proprietor is licensed and files tax returns, there are generally no other regulations relating to legal structure.

 Risks

- **The responsibility is all yours.** You bear sole responsibility for everything that happens in your business. You are the ultimate decision maker and bear all responsibility for the outcome. This disadvantage can be mitigated as you grow by utilizing advisors and designating certain tasks to employees with the proper skills. If you fail to grow past a one-person operation, you will have to cover all areas such as, accounting, marketing, and customer relations, as well as everything else related to offering your products and/or services.

- **You are liable personally for the debts of your business.** You will be personally liable for all business debts. This means that your personal assets (home equity, savings, vehicle, etc.) are at risk if your business becomes indebted beyond its capability to pay.

- **Financing may be difficult to obtain.** Because your business is dependent on one person only, a banker or investor may be less likely to give you a loan or invest funds in your company. If you do get funding, you will be personally liable for repayment.

- **The business is dependent on your ability to operate it.** If you do not have other people who are capable of carrying on the business in your absence, it can be disastrous. What's more, if you should die, the business ceases to exist as a legal entity.

2. Partnership

A partnership is the relationship between two or more persons who join together to carry on a trade or business with each person contributing money, property, labor, or skill, and each expecting to share in the profits and losses of the business.

Partnership profits are not taxed to the partnership. Each partner must take into account his or her distributive share of partnership profits (losses) on his or her own income tax return (whether distributed or not). The business files a Form 1065 for its tax years, but it is mainly an information return. Each partner's distributive share is usually included in figuring earnings from self-employment.

Partnerships can have General and Limited Partners.

- **General Partners** are active in the control of the business. They share financing, decision-making, and management responsibilities according to terms spelled out in the partnership agreement. They also share in the liability.

- **Limited Partners** are generally taken on by a company to raise capital for the business. As long as the limited partners do not participate in the management or control of the business, they do not share in the liability. Limited partnerships are by contractual agreement spelling out the terms for the capital infusion, return on investment, and exit terms.

Do not form a partnership without a partnership agreement. This is a good time to point out that every partnership should have a formal partnership agreement. The Uniform Partnership Act (UPA) is a law (adopted in all states except Louisiana) that established the most basic legal rules applicable to partnerships. In order to spell out specifics applying to the business relationship, it is imperative that the partners draw up and sign a partnership agreement. A general form can be downloaded on the Internet. If you don't want to consult an attorney, Nolo Press has a partnership legal self-help book that will take you through the process and help you to address the terms and provisions. Some of the things that need to be covered are: equity shares, financial contributions, distribution of profits and losses, contributed capital and assets, partners' managerial and work responsibilities, provisions for a partner's exit due to death, disability, or desire, methods for settling disputes, the duration of the agreement and terms for dissolution of the business.

Benefits

- **It is easy to form a partnership.** If you file a DBA (fictitious business name statement) and obtain a business license from your city or county government, your partnership is generally considered as having been established. As with a sole proprietorship, if a partnership files required information and other tax returns, there are generally no other regulations relating to legal structure.

- **Partners share the responsibility of the business.** Unlike sole proprietors, partners have the advantage of being able to divide the work load, blend skills, share ideas, and make joint decisions that will make the business more profitable.

- **Partnerships have more access to funding.** Having two or more individuals contributing money to operate the business is always helpful. In addition, if the partners' personal equity is significant, the partnership will probably be more successful in attracting funding from lenders or investors.

- **Partners – not the partnership – are taxed.** The business itself does not pay taxes. Distributive shares of the profits (losses) of a partnership are reported as earnings from a business on the partners' personal tax returns and are computed with their other earnings and deductions at the appropriate rate.

 Risks

- **Dissolution of a partnership can be difficult.** Although it is not required by law, it is wise to have a formal partnership agreement spelling out not only the contributions and responsibilities of each of the partners, but providing for a partner to exit the partnership by buying out or selling to other partners.

- **Partners with more equity or assets stand to lose more.** If the business fails, the partners with the most equity or the most personal assets stand to lose more.

- **Profits belong to all partners according to equity share.** The business will have to make earnings sufficient to support each of the partners. Partners must agree on when and what portion of their earnings should be retained to operate the company and when and what portion should be distributed as owner draws.

- **Partners are bound by each other's decisions.** The nature of a partnership is that all general partners have a right to act on behalf of the company. Unless spelled out otherwise in the partnership agreement, partners can individually make contracts, spend money, borrow money, etc. and the other partners will be bound by those decisions.

3. Corporation

A corporation is a distinct legal entity, separate from the individuals who own it. It is formed by the authority of the state government, with approval from the secretary of state. If business is conducted in more than one state, you must comply with the federal laws regarding interstate commerce. Federal and state laws may vary considerably.

Forming a corporation involves a transfer of either money, property, or both by the prospective shareholders in exchange for capital stock in the corporation.

Every corporation unless it is specifically exempt or has dissolved, must file a tax return, even if it has no taxable income for the year and regardless of the amount of its gross income. Corporate profits normally are taxed to the corporation. When the profits are distributed as dividends, the dividends are then taxed to the shareholders.

 Note: *The cost and complexity of the corporate legal structure often make it an unrealistic option for many small businesses. S corporations or Limited Liability Companies (LLCs) may provide less complex alternatives with some of the same advantages.*

Articles of Incorporation. Due the complexity of the corporation, you should consult an attorney and/or accounting professional to draft the company's articles of incorporation and handle the filing of its Certificate of Incorporation.

The following is a summary of the types of information that will be needed to complete the Certificate of Incorporation. Your legal advisor can provide more detail and work with you adequately address requirements.

- Corporate name of the company
- Purposes of the corporation
- Length of time the corporation will exist
- Names and addresses of incorporators
- Location of the registered office of the corporation in the state of incorporation
- Proposed capital structure
- Management
- Director (person who will serve until 1st stockholder meeting)

If the designated state official determines that the corporation name is available, the certificate has been completely and properly executed, and there has been no violation, the charter will be issued. However, the incorporation process will not be complete until the stockholders meet, elect a board of directors, and adopt bylaws. The board of directors will in turn elect the officers (generally including a president, secretary, and treasurer) who will actually have charge of operating the corporation. In small corporations, the officers may be selected from the board of directors.

Bylaws. The bylaws are the governing rules of the corporation. They generally address and provide for the following: the location of the principal office and other offices; time, location, and notice of stockholder meetings, number of directors, their compensation, terms of office, method of election, and the filling of vacancies; time and location of directors' meetings; quorum and voting methods; insurance and form of stock certificates; methods of selecting officers and designating their titles, duties, terms of office, and salaries; method of paying dividends; decisions regarding the fiscal year; and procedure for amending the bylaws.

 Benefits

- **Liability rests on the corporation.** The corporation is a separate legal entity responsible and liable for its debts. It has an existence apart from the people who own it. Its shareholders are liable only for the amount of money they have invested.

- **Ownership is readily transferable.** Stock can be purchased, sold, or transferred. The corporation does not cease to exist with the death of an owner.

- **There is increased access to business expertise.** The corporation can draw on the experience and expertise of its board of directors, officers, advisors, and managers.

- **There is increased opportunity for raising capital.** The corporation can substantially increase its capital through the sale of stock.

 Risks

- **There is an increased tax burden.** Income tax is paid on the corporate net income (profit). Individual salaries and dividends are also taxed.

- **Corporations are difficult – and expensive – to form and maintain.** Some of the costs unique to corporations are the fees for setting up a corporate structure, costs of holding stockholders' and board of directors meetings, increased costs for documentation requirements, and legal and accounting fees.

- **They must conform to extensive government regulations.** Corporations are complex to manage and highly regulated. Burdensome local, state, and federal reports must be filed, and regular stockholder meetings must be held.

4. S Corporation

Some corporations may elect not to be subject to income tax. If a corporation qualifies and chooses to become an S corporation, its income usually will be taxed to the shareholders.

Formation of an S corporation is only allowable under certain circumstances.

- It must be a domestic corporation either organized in the United States or organized under federal or state law.

- It must have only one class of stock.

- It must have no more than 100 shareholders.

- It must have as shareholders only individuals, estates, and certain trusts. Partnerships and corporations cannot be shareholders in an S corporation.

- It must have shareholders who are citizens or residents of the United States. Non-resident aliens cannot become shareholders.

The formation of an S corporation can be an advantageous form of legal structure. However, if you enter into it without careful planning, it can result in more taxes – instead of less, as anticipated.

Benefits

- **S corporations have the limited liability of a corporation.** The S corporation is a separate legal entity and has an existence apart from the people who own it. The corporation is responsible and liable for its debts. Shareholders are liable only for the amount they have invested.

- **Income is generally taxed to the shareholders.** As with a partnership, the business itself does not pay taxes. The corporation files a Form 1120S income tax return. Each shareholder is provided with a Schedule K, summarizing the corporation's income, deductions, credits, etc. reportable by the shareholders. Schedule K-1 shows each shareholder's separate share and each individual shareholder's earnings are reported on their personal tax returns and taxes are computed with their other earnings and deductions at the appropriate rate.

- **S corporations are likely to have more access to funding.** If the S corporation's equity is significant, it will probably be more successful in attracting funding from lenders or investors.

Risks

- **Specific rules and conditions must be met.** As with any corporation, rules and regulations are more stringent. The S corporation must operate under specific rules and conditions to maintain its S corporation status.

- **There are limits on the origin of gross income.** No more than 25% of the corporation's gross income can be derived from passive investment activities.

- **Deductions are limited.** The corporation may not deduct the cost of fringe benefits provided to employee shareholders who own more than 2% of the corporations. Shareholders may not deduct corporate losses that exceed the amount of the investment in the company minus a few adjustments.

5. Limited Liability Company (LLC)

A Limited Liability Company (LLC) is a relatively new business structure allowed by state statute. LLCs are popular because, similar to a corporation, owners have limited personal liability for the debts and actions of the LLC.

Other features of LLCs are more like a partnership, providing management flexibility and the benefit of pass-through taxation.

Owners of an LLC are called members. Since most states do not restrict ownership, members may include individuals, corporations, other LLCs and foreign entities. There is no maximum number of members. Most states also permit "single member" LLCs, those having only one owner.

A few types of businesses generally cannot be LLCs, such as banks, insurance companies and nonprofit organizations. Check your state's requirements and the federal tax regulations for further information. There are special rules for foreign LLCs.

To set up an LLC, you follow a path similar to the formation of a corporation. You must submit an article of organization and the appropriate filing fees to the secretary of state in the state where your business is organized. Because states differ in the information required, it is wise to consult your attorney or accountant if you think the limited liability company form of legal structure is right for your business.

 Benefits

- **LLCs offer greater flexibility than S corporations.** You can accomplish the goals of limited liability and pass-through taxation. It offers its owners greater flexibility in allocating profits and losses and is not subject to the many restrictions of an S corporation.

- **Loss deductions are more liberal for LLCs.** The owners of an LLC do not assume liability for the business's debt, and any losses can be used as tax deductions against active income. Loss deductions are more limited under an S corporation.

- **There is less restriction on participation.** An LLC can be formed with just one person in every state except Massachusetts, which requires at least two owners. There is no maximum number of owners allowed.

- **LLCs can offer more stock options.** Unlike an S corporation, and LLC can offer several different classes of stock with different rights.

 Risks

- **Different rules apply in different states.** An LLC is a state entity and the business is governed by the code of that state. In some states, the business is dissolved on the death, retirement, resignation, or expulsion of an owner. Be sure to check your state's code to see if an LLC is the best form of legal structure for your business.

- **It may be difficult to operate in other states.** Expansion of the business out of state may be inhibited. If a company doing business as an LLC wished to do business in another state without similar legislation, there is no provision for it to legally register to conduct business in that state.

- **Converting an existing business may have tax implications.** Special rules may apply when your LLC has an operating loss. The amount of loss you can deduct may be limited because of your limited liability for LLC debts. Passive Activity Loss limitation may restrict the amount of loss you can deduct. Also, if you convert an existing business, such as a corporation, into an LLC, the conversion may result in a taxable gain. Employment tax wage bases may also be affected.

Changing Your Legal Structure

Most small businesses will initially operate as sole proprietors. As the business grows and complications set in, you may wish to change your legal structure. You may choose to take on partners to help you shoulder the load. If you need to expand your financial opportunities and decrease your financial liabilities, you may wish to form a corporation.

If you change the legal structure of your existing business, you must notify the Internal Revenue Service and your state tax agency.

- **Sole proprietorships and partnerships** are required to change legal form through the business license bureau.

- **Corporations** must register with the office of the secretary of state.

If you are unsure as to how to legally accomplish a desired change in legal structure, consult an attorney or accounting professional. It is better to be safe than sorry.

Summary

Choosing the legal structure for your business requires careful consideration of the available options. Your choice should match the short- and long-term personal and business goals.

What assets do you own and how much are you willing to risk? How much money will you need to run your business and where will the money come from? What are your own industry and managerial skills? Can you run your business by yourself – or will you need to bring other people into the business as owners or shareholders? What would happen to your business if you were not able to run it? Why did you start your business and what is your vision for its future?

Tech Tip

Tax Information on Legal Structures

The Internal Revenue Service provides specific business tax information for each form of legal structure. Go to the IRS Web site: www.irs.gov

Click on businesses under contents. You will be able to access information on tax considerations by legal structure. You can download general publications, tax worksheets and forms for each legal structure. You will also have access to online workshops.

Additional research sites
By going to any of the major search engines, you can type in the various types of legal structure. You will be provided with links to any of a number of sites where you can gain an instant education on this subject.

CHAPTER 8

Get a Business License

Why do you need a business license? The answer is simple. If your company is going to operate within the law, the city or county in which you will be doing business will require you to obtain a license or permit.

If that business is service-related and performs any portion of its work in other cities outside of its operational center, you may also be required to buy licenses in those cities. For example, if you have a repair service and you make several calls to homes away from the city where your shop is located, you could be obligated to purchase business licenses in the cities you service. For occasional work in another city, you may only be required to obtain a permit for those days on which you perform the work.

Business licenses are serious matters in most cities. They provide a source of revenue for the city or county. Licensing is also a means of controlling the types of businesses that operate within their jurisdictions.

It is true that many businesses are currently operating without licenses. A crackdown in one major city showed that almost 50% of its businesses had failed to produce current business licenses. Fines were imposed and ultimatums issued that failure to secure licenses would result in shutdowns. A business license is inexpensive and lends credibility to your operation. Without one, you, too, run the risk of being discovered and fined and/or barred from doing any business at all.

Location Considerations

In Chapter 5, "Decide on Your Business Location" you learned the basics of selecting the site of your business. Selecting your location and getting your business license is an interactive process. A business license is granted for a specific location and the selection of the location must take into account licensing restrictions.

Contact the City or County Clerk's Office in the city or county where you wish to locate your base of operation. They are an excellent source of information regarding police, fire and health permits needed for your business. Since any business location must fall within the zoning regulations, you may obtain verification from the zoning commission to determine if your business is approved for the location you have chosen. The local business license bureau can also help you with your decision by giving you information on any special restrictions as to types of businesses allowed or disallowed at any location.

If you have decided to locate in a shopping center or industrial area or other commercial location, call the chamber of commerce or city and ask for any publications with listings of facilities available showing number of square feet, price per square foot and other pertinent information.

You can also contact the management of the commercial or industrial complex you are considering and request written information about that location and current availability of leasing space. You should be able to get detailed information as to lease terms, restrictions, traffic patterns and other demographics. Be sure to read carefully and understand all the terms contained in a lease agreement. They vary and may well spell the difference between profit and loss for your business.

Licensing a Home-Based Business

If you have elected to have a home-based business, restrictions may not permit you to get a business license to operate in your city. You may be forced to move your business outside the home or operate outside of the law. If your family happens to be moving and you are a seasoned entrepreneur, you may wish to select your home partly on the basis of whether or not that city's ordinances will allow you to operate your business – or any business – out of your home.

If you are thinking of living in a planned community, don't forget to check into any restrictions that the association may have that relate to business use of your home. Even if the city will allow you to operate your business, the association may preclude that option.

The passage of the Model Zoning Ordinance did much to help protect the legalities of working from home. However, different types of businesses may be subject to special restrictions by the city or county. For instance, a mail-order business may be allowed in your home, but a direct-sales operation may be prohibited. Repair services may be allowed, but only if they do not involve the use of toxic chemicals. Food services will probable be disallowed, but the city may allow you to use your home as an administrative office for your business.

In most cities and planned communities, home-based businesses are not permitted to change the appearance of the neighborhood and, therefore, the use of advertising or equipment that can be viewed from the street may be prohibited. Very often, police or fire inspections will be conducted to see that your business does not violate any of several restrictions.

Doing some diligent ground work ahead of time may eliminate the possibility of selecting a business location only to find later that it was not an appropriate and/or legal choice.

Applying for a Business License

Once you have determined that your business meets all the specific requirements for operation within the city or county you have chosen, you are ready for a trip to the Business License Bureau or the City or County Clerk's Office to legalize your business.

You will be asked to fill out an application. Call ahead to find out what information you will need to complete the application. This will save you time and ensure that you have all of your information on hand when it is needed.

The application is usually fairly simple and will require only general information. You will probably be required to supply such specifics as:

- business name and address

- owner names and contact information

- organization information (manufacturing, wholesale, retail, service)

- type of legal structure

- nature of the business

- expected number of employees

- Federal Employer ID (FEIN) and State Sales Tax No. (Resale)

- expected gross

- other relevant information.

A typical fee for a business may be as little as 10 cents per $1,000 of projected revenues. We have also seen specific license fees applied to certain kinds of business. For instance, in one eastern city the charge for a home business license is $350.

You will probably be asked to submit your completed application together with one year's fee (frequently based on projected gross revenues). Your application will be reviewed by the proper agents and a license will either be issued or refused within a few days.

Business licenses are renewed annually, subject to that city or county's codes and regulations. Your renewal notice will be sent to you, but it is your responsibility to see that you renew should you fail to hear from the licensing agency.

Tech Tip

Business License Applications and Information for many cities is available via the Internet. The example in this chapter was downloaded as a PDF file for Adobe Acrobat Reader by searching the words, Virginia Beach, VA, and following the links to the official site for the city and to its business license information.

You can also research most city websites for other licenses and permits needed for your specific type of business.

Always Post Your Business License

Having a business license is a way of assuring customers that yours is a legal business. Your business license should be posted in a visible place at your business location. If you are exhibiting or selling at a trade show, you should (in fact, may be required to) have a copy on display. A copy of your business license may also be requested to establish accounts with venders or to gain admission to trade and industry shows.

Example Application

To give you an idea of some of the types of information that may be requested, a sample of a business license application can be seen on the next two pages. Applications will vary according to your city or county.

City of Virginia Beach, VA
Business License Application

Commissioner of the Revenue

City Hall
Virginia Beach, VA 23456-9002

Philip J. Kellam
Commissioner

BUSINESS LICENSE APPLICATION

VBgov.com/cor

ACCOUNT NUMBER: _____

THIS SECTION MUST BE COMPLETED BY ALL APPLICANTS
PHOTO IDENTIFICATION IS REQUIRED FOR ALL APPLICANTS.

BEGIN DATE _____, 20 _____   EXPIRES: DECEMBER 31, 20 _____   ☐ SSN (OR) ☐ EIN: _____

INDICATE APPLICANT TYPE: ☐ INDIVIDUAL   ☐ PARTNERSHIP   ☐ CORPORATION   ☐ LLC

APPLICANT NAME: _____   Is the applicant a U.S. Citizen? ☐ Yes ☐ No

BUSINESS ENTITY NAME: _____

INTENDED BUSINESS NAME (TRADE NAME): _____

MAILING ADDRESS: _____

BUSINESS ADDRESS (PHYSICAL LOCATION): _____

TELEPHONE: _____   FAX: _____   E – MAIL ADDRESS: _____

PLEASE ANSWER THE FOLLOWING QUESTIONS AS ACCURATELY AS POSSIBLE:

Do you have any other business entities currently licensed in Virginia? Yes ☐ No ☐   *If yes, please list the owner entity name, trade name and locality:*

_____

_____

Briefly describe your prospective customers: ☐ *individuals* ☐ *other businesses* ☐ *government* ☐ *other:*_____

Briefly describe the nature of your compensation: ☐ *fees* ☐ *commissions*   ☐ *product sales*   ☐ *other:*_____

Will you use any licensed vehicles in your line of business?   ☐ *Yes*   ☐ *No; If yes, provide number of vehicles:* ____   *Indicate percentage of business use:* ____

Will you be conducting this business from your home?   ☐ *Yes*   ☐ *No*

   If yes, submit Restrictions for Use of Home Form with application. Submitted ☐   *If no, submit Fire Code Permit Form with application. Submitted ☐*

Provide a detailed description of business activity: _____

_____

_____

Provide an estimate of gross receipts between beginning date of business and December 31: _____

FOR OFFICE USE ONLY – BUSINESS LICENSE

BUSINESS CLASSIFICATION	NAICS #	BASIS*	TAX	TOTAL**
Trade Name Registered? Yes ☐ Not applicable ☐ Already registered ☐	-0000	* Basis is total gross receipts		** Penalty & interest is applied in accordance with state and city codes

The Virginia Beach City Code Section 18-21 requires the Department of Planning to regulate business activities in accordance with the city's zoning ordinance. The Department of Planning is located in Building 2, Room 100.

Zoning approval by:_____   Date approved:_____

Application
Revised 11.17.2011

City of Virginia Beach, VA
Business License Application
page 2

FOR OFFICE USE ONLY – OTHER STATE/CITY REGULATIONS (BASED UPON BUSINESS ACTIVITY)

AGENCY	LOCATION	REGULATED AREA AND CORRESPONDING CODE		REQUIREMENT	INITIAL
Agriculture	1444 Diamond Springs Rd	Home Bakery/Equipment	☐	Referral to Dept. of Agriculture	
City Attorney	City Hall 2nd Floor	Equipment Rental (18-22.1/18-60)	☐	Valid Insurance Policy	
Clerk of the Circuit Court	Building 10 B	Trade Name Registration (59.1-69)	☐	Proper Identification	
Commissioner of the Revenue	City Hall, 1st Floor	Alcohol Beverage Control (18-49 c)	☐	Proof of License	
		Fats, Oils & Grease Form	☐	Form Completed	
		Massage Therapists (18.5-2)	☐	State Certificate	
		State Contractors License (54.1111)	☐	License, Certification or Affidavit	
		Workman's Compensation (58.1-374)	☐	Form Completed by Contractor	
Criminal Justice Services	Richmond	Detective / Security Services (18-77)	☐	Proof of License	
		Bondsmen (18-65)	☐	Proof of License	
Environmental Health	4452 Corporation Lane	Prepared Foods	☐	Health Dept. Application	
		Body Piercing (18-64.1)	☐	Annual Permit	
		Tanning Booth/Beauty or Barber Shop/Nail Salon (18-56)	☐	Annual Permit	
		Tattoos or Permanent Make-up (18-104.2)	☐	Annual Permit	
Police Department	Building 11, Room 150	Billiards/Pool (18-62)	☐	Police Permit	
		Book & Magazine Agents (18-47) (26-31)	☐	Police Permit & Bond	
		Taxicabs (36-114) (18-105)	☐	Inspection	
		Solicitor/Peddlers (26-26) (18-95)	☐	Police Permit	
		Pawnbrokers (18-76.1 & 18-92)	☐	Police Permit	
		Second-Hand Dealer (18-32 & 18-86)	☐	Police Permit	
Risk Management	Building 22	Towing Operators Insurance (18.55.1)	☐	Valid Insurance Policy	
Treasurer	City Hall, 1st Floor	Carnivals (18-68 a)	☐	Bond	
		Coin Machine Operators (18-72)	☐	Bond	
VDACS	Richmond	Health Spas/Fitness Centers (59.1-296.1)	☐	Proof of Registration	

FOR OFFICE USE ONLY – TRUSTEE

☐ Meals   ☐ Cigarette   ☐ Lodging   ☐ Utility Service

☐ Admissions   ☐ Daily Rental   ☐ Lodging (Flat)   ☐ Utility Consumption

☐ Participatory Sport   ☐ Heavy Equipment Rental   ☐ Sandbridge SSD   ☐ Water (Commercial/Residential)

                                               ☐ Sandbridge SSD (Flat)

Is this business seasonal? ☐ Yes ☐ No   If yes, what months does the business operate? _____   Trustee account added by: _____

Responsible party for trustee tax: _____   Contact Number: _____

THIS SECTION MUST BE COMPLETED BY ALL APPLICANTS

Registered Agent for Business _____   Address _____

Accountant's Name _____   Address _____

Please read and sign the statement below. Signature must be owner of business, an officer of the Corporation or member of the Limited Liability Company.

I, the undersigned, so swear (or affirm) that the forgoing figures and statements are true, full and correct to the best of my knowledge.

Print Name	Sign Name	Title	Date

Notary Signature (if applying by mail)	Commission Expires Date	Date Acknowledged & Sworn

Signature of Deputy	Date

Application
Revised 11.17.2011

Register Your
Fictitious Business Name
(File a DBA)

What is a Fictitious Business Name (DBA)?

A fictitious business name is commonly referred to as a DBA, which stands for "*Doing Business As*". A fictitious name is any business name that does not contain your own name as a part of it. In some states, that means your legal name (frequently first and last).

If you are not a corporation and you plan to conduct business under a fictitious name, you must file a DBA. If you are a corporation, ownership of your name is ensured when you incorporate. Also, if your legal name is considered very common, you may be required to file a DBA.

The following are examples to illustrate this point:

✓ *Peak Rescue - DBA required*

✓ *Glenn's Peak Rescue - DBA required*

✓ *Pinson's Peak Rescue - DBA probably required*

✓ *Glenn Pinson's Peak Rescue - No DBA required*

✓ *Jim Smith's Peak Rescue - DBA may be required (because name is common)*

✓ *Peak Rescue, Inc. - No DBA required (corporation)*

Filing your DBA is one of the first tasks to be undertaken because every other piece of paperwork requires the business name. Your bank will also require a copy of your DBA before they will open a business account under that name. This is the only authorization they have for depositing or cashing checks made out to that business name or written against its account.

Your business name should be free of conflict with names already registered in your area. Find out if a corporation has staked a claim to your name by calling your state's office of name availability.

You may also wish to check the DBA books at the county clerk's office. Finding out at a later date that your name is already legally registered to another business will result in your having to redo all of your paperwork.

 Note: You may wish to refer back to Chapter 3, "Start Branding Your Business", for further information on researching your business name.

If You Fail to File

Registering a business name is very important for your own protection as well as for compliance with the law. Registration of that name gives you exclusive rights to it. It also keeps others from filing the same or a similar name and capitalizing on the hard work and investments you have made in your business.

Unfortunately, there are individuals who lurk in the shadows waiting for just such an opportunity. I had a business owner in one of my classes who had built a very successful electronics firm. However, he failed to file a DBA. Someone else discovered his error, filed under his business name and offered the option of either paying to buy the name back or ceasing to do business under that name. The business owner refused to pay the blackmail and chose to re-establish under a new name. However the continuity of his business was set back and he lost a large amount of business trying to re-establish under the new name.

The time and money required to file a DBA is very small compared to the benefits you will derive from becoming the legal owner of your business name.

How to File a DBA

Assuming that you have chosen a fictitious name, it is time to register it (or file it) with the city or county in which you are doing business. This is a two-part process: first you must file that name with the county clerk and; second you must publish your fictitious name through a general circulation newspaper.

1. **Filing with the county clerk.** You will have to file a fictitious business name statement with the City or County Clerk. You may do so in person at the office or by mail — or you may be able to file online. If you file by mail, a certified copy of the filed statement will be sent to you. Fees for filing a DBA vary, but generally run between $15 and $50.

2. **Publishing your fictitious business name.** Your fictitious business name must be published in a general circulation newspaper in your area within 30 days of filing your statement. Some counties require the fictitious name to appear in four consecutive editions. When your fictitious name is published, the newspaper will send you a copy of the publication and issue a Publication Certificate. It is your responsibility to see that the certificate is also filed with the County Clerk. The fee is generally between $20 and $75.

 Note: Some newspapers will file the publication certificate for you after publishing. This will save you a trip to the County Clerk's office. Others publish only and require that you do your own filing. As you can see above, there is also a lot of variation in the fees that are charged for this service. Local newspapers frequently charge less and are easier to access.

It would be wise for you to do some calling to various newspapers and ask the following questions:

- Do you publish new fictitious business names (DBAs)?

- What is your charge for the publication of a DBA?

- Do you (the newspaper) also file the proof of publication with the City or County Clerk? If so, is there an additional charge?

- What information do I need to bring with me? Do you need a copy of my filled in application for a Fictitious Business Name?

Tech Tip

Access Applications via the Internet

Fictitious Business Name Statement forms can be filled in and processed via the Internet from the official websites of most counties. Alternately you may have the option to download and fill in the application. You can send it in by mail or take it in person to the responsible agency.

The example at the end of the chapter was filled out online and then downloaded by inputting the following keywords in the search box: Fictitious Name Statement, Orange County, CA. We then followed the links to the Orange County, CA official website and subsequently chose links for filing a Fictitious Business Name.

Renewal of Your DBA

You will be required to renew your DBA at certain intervals -- such as every five years. You will be notified by the filing agency when it is time to renew. Again, it is your responsibility to know when it must be done and to protect yourself by inquiring if you do not receive your renewal notification. Renewal does not require republishing, but will involve a fee to the City or County Clerk. You can renew your DBA in person by going to your City or County Clerk's office. Alternatively, you can print out and complete the renewal application form, and then mail it to the City or County Clerk's office. The form will be mailed back to you with the official City or County Clerk's seal.

Warning!

There are many companies that keep track of expiring DBAs and send you official-looking notices(with forms) to refile. They also build in a hidden fee for themselves. Refiling is very simple. Be sure your notice is the official one from the County Clerk. If, for some reason, you do not receive notification from the County Clerk before your DBA is due to expire, it is your responsibility to contact them and request a renewal form.

Example Forms

The next two pages contain examples of a Fictitious Business Name Statement and a Proof of Publication that has been filed in the State of California with the County of Orange (pages 67 and 68).

Fictitious Business Name Statement
Orange County, California

HUGH NGUYEN
CLERK-RECORDER
12 CIVIC CENTER PLAZA, ROOM 106
POST OFFICE BOX 238
SANTA ANA, CA 92702-0238   FBN01151707

FICTITIOUS BUSINESS NAME STATEMENT

THE FOLLOWING PERSON(S) IS (ARE) DOING BUSINESS AS:

1.	Fictitious Business Name(s) Ace Sporting Goods (optional) Business Phone No.

1A	[x] New Statement [ ] Refile - list previous No. [ ] Change

2.	Street Address, City & State of Principal place of Business (Do not use P.O. box or P.M.B.) City State Zip Code County 12345 Edwards Street Anytown, California 93456 ORANGE

3.	Full name of Registered Owner (If Corporation, enter corporation name) If Corporation / LLC State of Incorporation or organization John Robert Smith Res. / Corp. Address (Do **NOT** use a P.O. Box or P.M.B) City State Zip Code 2345 Newstreet Drive Anytown Californ 93456 INFORMATION ONLY. THIS FORM WAS NOT FILED.

4.	(CHECK ONE ONLY) This business is conducted by: [ ] a trust [ ] a state or local registered domestic partnership [x] an individual [ ] a general partnership [ ] a limited partnership [ ] an unincorporated association other than a partnership [ ] a corporation [ ] a Limited Liability Partnership [ ] co-partners [ ] a married couple [ ] a joint venture [ ] Limited Liability Co.

5.	Have you started doing business yet? [x] Yes Insert Date: 02/07/2014 [ ] No	Notice: This Fictitious Business Name Statement expires five years from the date it was filed in the Office of the County Clerk-Recorder. The statement expires 40 days after any change in the facts is made other than a change in the residences address of the registered owner. A new Fictitious Business Name Statement must be filed before either expiration. When ceasing to transact business under an active Fictitious Business Name Statement, Abandonment shall be filed. The filing of this statement does not of itself authorize the use in this state of a Fictitious Business Name in violation of the rights of another under federal, state or common law (see section 14411 et seq., Business and Professions Code).

6.	If the registered owner is NOT a corporation, sign below:
	(See Instructions on the reverse side of this form)
	
	Signature: _____
	
	John Smith
	_____
	(Type or Print Name)
	
	I declare that all information in this statement is true and correct. (A registrant who declares as true any material matter pursuant to Section 17913 of the Business and Professions Code that the registrant knows to be false is guilty of a misdemeanor punishable by a fine not to exceed one thousand dollars ($1,000).)
		If the registered owner is:
		    a corporation, an officer of the corporation signs below.
		    any type of partnership, the general partner signs below.
		    a limited liability company, a manager or an officer signs below.
		
		_____
		Limited Liability Company/Corporation/Partnership Name
		
		_____
		Signature and Title of Officer/Manager or General Partner
		
		I declare that all information in this statement is true and correct. (A registrant who declares as true any material matter pursuant to Section 17913 of the Business and Professions Code that the registrant knows to be false is guilty of a misdemeanor punishable by a fine not to exceed one thousand dollars ($1,000).)
		
		_____
		Print Name of Officer/Manager or General Partner

These fees apply at time of filing (Please provide a self-addressed, stamped, return envelope if mailed):
Filing fee $23.00 for one business name
$7.00 for each additional business name
$7.00 for each additional partner after first two

Example
Proof of Publication Certificate

PROOF OF PUBLICATION
(2015.5c.c.p.)

STATE OF CALIFORNIA

COUNTY OF ORANGE

I am a citizen of the United States and a resident of the County aforesaid; I am over the age of eighteen years, and not a party to or interested in the above-entitled matter. I am the principal clerk of the printer of the the Orange Big News, a newspaper of general circulation printed and published weekly in the City of Orangetown, County of Orange, and which newspaper has been adjudged a newspaper of general circulation by the Superior Court of the County of Orange, State of California, under the date of April 14, 1987, Case Number A-62222, that the notice of which the annexed is a printed copy (set in type not smaller than nonpareil), has been published in each regular and entire issue of said newspaper and not in any supplement thereof on the following dates, to wit:

3/07 3/14 3/21 3/28

all in the year 20 14.

I certify (or declare) under penalty of perjury that the foregoing is true and correct.

Dated at Orangetown, California, this.....28th.........day

of.................March................., 20.14....

Arlene S. Herzog
Signature

ORANGE BIG NEWS
533 W Harper
Orangetown, California 92622

OCH FORM NO. 0023-6/78-621-2M

This space is for the County Clerk's Filing Stamp

FILED
MARCH 28 2014
PETER M. JONES, County Clerk
By_____DEPUTY

Proof of Publication of

FICTITIOUS BUSINESS NAME STATEMENT
F5987003

The following person(s) are doing business as:
Ace Sporting Goods
12345 Edwards St.
Anytown, CA 93456

1. JOHN R. SMITH
2345 Newstreet Drive
Anytown, CA 93456
This business is conducted by an individual.
The registrant commenced to transact business under the fictitious business name or names listed above on February 7, 2014.
Published: Orange Big News
March 7, 14, 21, 28, 2014

PROOF OF PUBLICATION

F-_____

Obtain a Seller's Permit

Anyone who purchases items for resale or provides a taxable service must obtain a seller's permit number. This number is required in all states where sales tax is collected.

Applying for a Seller's Permit

Information regarding sales tax and getting a seller's permit can be obtained through your state's Department of Revenue or Board of Equalization. Applications can be made online using the electronic registration system or in person at your local state offices. You can also send your application in by mail. After filling out and submitting your application, a seller's permit will be issued to you. It can take up to two weeks to get your permit. There is no fee required to obtain a seller's permit. However, some states may require a security deposit that will be used at a later date to cover any unpaid taxes, if the business closes.

 Example Form. An example of an Application for a Seller's Permit for the State of Texas is included in the last part of this chapter (page 75).

Purpose of a Seller's Permit

A sales tax is imposed upon retailers for the privilege of selling tangible personal property at retail within a state. The retailer, not the customer, is the person liable and responsible for paying the sales tax. Consequently, every seller engaged in the business of selling a tangible product or providing a taxable service in a state where sales tax is collected is required to hold a seller's permit for the purpose of reporting and paying their sales and use tax liability. The seller's permit is more commonly referred to as a ***resale tax number.***

Because of the complications involved in the sales tax process, it may be difficult to determine which of your products and services will be taxable. You may request information sheets from the State Department of Revenue or your local State Board of Equalization that will explain the sales tax regulations on your particular type of business. You may also request a ruling to determine whether or not your product or service is taxable under a particular circumstance. Later, you must be sure to keep abreast of any changes that are made regarding the taxing of sales for your particular industry.

Your request must be on the basis that your business will be selling taxable items to your customers or providing a taxable service. Any other reason for your request will be grounds for denial. For example, many food services are not taxable unless they are provided at an event that charges admission. Therefore, a resale tax number would not be warranted.

 Note: *If your business will operate in multiple places, you will need a separate sellers permit for each location. Each permit will have the same taxpayer identification number, but different outlet or sequence numbers.*

State Laws Vary

The laws governing the collection of sales tax in any state can be complex. They also vary from state to state. There have been many attempts to come up with a uniform sales tax system that would be fair to the consumer and, at the same time, guarantee collection of tax on all applicable sales. Individual states are also working to ensure that out-of-state companies servicing their companies in state and selling their products through local outlets are collecting and reporting sales tax.

Some states have laws that require buyers of out-of-state goods to pay a use tax – a law that would increase state revenues significantly, but is difficult to monitor or enforce.

Finally, there is the never-ending debate regarding the legalities of selling via the Internet without collecting or reporting sales tax. Brick and mortar businesses feel that selling tax-free via the Internet gives online sellers an unfair advantage. Internet sellers think they should not have to collect sales taxes. According to a 1992 Supreme Court Ruling, online retailers are not required to collect sales tax unless they have a physical presence in the state.

Misuse of Your Seller's Permit

Once you have been issued a resale tax number, it is imperative that you use it only for the purpose for which it was intended. Many tax numbers have been used to avoid paying sales tax on business-related purchases as well as tax on personal items. Purposeful misuse of a seller's permit has long been a laughing matter with many users. If you get caught, however, it may cease to be something to brag about. Most states are expanding their efforts to catch offenders. The penalties for misuse are serious and may involve a heavy fine and/or jail sentence. The rule of thumb is: If you do not intend to resell your purchase through your business, do not use your resale number in order to buy it without paying sales tax.

At this point, it is only fair to say that there is some validity to using your resale number to purchase wholesale. Many wholesalers do ask you to file a resale card with them before they will sell to you at wholesale prices. However, this does not mean you are not required to pay sales tax if you are not purchasing for resale. It may only be a means of adding credibility as a business owner. In fact, if the seller does not collect from you at the time of the sale, you will be required to include the purchase in you periodic sales tax report and pay the sales tax at that time.

Resale Certificate

If you are purchasing goods for resale, the supplier or manufacturer will ask you to fill out a resale certificate that may be kept on file to validate selling to you on a tax-free basis. By the same token, when you sell to another dealer, you must also have him or her fill out a resale card for your files. If the state later questions your nontaxable sales, you will have documentation as to why you did not collect tax on the sale. Pads of resale certificates may be purchased at almost any office stationery supply store.

 Example Form. A copy of a Texas Sales and Use Tax Resale Certificate can be found at the end of this chapter (page 78).

Reporting Sales Tax

As previously stated, the purpose of a seller's permit is to provide the state with a means of collecting sales tax. To accomplish this, the sales tax must be accounted for by the final seller and sent to the state along with a report of the sources of those taxes. For this reason, the seller must keep accurate records on the types of sales made and the amount of sales falling within each of the following categories:

- Gross sales
- Purchase price of property you bought without paying sales tax and that you used for purposes other than resale

- Sales to other retailers for purposes of resale
- Nontaxable sale of food products
- Nontaxable labor (repair and installation)
- Sales to the U.S. government
- Sales in interstate or foreign commerce to out-of-state consumers
- Bad debt losses on taxable sales
- Other exempt transactions

Note. Sales tax rates may vary from county to county. When you are selling out of your local area, you will collect sales tax based on the current rate in that area. You will also be required to keep an accurate record of those sales. In many cases a portion of your state's sales tax may be designated as belonging to a transit district, special assessment, etc. For instance, the State of California has many transit districts that are allocated one half of one percent to support their mass transportation systems. Therefore, a retailer from Los Angeles selling at a trade show in San Francisco will have to report the amount of those sales so the fund may be properly divided by the state agency.

The state will require you to file a quarterly report in which you summarize your sales for the period. If your taxable sales are unusually small, you may only have to report annually. If they are excessive, you may be required to place a bond and report monthly.

The reporting forms will be sent to you by the Department of Revenue or State Board of Equalization. You must complete the report and mail it to the state, along with your check in the amount of sales tax due, by a certain date (usually at the end of the month following the reporting period).

A note of caution about responsibility for reporting
If you do not receive a report form in the mail, it will be your responsibility to call the Department of Revenue and request that officials send you one.

When you receive this report, you will also receive a tax information sheet with featured articles on sales tax regulations and crackdowns. Take the time to read it carefully, especially the information that may pertain to your particular industry.

Failure to properly report may result in loss of your resale privilege as well as the more serious penalties mentioned above.

 Sample Report Form: A copy of a Texas Sales and Use Tax Return form is included on page 77. The form for your state will probably be similar.

Tech Tip

Keeping Track of Sales for Easy Sales Tax Reporting

Sales tax reporting can be a long and tedious process—or you can do it at the click of a mouse! The secret is to utilize your accounting software to generate the information you need for your report to your local sales tax authority.

In order to generate the right information, you will have to think in terms of sales tax reporting when you set up your chart of accounts. This means that revenue accounts will need to be divided not only by the types of products and services you sell, but also according to their applicability to sales tax reporting responsibility.

Example: If you are in the business of selling two taxable products and your state requires sales information on taxable sales, out-of-state sales, sales to resellers, and sales tax payable, revenue accounts in your chart of accounts could be set up as follows:

Taxable Sales	Out-of State Sales	Reseller Sales
Product #1	Product #1	Product #1
Product #2	Product #2	Product #2

When deposits are made, they are "split" deposits and revenues are allocated among the appropriate accounts. The sales tax will be automatically calculated on taxable sales.

The Benefit: At any given time, you will be able to generate a report that will give you the numbers you need for your state's sales tax report.

Sales Tax Flowchart

The Sales Tax Flowchart will help you to understand the chain of sales tax responsibility. As illustrated, the final seller has the responsibility to collect sales tax (if applicable) and to report and pay taxes collected to the State.

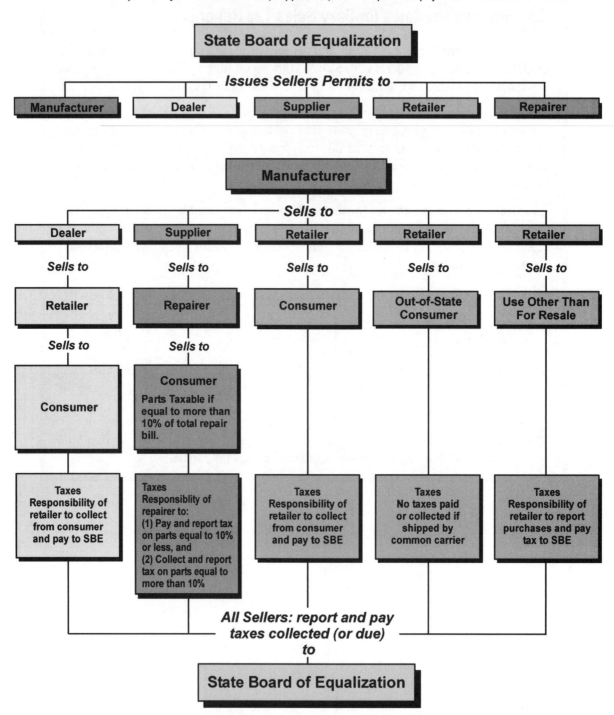

Note: When a manufacturer sells to an out-of-state retailer who, in turn, sells to a consumer in that state, the sales tax is collected by the retailer and paid to that state. If mailed directly to the out-of-state consumer (via common carrier), no sales tax is collected or paid on the product.

Application for a Seller's Permit

page 1

SUSAN COMBS

PRINT FORM CLEAR FORM

Texas Application

- **Sales Tax Permit • Use Tax Permit • 9-1-1 Emergency Communications**
- **Prepaid Wireless 9-1-1 Emergency Service Fee • Fireworks Tax**
- **Off-Road, Heavy Duty Diesel Powered Equipment Surcharge**

TEXAS COMPTROLLER *of* PUBLIC ACCOUNTS

ENTITY INFORMATION

If you are a sole proprietor, start on the next page, Item 10 –

1. Business Organization Type
   - ☐ Profit Corporation (CT, CF)
   - ☐ Nonprofit Corporation (CN, CM)
   - ☐ Limited Liability Company (CL, CI)
   - ☐ Limited Partnership (PL, PF)
   - ☐ Professional Corporation (CP, CU)
   - ☐ Other *(explain)* ____
   - ☐ General Partnership (PB, PI)
   - ☐ Professional Association (AP, AF)
   - ☐ Business Association (AB, AC)
   - ☐ Joint Venture (PV, PW)
   - ☐ Holding Company (HF)
   - ☐ Business Trust (TF)
   - ☐ Trust (TR) Please submit a copy of the trust agreement with this application.
   - ☐ Real Estate Investment Trust (TH, TI)
   - ☐ Joint Stock Company (ST, SF)
   - ☐ Estate (ES)
2. Legal name of corporation, partnership, limited liability company, association or other legal entity
3. Federal Employer Identification Number (FEIN)........ __ - _______
   (assigned by the Internal Revenue Service for reporting federal income taxes)
4. ☐ Check here if you DO NOT have an FEIN.
   3
5. Please list any current or past 11-digit Texas Taxpayer Number for reporting any taxes or fees to the Texas Comptroller of Public Accounts. ....
6. Have you ever received a Texas vendor or payee number (Texas Identification Number/TIN)? .... ☐ YES ☐ NO If "YES," enter number...
7. Enter the home state or country where this entity was formed and the formation date........ State/country Month Day Year

   Enter the home state registration/file number........ File number

   Non-Texas entities: enter the file number if registered with the Texas Secretary of State........ File number
8. If the business is a corporation, has it been involved in a merger within the last seven years? .... ☐ YES ☐ NO If "YES," attach a detailed explanation. *(See instructions.)*
9. Please list all general partners, officers or managing members ***(Attach additional sheets, if necessary.)***

   Name | Phone *(area code and number)* ( ) -

   Home address | City | State | ZIP code

   SSN - - | FEIN - | Percent of ownership ____ % | County *(or country, if outside the U.S.)*

   Position held: ☐ General Partner ☐ Officer/Director ☐ Managing Member ☐ Other ____

   Name | Phone *(area code and number)* ( ) -

   Home address | City | State | ZIP code

   SSN - - | FEIN - | Percent of ownership ____ % | County *(or country, if outside the U.S.)*

   Position held: ☐ General Partner ☐ Officer/Director ☐ Managing Member ☐ Other ____

Proceed to Item 15 if you are not a sole proprietor –

Application for a Seller's Permit

page 2

AP-201-2
(Rev.7-11/16)

Texas Application for
Sales Tax Permit and/or Use Tax Permit

Page 2

You have certain rights under Chapters 552 and 559, Government Code,
to review, request and correct information we have on file about you.
Contact us at the address or numbers listed on this form.

• TYPE OR PRINT   • Do NOT write in shaded areas.

If you are a sole proprietor, start here –
(If you are NOT a sole proprietor, skip to Item 15, below.)

SOLE PROPRIETORS

10. Legal name of sole proprietor *(first, middle initial, last)*

11. Social Security number (SSN) .... ☐ Check this box if you DO NOT have a Social Security number (SSN).

12. Please list any current or past 11-digit Texas Taxpayer Number for reporting any taxes or fees to the Texas Comptroller of Public Accounts. ....

13. Have you ever received a Texas vendor or payee number (Texas Identification Number/TIN)? .... ☐ YES   ☐ NO   If "YES," enter number ....

14. Federal Employer Identification Number (FEIN), if you have one, assigned by the Internal Revenue Service for reporting federal income taxes. ....

All applicants continue here –

BUSINESS

15. Mailing address of **taxpaying entity** - This address is for an individual or the party responsible for making decisions regarding address changes and banking changes and who is responsible for overall account management and account security. Please provide complete address including suite, apartment or personal mailbox number. Indicate whether the address is on a street, avenue, parkway, drive, etc., and whether there is a directional indicator (e.g., North Lamar Blvd.).

Street number and name, P.O. Box or rural route and box number   Suite/Apt. #

City   State/province   ZIP code   County (or country, if outside the U.S.)

16. Daytime phone number *(area code and number)* ....

17. FAX number *(area code and number)* ....

18. Mobile/cellular phone number *(area code and number)* ....

19. Business website address(es) ....

20. Contact person for business records
Name   Email address

Street address *(if different from the address in Item 15)*   Phone number *(area code, number and extension)*

21. Alternate contact person for business records
Name   Email address

Street address *(if different from the address in Item 15)*   Phone number *(area code, number and extension)*

22. Name of bank or other financial institution *(Attach additional sheets, if necessary.)*

☐ Business   ☐ Personal

23. If you will be accepting payments by credit card and/or through an online payment processing company, enter the name of the processor.   Merchant identification number (MID) assigned by processor

Sales and Use Tax Return

Comptroller of Public Accounts FORM 01-114 (Rev.4-13/37)

DDDD

b. ■

PRINT FORM   CLEAR FIELDS

Instructions in English

Texas Sales and Use Tax Return

a. ■ 26100

See instructions, *Form 01-922.*

Page 1 of ____

- Do not staple or paper clip.
- Do not write in shaded areas.

c. Taxpayer number

d. Filing period

e.

f. Due date

Taxpayer name and mailing address

g.

- Blacken this box if your mailing address has changed. Show changes by the preprinted information. _____ 1. ■
- Blacken this box if you are no longer in business. Write in the date you went out of business. _____ 2. ■
- Blacken this box if one of your locations is out of business or has changed its address. _____ 3. ■

You have certain rights under Chapters 552 and 559, Government Code, to review, request and correct information we have on file about you. Contact us at the address or phone numbers indicated in the instructions.

h.

i.

Return MUST be filed even if no tax is due.

j. Are you taking credit to reduce taxes due on this return for taxes you paid in error on your own purchases? *(Blacken appropriate box)* _____ YES 1 / NO 2

k. Did you refund sales tax for items exported outside the U.S. based on a Texas Licensed Customs Broker Export Certificate? *(Blacken appropriate box)* _____ YES 1 / NO 2

If you answered yes to either question j or k, you must complete Form 01-148 and submit it with your return.

I. NO SALES - *If you had zero to report in Items 1, 2 and 3 for ALL locations for this filing period, blacken this box, sign and date this return and mail it to the Comptroller's office.* ▶ 1 ■

PLEASE PRINT YOUR NUMERALS LIKE THIS 0 1 2 3 4 5 6 7 8 9

6. Physical location (outlet) name and address *(Do not use a P.O. box address.)*   Outlet no. ■

1. TOTAL SALES *(Whole dollars only)* ■

2. TAXABLE SALES *(Whole dollars only)* ■

3. TAXABLE PURCHASES *(Whole dollars only)* ■

4. Amount subject to state tax *(Item 2 plus Item 3)* ■

5. Amount subject to local tax *(Amount for city, transit, county and SPD must be equal.)* ■

7. AMOUNT OF TAX DUE FOR THIS OUTLET *(Dollars and cents)* *(Multiply "Amount subject to tax" by "TAX RATE" for state and local tax due)*

TAX RATES

X ■ 0.062500 = 7a. State tax *(include in Item 8a)*

X ■ = 7b. Local tax *(include in Item 8b)*

■ 26180	■ STATE TAX - Column a	■ LOCAL TAX - Column b
8. Total tax due *(from all outlets or list supplements)*		
9. Prepayment credit ___ −		
10. Adjusted tax due *(Item 8 minus Item 9)* =		
11. Timely filing discount (0.005) −		
12. Prior payments −		
13. Net tax due *(Item 10 minus Items 11 & 12)* =		
14. Penalty and interest *(See instructions)* +		
15. TOTAL STATE AND LOCAL AMOUNT DUE *(Item 13 plus Item 14)* =	15a. Total state amount due	15b. Total local amount due

01-114 (Rev.4-13/37)   DDDD

Mail to: **Comptroller of Public Accounts** P.O. Box 149354 Austin, TX 78714-9354

■ T Code   ■ Taxpayer number   ■ Period

26020

16. TOTAL AMOUNT PAID *(Total of Items 15a and 15b)*

Taxpayer name

n. ■

I declare that the information in this document and any attachments is true and correct to the best of my knowledge.

sign here ▶   Taxpayer or duly authorized agent   Date   Daytime phone *(Area code & number)*

Make check payable to: **STATE COMPTROLLER.**

Resale Certificate

 Comptroller 01-339
of Public
Accounts
Form   (Rev.4-13/8)

| SAVE A COPY | CLEAR SIDE |

Texas Sales and Use Tax Resale Certificate

| Name of purchaser, firm or agency as shown on permit | Phone *(Area code and number)* |

Address *(Street & number, P.O. Box or Route number)*

City, State, ZIP code

Texas Sales and Use Tax Permit Number *(must contain 11 digits)*

Out-of-state retailer's registration number or Federal Taxpayers Registry (RFC) number for retailers based in Mexico

(Retailers based in Mexico must also provide a copy of their Mexico registration form to the seller.)

I, the purchaser named above, claim the right to make a non-taxable purchase (for resale of the taxable items described below or on the attached order or invoice) from:

Seller: _____

Street address: _____

City, State, ZIP code: _____

Description of items to be purchased on the attached order or invoice:

_____

_____

_____

Description of the type of business activity generally engaged in or type of items normally sold by the purchaser:

_____

_____

The taxable items described above, or on the attached order or invoice, will be resold, rented or leased by me within the geographical limits of the United States of America, its territories and possessions or within the geographical limits of the United Mexican States, in their present form or attached to other taxable items to be sold.

I understand that if I make any use of the items other than retention, demonstration or display while holding them for sale, lease or rental, I must pay sales tax on the items at the time of use based upon either the purchase price or the fair market rental value for the period of time used.

I understand that it is a criminal offense to give a resale certificate to the seller for taxable items that I know, at the time of purchase, are purchased for use rather than for the purpose of resale, lease or rental, and depending on the amount of tax evaded, the offense may range from a Class C misdemeanor to a felony of the second degree.

| **sign here** ▶ Purchaser | Title | Date |

This certificate should be furnished to the supplier.
Do _not_ send the completed certificate to the Comptroller of Public Accounts.

Establish a Business Bank Account

The selection of the bank with which you will do business should be undertaken with a great deal of consideration. Banks vary greatly in the services they offer, as well as in the charges for those services. You will want to think about such factors as service charges, transaction fees, interest rate paid on accounts, holding periods on deposited funds, locality, hours of operation, loan policies, online banking, merchant credit services, etc.

Basic Information to Think About

The following will give you some basic information to think about when you are deciding which bank to select:

1. **Have you already established a personal relationship with your banker?** If you already know the key management and personnel at your bank, you will have a head start when you need special consideration.

2. **What kinds of loan programs are available through the bank?** Does this bank make business loans or does it confine itself to personal financing? Is the bank a participating SBA guaranteed lender? Does it participate in any other programs aimed at helping small business owners? Either now or sometime in the future, you may need additional funds to operate or expand your business. It is easier to go to your own banker than to have to approach an unknown lender.

3. **Does the bank have merchant credit card services?** You may find that your business will be more profitable if you can offer VISA, MasterCard, Discover or American Express services to your customers. We are now living in an age in which buyers of products and services do not carry cash and expect to pay with a credit card. The merchant now has the advantage of being able to instantly authorize the purchase and have funds deposited to the business account within 24-48 hours. The bank generally charges the merchant between 1.5% and 3% (plus or minus) of the purchase amount for the service, but having the capability may significantly increase your sales.

    Instant online credit card authorization has made selling over the Internet an important source of business income. If your bank offers online merchant accounts, you will need to be sure that your shopping cart system will work seamlessly with the bank's authorization and deposit system.

    When considering credit card processing machines, think about the nature of your business. If you will be operating from a business office, you will need a standard credit card processing machine. If you run a business that requires you to be out in the public, such as a food truck, you will want to consider a mobile credit card processing system. BluePay is one of the most popular mobile systems to consider. It allows a merchant to process credit cards on their iPhone or iPad. Services are also available that allow you to process credit cards online.

     Warning! *If you are considering credit card services, do some careful planning before you commit your business to a program. You will get calls from lots of third-rate companies wanting to set you up with merchant services. Their salespeople are trained in the "fast sell". They thrive on signing up new small business owners. However, the costs to you can far outweigh the advantage gained by having the service. Ask for (and review in writing) all of the costs involved in setting up the service and the monthly charges for maintaining the service. Also determine the cost, should you decide to discontinue services after a period of time.*

    One company rented their "Brand-X" machine for $10.00 per month. However, if you quit in six months, you would owe $1,750 for the machine. The irony -- the "Brand-X" machine cost only $200 to $300 to purchase from most reputable banks. Also, most banks will rent and update machines for a few dollars a month with no cost to you should you discontinue your merchant account. Watch for non-refundable application fees and other miscellaneous charges — as well as restrictions on types of purchases that you may accept (telephone orders, etc.)

4. **What does the bank offer in the way of a business bank account?** Is there a holding period on your deposits? Can it be waived? What are the service charges? What is the policy regarding returned checks? Do they have overdraft protection? What other kinds of accounts does the bank have that will allow you to divert temporary funds where they can earn more and still stay liquid? Is there a monthly transaction limit? What type of statements and information is provided to you about your account?

5. **Is the bank a federal depository bank?** If your business has employees and you are paying any of those employees over a certain amount, you will have to deposit funds in a separate depository account on a regular basis. It will be more convenient if you can do all of your banking in the same place.

6. **What additional services are available at the bank?** Do they have branches available in several locations? What hours are they open? Do they have 24-hour ATM services? Do they have safe deposit boxes? Do they have notary services? Is the bank an SBA Lender? What other services does the bank have that might be required by your business?

7. **Does the bank provide online banking services?** Many banks now offer online banking services. You can quickly access account information, make deposits, transfer money, pay bills and more – all from the convenience of your computer.

   Some banks also offer mobile banking, which allows you to access and manage your business account on a mobile device. A new mobile feature offered by some banks is text banking. Using your phone, you can check account balances or transfer funds between accounts. This service is typically free for business online banking users.

It might be beneficial for you to spend some time calling banks to gather information. It can also be helpful to talk to other business people and see which banks they use and whether or not they would recommend them for your needs. You can also check out banks on the Internet. There are online services such as www.bankrate.com that allow you to compare multiple banks for features such as service charges, transaction fees, etc.

Separate Business and Personal Finances

Many times, a new business owner will be tempted to run business finances through personal accounts. Do not mix the two by trying to use the same checking account for your home and business. It is imperative that you keep your personal and business finances separate.

The IRS does not look kindly on businesses that "co-mingle" personal and business monies. The fate of more than one small business owner has been determined based on this issue during an audit – and not in the business's favor. Mixing business and personal finances will also cause you many problems with your accounting and tax computations. The accounting process becomes very complicated and creates a confusing paper trail when you use business funds for personal obligations and vice versa.

Business accounts are necessary for credibility when dealing with other businesses. Many of your vendors will not accept a check unless it is preprinted with your business name and address. It may also be difficult, if not impossible, to establish an open account with a supplier or wholesaler if you do not have a business bank account.

Open a Checking Account

The first account you will need is a checking account. The following are some pointers that should help you to make needed decisions:

1. **Your DBA is required.** If your business name is an assumed one, you cannot open a checking account under that name without first having filed a DBA as discussed in the previous chapter. The DBA is a means for giving the bank authority to deposit and cash checks under your fictitious name. It should be noted here, that banking policies at most financial institutions preclude offering interest-bearing checking accounts unless your name is part of the company name. If you have filed a DBA, be sure to take your form with you when you open your checking account. The bank will require a copy for their records.

2. **Select a checkbook style.** When you open your checking account, you will be asked what style of checks you wish to order. You will have to decide between the book type and the wallet type. The smaller one is easier to carry, but the book type is the better choice. It will allow you to record more information about your checking transactions – information that can be invaluable during accounting procedures. There is a personal desk type checkbook that is smaller than the business size and still very adequate. You will have to ask about this particular style as it is not included under business checkbook selections.

3. **How many checks should you order?** Be sure to think ahead as to your needs before deciding on the number of checks to order. Reordering of checks can be costly. Start with a minimum order. In most cases there will be some change that needs to be made before long. You may get a new telephone number or decide to add or subtract a name.

Tech Tip

Computer Checks Can Save Time and Money

Many small businesses use software for their accounting (such as *QuickBooks Pro*). These software applications give you the option of printing your checks directly to computer check forms that are purchased from various office supply retailers.

The accounting software also maintains the check register and copies of the checks you have written. If you regularly send checks to the same payee, the address will automatically be printed on the check in a position that will align with windowed envelopes, saving you the time required to address envelopes.

4. **Arrange for overdraft protection.** It is best if you always maintain a healthy checking account balance for your business. However, there may be times that you have to make an unexpected purchase or that you make an arithmetic error that will cause your account to be overdrawn. Providing coverage for these instances can save you time and embarrassment.

5. **Get an ATM/Debit Card for your account.** This will allow you to deposit or withdraw funds during non-banking hours and it will allow you to access your funds at remote locations. Using a debit card is also the easiest way to pay for company purchases when you do not want to charge them.

Additional Accounts You May Wish to Consider

In addition to your checking account, you may also wish to consider other types of accounts such as savings, money market, CDs, etc. The interest rates are the lowest on regular savings accounts. They are usually higher on money market, C.D and other special accounts. Some have limits and withdrawals before specified dates may impose penalties. Some are more liquid and a limited number of checks can be drawn on the account without penalty as long as you maintain a minimum balance. The earnings are usually proportionate to the length of time for which your funds are committed.

Conclusion

Keep in mind that all accounts need not be at the same financial institution. However, it only makes sense that the amount of business you do with any one bank will be directly proportional to the benefits you will derive from it. Be sure to look at the stability of the bank you are considering. You will want to feel secure that tomorrow morning when you wake up that your funds will still be available to you.

A good banking record, along with the establishment of rapport with management and personnel of your bank, may get you special concessions. For example, the hold on your deposits may be waived if the management so desires or notary services may be extended for free as a courtesy. If you already have a bank with which you have been satisfied, you may wish to deal where you already have the advantage of being known by them as a valued customer.

Banking is serious business. Selection of the right bank and the right kinds of services will be a definite asset to your business.

 Worksheet: On the next page, you will find a filled-in example worksheet entitled *"Choosing a Bank".* It will help you to see how you can compare advantages and disadvantages of the financial institutions you are considering.

Choosing a Bank Worksheet

	Name of Potential Financial Institution		
	A. City Bank	**B. Home National Bank**	**C.**

1. Have you already established a Working relationship with
    a. the management?
    b. the personnel?
	Manager:
	J. Smith
	Personnel: great
	Tellers: friendly
		Manager:
		L. Jones
		(service-oriented)	

2. What kind of business bank accounts are available?	business checking + CDs, etc.	business checking + CDs, etc.	
3. Does this bank offer merchant credit card services?	no	yes	
4. Does the bank participate in business loan programs?	real estate only.	preferred SBA lender	
5. Is the bank a federal depository bank?	yes	yes	
6. Is the bank a stable financial institution?	27 years old	22 years old	
7. How many branches does the bank have?	7	103	
8. Is the location of the bank convenient for your business?	yes	yes	
9. What are the bank's hours of operation? Are they open on Saturday?	9-3 Mon-Thurs 9-6 F; 10-1 Sat	9-3 Mon-Thurs 9-6 F; 10-3 Sat	
10. Will the bank place a holding period on your deposits?	3 days	waived, except for 2nd party	
11. What will it cost you to have a business checking account?	free w/$500 min.	free w/$750 min.	

12. What other services does the bank have?
    a. online banking?
    b. safe deposit?
    c. notary public?
    d. electronic transfer?
    e. other?
	a. no
	b. yes (free)
	c. no
	d. yes
	e. ATM
		a. yes
		b. yes
		c. yes
		d. yes
		e. ATM; seminars	

13. What is your overall feeling about the bank?	nice bank, but doesn't fill needs	seems to be stable and fills all needs	

Plan for Your Insurance

At some point during the formation of a business, the question of insurance needs will necessarily arise. In fact, if you are writing a business plan, insurance will be one of the topics you cover in the Organizational Plan and interpret into costs in your Financial Documents.

Today's world of rapidly-expanding technology goes hand-in-hand with a society steeped in lawsuits. The most innocent business owner can find himself/herself involved in legal actions against the business. In addition to liability, there are many other insurance considerations such as fire, flood, earthquake, theft, auto, workers' compensation, health insurance, etc. that need to be addressed during the period of ownership.

The above are all concerns during the lifetime of the owner. What happens if the owner dies? There may be a need for life insurance and a buy-sell agreement to safeguard your beneficiaries.

Shopping for an Insurance Company

Shopping for an insurance company is like shopping for a bank. Careful research will help you to determine what company can best serve your needs and provide you with affordable coverage.

Call your current insurance company and see what they have to offer in the way of business insurance. Check with several other independent agents that you know or that have been recommended by your business associates. Ask them to discuss your business with you and recommend an insurance package that will give you the best coverage for the least number of dollars.

If your insurance needs are unique because of your type of business, you can look through your trade journals. Many times, business insurance companies will advertise in those journals, especially if the type of insurance they are advertising is not available with major companies.

For example, food industries have their own unique considerations. Coverage is very expensive and they must usually seek a specialized insurance company.

What are the Basic Kinds of Insurance?

As stated previously, there are many different kinds of insurance. In fact, there are so many kinds of insurance that most small business owners would go bankrupt if they were paying for the highest protection possible in all areas.

Most small businesses buy what is generally known as a Business Owner's Policy (BOP). The policy generally includes property, liability and criminal coverage and various specialty coverages needed by the business. The advantage of a Business Owner's Policy is that it usually costs less than if each of the types of coverage were purchased separately.

In the following pages, we will address some of the most basic types of insurance that should be considered. There are two general categories under which all business insurance falls. They are "Property & Liability Insurance" and "Life & Health Insurance".

Property and Liability Insurance

Property insurance covers buildings and their contents against losses due to such things as fire, theft, wind, earthquake, flood, etc. Some of those risks may be specifically excluded in your policy and may require the purchase of additional policies (earthquake, flood, ground water, etc.).

Liability protects a business when it is sued for injury or property damage to third parties. This type of coverage pays damages related to bodily injury, property damage and personal injury. These policies carry certain limits on the maximum that will be paid by an insurer for specific kinds of occurrences.

1. **General Liability.** Regular liability insurance pays for claims brought against your business because a customer or other person (the owner and employees are **not** covered) was injured on the business premises.

   It is a good idea to have this kind of liability insurance in force when you open your business. It's not uncommon for a customer to fall and file a lawsuit that will be difficult for you to pay. Regular liability insurance also generally includes coverage for damage to property that you do not own or rent for your business (such as a water leak from your property that damages property in an adjoining business).

2. **Property Damage Liability.** This policy covers damage to property that you lease or rent and property that belongs to your customers.

3. **Fire Insurance.** Protects your premises, fixed assets and inventory against fire. Fire liability covers fire damage to property you are leasing or renting.

4. **Earthquake Insurance and Flood Insurance.** If you live in an area that has a likelihood of being damaged by an earthquake or some other serious act of nature, you may be wise to obtain special insurance coverage. The premiums are usually high, but well worth it if you are hit by a disaster.

5. **Theft.** Protects against burglary and robbery at your place of business.

6. **Fidelity Bonds.** Protect a company against employee dishonesty.

7. **Surety Bonds.** Provide monetary compensation in the event a contractor fails to perform specific acts or complete work within the agree-upon period of time.

8. **Boiler and Machinery Coverage.** Protects against breakdowns of equipment that is essential to the business (for example: computer and telephone systems, production equipment, etc).

9. **Product Liability.** Protects against claims filed by anyone using your product after it leaves your business. In most cases you will be liable even if your product has not been used correctly. The cost of product liability is generally in proportion to the volume of sales and the degree of hazard involved.

10. **Workers' Compensation.** Most states require that an employer provide insurance that cover all employees in case of disability or illness related to the workplace. You can call you insurance carrier to get workers' comp or contact the State Employment Department for information on state-operated insurance. Although this is insurance that will cover employees, it is paid in full by the employer. The amount charged for workers' comp varies according to the number of employees you have and also according the degree of risk involved. If you are in a high-risk industry, the premiums can be very high.

    Workers' comp is one the most controversial issues today. Due to a high rate of fraud and the trend toward stress claims, many employers have literally been forced out of business because of their inability to pay increasing insurance costs. Many businesses have instituted safety-in-the-workplace programs and intervention programs to cut down on claims. There is also an emphasis being placed on fraud detection. To relieve stress-related claims, legislation is pending that will place a percentage value that must be attributable to those claims.

11. **Business Interruption Insurance.** Coverage can generally be added to your regular policy that will pay you an amount approximately equal to what you would have earned in the event that you have to close your business while your premises are being rebuilt or repaired. You can also buy **overhead insurance** that will pay operating expenses during that time. There are also additional types of coverage that can be purchased to cover business operations under separate circumstances such as hospitalization.

12. **Vehicle Insurance.** Most states require that you carry a certain amount of liability coverage if you are going to operate a vehicle. Your regular insurance carrier will probably be able to insure your business vehicle. If you use the vehicle for both personal and business purposes, you will need to see that a rider

is attached that will cover the business use. If you have employees that will be driving your business vehicles, be sure you have coverage that will be in effect in case of an accident.

13. **Umbrella Insurance.** A liability policy that protects the business against catastrophic losses. It provides for extra protection for accidents involving a number of people. It also extends liability limits on auto policies (usually in increments of $1,000,000).

Life Insurance

One of the concerns of spouses and beneficiaries of a business owner is the question of what happens to that business if the owner dies. With the death of an owner comes responsibility for providing for the disposition of the business. You may need life insurance and some kind of a buy-sell agreement. If you die without having made necessary provisions, your beneficiaries may be forced to sell or dismantle the business to pay the estate taxes that might be due. If, instead, you have planned ahead and have an adequate life insurance policy, your beneficiaries can use the insurance proceeds to pay the estate taxes and allow the business to continue to operate. If they decide to sell the business, they will still be left with something to sell.

Life Insurance can be an especially important consideration for a partnership. In many community-property states, if a partner dies, his or her spouse now owns that share of the business and has the authority to make that partner's decisions. This can create a situation that may be extremely unsatisfactory to either the surviving partner or the spouse. That is why it is important to have a partnership agreement that spells out what happens if one partner dies. A life insurance policy can be included as part of the partnership agreement with a provision designating that the policy payoff be used by the surviving partner to buy the deceased partner's share of the business.

The purchase of individual permanent life insurance by business owners can fund a deferred compensation program on a non-tax qualified basis allowing owners to set aside money for retirement or pay a death benefit to the surviving spouse. Key Life insurance can also be purchased to cover key people whose death might affect the company's sales and profitability. A term policy would pay to help replace the loss of the person. A permanent key person life insurance policy would also accumulate cash value to help fund that person's retirement plan.

Health Insurance

Health insurance has long been the nemesis of the self-employed. The costs are often prohibitive and the coverage poor. Many group policies are available through trade associations and insurance companies specializing in small business, but most of the premiums are fairly high.

The best advice we can give is to tell you that you should explore every avenue and continue to get quotes on new coverage being made available. If you have the opportunity to keep purchasing health insurance from a previous company you worked for, that may be your best avenue.

Employee Benefits

This is another issue requiring some important decisions if you are a small business owner. Your employees certainly need health insurance and are probably entitled to expect it. However, the prohibitive costs of group health plans have made it almost impossible for the small business owner to provide it for employees even if they wish to do so. Costs continue to rise due to a number of factors such as complexity of treatment, unnecessary care, stress claims and defensive medicine, and the implementation of the Affordable Care Act.

There has been much controversy about this area in the government sector. The Affordable Care Act coverage mandate requires businesses with 50 or more employees to provide health care plans for all employees working an average of 30 hours a week.

In order to get away from paying employee benefits many companies, including major corporations, are hiring personnel through temporary agencies. There are both state and IRS rules that apply to non-employee (or contract) services. Be aware that these restrictions exist and be sure that you are properly classifying your workers. Classifying an employee as contract services when he or she is actually an employee carries some heavy tax penalties.

Work with an Insurance Professional

Insurance coverage is a complicated subject and cannot be covered adequately in the space we have allotted here. We are not in the insurance business and therefore do not wish to have you consider this as advice in regard to the insurance you should purchase or from whom you should purchase it.

The material covered in this chapter is for the purpose of acquainting you with some general information regarding types of insurance that you should consider. See your insurance professional to determine what is available and what would be best for your business and for you. It would also be wise to consult with your tax planner, especially in the area of life insurance.

After You Have Your Information

When you have received information from several insurance companies regarding coverage and costs, you will have some last decisions to make. You will have to look at your insurance needs in terms of immediate needs and long-term protection. Know what is required by the federal and state government, by your lender or the title holder of your vehicles, etc. Also decide what kinds of insurance you will have to have to protect your business. Divide your insurance needs down into those that are required, necessary and desirable. Decide what you can purchase now, what you will purchase when financing allows and what you will put on hold until a future time.

 To Help You with Your Insurance Shopping
We have provided an insurance fact sheet on the next page that will help you when you are comparing insurance companies for coverage and costs. There is also an Insurance Update Form Worksheet for your use included in the blank forms in Appendix II at the back of the book (page 182).

Insurance Fact Sheet

I. Types of Business Insurance

A. Property and Liability

General Liability
Property Damage Liability
Fire Insurance
Earthquake/ Flood Insurance
Theft
Fidelity Bonds
Surety Bonds
Boiler and Machinery Coverage
Product Liability
Workers' Compensation
Business Interruption Insurance
Vehicle Insurance
Umbrella Insurance

B. Life and Health

Life Insurance

Disability Insurance

Employee Benefits

Group Insurance

Retirement Programs

Overhead Expense

II. Figure Out Your Insurance Priority Shopping List

A. Immediate Protection that is:

1. Required _____
2. Necessary _____
3. Desirable _____

B. Long-Term Protection that is:

1. Required _____
2. Necessary _____
3. Desirable _____

III. Key Points

A. Insurance is and should be a major factor to consider in forming a business.

B. First year property & liability premiums will sometimes be higher than other years due to frequency of misstatement by the insured and high risk to the insurance company.

C. Choosing your insurance agent/broker (consultant and buyer) is one of the most important decisions you can make.

IV. Five Steps to Prevent Your Business from Failing Due to an "Insurable" Cause

A. Recognize risks you will be facing.

B. Follow guidelines from covering them economically.

C. Have a plan in mind.

D. Get advice from experts.

E. Insure your business now !

Using the Internet

The Internet is a powerful resource that has transformed several areas of business. It can make your business more productive and profitable. The Internet is a vast collection of interconnected computers and networks. It allows your computer to communicate with any other computer, as long as both are connected to the Internet, allowing you to access millions of websites on what is known as the World Wide Web.

The Internet can help you streamline business activities and reduce expenses. Some of the ways you can use it are to:

✓ *Communicate with current and potential customers as well as vendors*

✓ *Look for information, products, and services that you need*

✓ *Develop a website to distribute information and/or sell your products and services*

✓ *Store and share information*

Connecting to the Internet

The first thing you will have to do before getting on the Internet is to establish a connection. In order to do that, you will need an Internet service provider, or ISP. An Internet service provider is a company whose service gives you access to the Internet. To begin with, you will have to sign up for an account with them, just as you do for other services such as telephone.

Internet service providers are typically phone companies such as AT&T, SBC, Verizon, and CenturyLink. They provide a DSL or fiber optic connection. They may also be TV providers, such as Comcast, Time Warner, Cox Cable, and Charter Communications that give you a cable or satellite connection. To connect to the Internet you will need a modem. This may be included as part of the setup hardware from your Internet service provider when you sign up for an account or you may have to buy one separately. If you plan to share Internet access with multiple computers, you will also need a router. In some cases, a modem and router are combined in one device.

Establishing Your E-mail Account

Now that you have an Internet service provider and are connected to the Internet, you can set up your e-mail. You can do that by using the e-mail tools provided by your Internet service provider. Alternatively, you can use the free services that are offered by various e-mail providers such as Hotmail, Yahoo, and Google. Logging on to your e-mail service will allow you to compose and send e-mails as well as retrieve any new and old messages.

To set up your e-mail, you will have to click the sign up as a new user option and provide the necessary personal information, create a user name and password, provide an answer to a security question that will be used in the event you forget your password, and agree to the "Terms of Service" as designated by the e-mail service provider. If the user name selected is being used by another user, you will be prompted to select another name. The user name you choose together with the e-mail provider's extension will then become your e-mail address (e.g., johnjones123@hotmail.com).

Communicating with Customers and Vendors

Now that you are connected to the Internet and have set up your e-mail, you will have the ability to send and receive e-mail communication and surf the World Wide Web.

Using e-mail to communicate with your customers and vendors has a significant advantage over snail mail (sending letters, etc.). It speeds across the information super highway and does not require paper, envelope, or postage. Email provides instant communication allowing for timely decision making. Using your e-mail, you will also be able to send documents and pictures in the form of a file attachment. Your e-mail can also be used as an Internet marketing tool because it is fast, easy to use, and inexpensive. It will allow you to deliver your message directly to your customers or prospective customers.

Be aware that you will also receive a lot of unwanted e-mail, commonly know as "spam." You can minimize spam by using filters provided by your e-mail service provider.

Another communication method you can use is instant messaging, or IM. A component of many e-mail services, instant messenger runs in the background while you are online and alerts you when you have a message or someone wants to talk to you. Instant messenger also allows you to set up a temporary chat room if you want to talk to two or more people. It also allows you to pass files and move data quickly.

Video chat is a medium you can use to hold meetings with customers and vendors. This will save your business time and money as you will not have to pay any travel related expenses. The most popular video chat services are Skype and ooVoo. It is free to set up an account, and with both services, you can connect multiple people in different locations, if necessary. GoToMeeting is a paid service that you can also use to hold meetings. In addition to video conferencing, it allows the organizers to share their screens with attendees so that they can see the information that is being discussed. Mac devices have an application called FaceTime. FaceTime allows you to conduct a video call with another person who is also on a Mac device.

Searching for Information on the Internet

The Internet can be used to search for information of all types. This includes general information, specific subject matter, and information about a person or people.

Search Engines

The most commonly used resources for searching for information are search engines. A search engine is a company with specialized tools that will allow you to search the World Wide Web for information on any topic. Each search engine has its own web address.

> **What is a Web Address?** – *Much like the physical address for your office, each site on the Internet has a specific web address called the Uniform Resource Locator (URL). The URL appears in the address box of your browser when you visit a website. A web address looks like this: http://www.business-plan.com. The company's domain name is "business-plan.com." It identifies the specific address (or location) of the website on the World Wide Web.*

Your search request will consist of keywords related to what you are looking for. Keywords are words or short phrases that you type into a search box that will enable the search engine to produce web pages with the information you are looking for. Upon receipt of your search request, the search engine goes out and searches the World Wide Web for matches. It then returns the results to you on web pages that it assembles with descriptive lists and direct links to web addresses, where you can access the requested information.

 Note: Be specific when selecting keywords. You may also have to try several keywords or combinations of words before you find what you are looking for.

Metasearch Engines

A metasearch engine is a search tool that will send your search request to other search engines and/or databases and compile the results in a single list. This enables you to enter one search criteria but have access to multiple search engines simultaneously. This will save you from having to search several different engines separately. Examples of metasearch engines include info.com, search.com, and metacrawler.com.

Industry Specific Websites

In addition to using search engines to find the information you are looking for, you can use specific industry websites or portals. With few exceptions, large corporations, industry associations, organizations, schools, newspapers, magazines, political groups, etc. have their own websites.

Many of the addresses can be accessed by putting the name of the company or group in the address section of your web browser and selecting "Go." For instance, you can reach United Airline's website by inputting "United Airlines" in the address bar, which will either take you to the company's site or to direct links to the site.

Tech Tip

Find Information Via Search Engines

The most popular search engines (in alphabetical order) are:

- **Ask**   www.ask.com
- **Bing**   www.bing.com
- **Google**   www.google.com
- **MSN**   www.msn.com
- **Yahoo**   www.yahoo.com

The most popular metasearch engines alphabetically) are:

- **Info**   www.info.com
- **Metacrawler**   www.metacrawler.com
- **Search**   www.search.com

Newsgroups (Forums)

You can also use newsgroups or forums. These are industry- or topic-related electronic bulletin boards where you can post a message, reply to a message, or read messages posted by others.

Newsgroups allow you to discuss or view discussions on any subject matter that you are interested in. For example, if you are interested in computers and would like to discuss the latest computer technology, you can go to a technology newsgroup. If you have a question about a particular topic, you simply post it on the board and other users will respond. Be aware that newsgroup responses do not take place in real time. When you post a message, you will have to return from time to time to the newsgroup to check for responses.

One of the most common places to find newsgroups is on Google. You can access the newsgroup site at http://groups.google.com. To access a newsgroup, click on one of the industries listed on that site and then find the group of your choice. Alternately, you can enter keywords in the search box to bring up a list of related newsgroups.

Web Directories

A web directory is another resource you can use for searching for information. It is not a search engine. A web directory lists websites by category and subcategory. The scope of most directories is general in nature, providing sites from an array of categories. There are some niche directories that list websites in specific categories. Examples of web directories include IPL2 and Infomine. IPL2 features a searchable, subject-categorized directory of authoritative websites. Infomine is a comprehensive virtual library and reference tool for academic and scholarly Internet resources.

Buying Products and Services Online for Your Business

The Internet is a virtual marketplace and an important channel for buying products and services.

Shopping Online

Instead of going to a store and walking down the aisle, you are in a virtual store where you shop and complete your purchase by using your credit card. Unlike a brick-and-mortar store, the Internet offers 24-hour access to millions of merchants and manufacturers and their products and services. You will also benefit from the convenience, selection, and product information available from shopping online.

However, shopping online may present a problem. You will need to sort through the large volume of information and choices. Do not despair; you have help. Some websites offer online price comparison services.

Examples of online price comparison services include Pricegrabber.com, MySimon.com, Shopping.com, and Shopzilla.com. These websites allow you to research and compare products from various vendors for price, features, customer reviews, etc. Using comparison-shopping services will help you to make better-informed shopping decisions.

- **Products.** Once you have found the merchant of your choice, you will have to search through their online catalog for the specific products you are looking for. As you find the products you wish to purchase, you add them to your online shopping cart. When you indicate that you have finished shopping, typically by hitting the "Check Out" button, your purchases are added up. You are then given some choices for shipping options and those costs are added to your total purchase. Your credit card information is entered and processed and you will be provided with an order confirmation and follow-up emails.

- **Services.** Looking for travel deals, cell phone services, or business plan consulting? These are only three of a vast number of services that can be accessed via the Internet. Using the Internet, you can learn about the company, the services it offers, and in some cases view samples of its work. It is very important that you conduct due diligence on the company providing the service, especially if it is located in another city or state. This includes getting and verifying references and talking to past customers about their services and satisfaction levels. Be sure to do this prior to retaining the services of a company or individual online. This will prevent unnecessary harm to you down the road.

Does Your Company Need a Website?

The Internet gives merchants the ability to reach large audiences of potential customers. However, some businesses may not find it cost-effective to maintain a website. For example, if you have a local business where all communication with potential and current customers needs takes place on a personal level, then you may not need a website. So, the first thing you will have to do is to decide whether or not you need a website.

How Will Your Business Use a Website?

You have decided that you do need a website for your business. Before you develop the site, you need to map out the goals that you want to accomplish. Websites can be used for providing information and/or selling products and services.

- **Information Website.** You can provide information aimed at educating consumers on a particular subject matter. The information can be provided in the form of content on the website, newsletters, articles written by industry experts, and links to other industry related websites. In addition to industry information, your site can provide information about your company. This will give you more exposure than a regular brochure.

  You can also use the website to provide product specifications and technical information. For example, a dentist might use a website to list services and post pertinent articles and information that would prove helpful to current and prospective patients. In essence, the information would boost confidence in the practice and act as a selling tool for its services. Website content can be updated instantly, making it easy to provide site visitors with the most current information.

- **Selling Website.** A website enables you to showcase your products and services, thereby stimulating sales to current and prospective customers. To sell products on the Internet, you will have to develop a secure e-commerce website.

  An e-commerce site contains web pages with your products and a shopping cart feature. The shopping cart allows the online consumer to select the product and "buy now" by inputting shipping and credit card billing information at a secure (encrypted) web page location. The credit card charge is authorized within seconds. The customer gets a printable receipt and the seller receives and fulfills the order. The best part is that the sale can take place at the customer's convenience at any time—day or night.

To sell online, you will need a merchant account. A merchant account gives you the ability to accept credit card payments online. Merchant accounts can be set up through banking institutions or private companies. A merchant account has several fees associated with it. Fees will vary depending on the merchant account provider you choose. You may have to pay an application fee and setup costs. Some service providers waive these up front fees and costs. Once you are up and running, you will be responsible for a monthly service fee. Your company will also be charged a transaction fee that typically ranges from 1.5% to 3% (plus or minus) on each customer's purchase. For example, if a customer buys a product for $100, the merchant account provider will take $2 to $3, leaving you $97 to $98.50.

Developing Your Company's Website

Building a successful company website is a major effort requiring a lot of time, talent, and dollars. You will have to choose a domain name, find a host, design your site pages, and then figure out how to drive traffic to your site.

Choosing a Domain Name

Your first task will be to choose, research availability for, and register a domain name for your website. Your domain name is the descriptive name you choose for your site combined with one of the common extensions (.com, .net, .org, etc.).

Most companies use their company name or a name that is descriptive of their products or services. Dot-com (.com) is the most desirable extension for a private business, followed by dot-net (.net). Other extensions are particular to schools (.edu), government agencies (.gov), organizations (.org), etc.

When you have decided on the domain name you would like for your company's website, you will have to research the name availability and gain ownership of the name for a period of time by registering it with InterNIC for a modest fee.

There are several sites that you can use for this service. Among the most frequently used are http://www.godaddy.com, http://www.web.com, http://www.networksolutions.com, and http://www.justhost.com.

Finding a Website Host

You will have to find a company that will host your site. A web hosting company provides a service (hosting) that allows you to post the pages of your website to the Internet. Hosting companies (such as Verio) have the technology to keep your site up and running 24 hours a day. For their services, you will pay a hosting fee. Hosting fees are typically paid on a monthly basis or an annual basis. Fees will vary according to the size of your website and the specialty services that you require.

Designing Your Website

You will have to decide whether you will design and develop your own web pages or use the services of a professional web developer. If you decide to do it yourself, there are several software applications that you can use (e.g., WordPress and Adobe Dreamweaver have been two of the most popular applications). There are also service providers that offer to help you produce instant websites. Be aware that these opportunities will result in generic websites that do not provide for the customization necessary for a real working business site.

If you can afford it, the best answer is to hire a professional website developer to design your site and to act as webmaster to maintain it for you. Your job would be to work directly with the site developer to provide needed information and to see that the web pages reflect the vision of your company that will best serve its current and potential customers.

Driving Traffic to Your Website

Just having a website will not generate traffic. You will have to develop strategies to drive visitors to your website. Be aware that you will be inundated with solicitations from companies claiming that they can get you millions of customers. Most of them do not produce results.

There are several valid ways to drive traffic to your website.

- **Search Engine Registration.** This accounts for a large volume of traffic driven on the Internet. Your site should be submitted periodically with all of the major search engines. In addition, you can pay for positioning of your website information on some search engines (e.g., Yahoo and Google), on a pay-per-click basis. Under this setup, you pay the search engine every time a customer clicks through to your website. Typically, your credit card is charged at the end of the month for the number of "click throughs." Placing paid ads on the Internet is also a great way to drive traffic to your site and increase sales. Make sure you are getting the most out of your paid ads by tracking the sales from your ad campaign.

  To generate substantial traffic to your site through search engines, make sure that it has a high ranking. We recommend that you work with an Internet consultant who will submit your website to search engines and use various techniques to improve your ranking. The consultant will work with you to place meta tags on the pages of your site. Meta tags are codes that provide a summary of the content on a web page as well as keywords related to the page.

- **Link Exchanges.** You can drive traffic to your site through links. This means you can establish an alliance with other websites that will place a link to your site on their own site. You may also carry a link to their website on your site. This is called a link exchange. In exchanging links with other websites, look for companies with whom you share something in common.

- **Affiliate Programs.** You can also drive traffic by developing an affiliate program. Affiliate programs will also serve to increase sales. Affiliates promote your products and services on their website. For any sales that are generated through the affiliate's site, you pay a commission agreed to with the affiliate. Having an affiliate program creates an additional sales force, one that you do not have to account for on your payroll.

- **Banner Ads.** Online, you can place banner ads on other websites. You can measure the effectiveness of your banner ad by the number of clicks you get on your site from that ad. This is referred to as click-through ratio. Rich media (or multimedia) banner ads are believed to be three to five times more effective than standard ads, because they can be designed to be more creative and interactive. You need to understand your target market and their needs before you invest in this option.

- **Marketing Materials.** Listing your website on all your marketing materials, such as brochures and business cards, is another way to drive traffic to your site.

- **YouTube Advertising.** YouTube has become one of the most popular and creative ways to promote your business. It allows you to showcase information about your company through the use of videos. Examples include videos featuring product information that will help solve a problem or videos of your business events that allow non-attendees and other pertinent business associates to share in the experience. Be sure to include links to your website in all of your videos.

- **Blog.** Creating your own blog is an excellent way to promote your products and services because it allows you to show yourself as an expert in a particular subject matter. A blog can be set up and run directly from your website. This will also help your site with search engine rankings. Make sure the content you put out is directly related to your products and services and is posted frequently.

- **Email marketing.** You can reach out to existing and potential customers by email on a regular basis through the use of email marketing services such as iContact and Constant Contact. Both are paid services. They allow you to track the number of emails sent, emails opened, and click throughs to your website. They also keep track of people opting out as they may consider your emails to be spam. Be sure to get permission before adding people to your mailing list.

- **Forum Marketing.** While forums are a great resource when searching for information, they can also be valuable in marketing your business and getting traffic to your website. Because each forum has its own specific area of focus, you will receive targeted traffic. You can gain traffic to your site by contributing helpful information on forums.

- **Social Media.** Developing a social media presence will greatly enhance your business and help to drive traffic to your website. Research shows that almost two-thirds of people looking for a product or service in their community are more likely to use a business that displays information on a social media site. Some of the social media sites you can use for your business include LinkedIn, Facebook, Twitter, Pinterest, and Instagram.

Information Storage and Sharing

It is very important to back up your information as computers are subject to random mishaps, file corruption, or hacking. This can be done by storing your data on an external hard drive. However, you can also store your files and information on the Internet (typically called "in the cloud"). This will also allow you to access your information anytime and anywhere you have Internet access. There are several websites that offer this service for free while others offer it for a monthly fee.

By giving access to other users, you can quickly share files and information using these online storage services. You can also access your information on the Internet by creating an FTP site. FTP stands for File Transfer Protocol. Each authorized user will be able to login to the site and upload or download information, as necessary. To access the information, you will need some kind of an application, and one of the most common ones is called WS_FTP. In addition to storing general information, your FTP site will store all the files related to your website, allowing you to easily access them for edits and updates.

Tech Tip

Information Storage and Sharing Resources

The most popular resources (in alphabetical order) are:

- **Box**   www.box.com
- **Carbonite**   www.carbonite.com
- **Dropbox**   www.dropbox.com
- **Flip Drive**   www.flipdrive.com
- **Google Drive**   www.google.com
- **SkyDrive**   www.skydrive.live.com
- **Xdrive**   www.xdrive.com

Summary

In today's world, you can access the Internet from anywhere with a wireless connection, commonly known as Wi-Fi. Many places now offer free Wi-Fi service, allowing you to work on your business from anywhere. You can connect to the Internet using mobile devices such as cell phones (smartphones) and tablets or your laptop. We hope this chapter has helped to introduce you to the benefits available through the use of the Internet for your business. The important thing is for you to decide what will or will not benefit your business. Choose well and the Internet can help you reach your goals and enhance your profitability.

Determine Financing Needs for Your Business

When you are planning to start a new business (or expand your current operation), four very important questions arise relating to finance.

In order to make an intelligent decision on a timely basis, you will need to address all four of these questions. If you fail to do so, the lack of sufficient and ready capital can quickly lead to business failure.

> ✓ *Do you need financing?*
>
> ✓ *If you need outside financing, how much do you need and when will you need it?*
>
> ✓ *What are the sources of funding available to meet your needs?*
>
> ✓ *How much will it cost?*

Do You Need Financing?

The first step is to ask yourself some questions that will help you to make the right decision – questions that will help you to realistically understand your financial needs and keep you from making costly errors that may ultimately bankrupt a potentially viable business.

To determine whether or not you will need outside financing, some of the questions you might ask yourself are:

1. **Have I written a business plan** so that I can make financial decisions based on achieving the desired goals for my business? If you haven't written one, do so.

2. **Am I willing to risk my own money on my venture?** What are the risks? What are my own sources of available capital? If you are not willing to take a risk, don't expect someone else to.

3. **Do I really need additional financing** or do I just need to manage my present cash flow more effectively?

4. **What do I need the money for?** If I borrow, can I realistically project increased revenues? If so, when will those increased revenues justify the debt?

How Much Money Do You Need – and When do You Need It?

If you have decided that you will need additional financing, you will then need to carefully assess your needs and determine not only the amount you need, but when you will need it. Many business owners overestimate or underestimate their capital requirements and/or do not time their financing to the best advantage. Either can lead to serious problems.

The first thing you need is a realistic *business plan* and one that you intend to follow as closely as possible. The only way to look at every aspect of your business is through the planning process. It will force you to create an organizational plan and a marketing plan and quantify your concepts through the development of projected financial statements whose numbers can then be analyzed and used in the decision making process. Those projections give you an educated estimate of your financial needs and tell you when they will most likely occur. Your business plan will answer such questions as:

- What are my most critical needs?

- If I need the money for immediate operating capital, how much will I need to operate my business until it becomes self-sustaining?

- If I need the money to buy fixed assets for my business, has my research shown that I can reach the target market that will justify the purchase of those assets? If not now, when would be the optimum time to add those assets?

- If I need the money for marketing, what are the most effective ways to reach my target market? How much will it cost to advertise? Will the increased marketing be reflected in even higher increases in revenues? According to my industry trends, what are the best selling periods and when will I need financing in order to have the lead time to advertise for the best results?

What are The Sources Available to You?

I get calls almost every day asking for direction to sources of start-up capital. Sources of financing available to prospective and expanding businesses fall into two broad categories, which we will discuss in the remainder of the chapter:

- **Debt financing** (dollars borrowed)

- **Equity financing** (ownership dollars injected into the business)

Debt Financing

Debt financing is generally obtained from one of two sources. It can come either from a non-professional source such as a friend, relative, customer or colleague or from a traditional lending institution such as a bank, commercial finance company or, on special occasions, directly from the U.S. Small Business Administration (SBA).

1. **Friends or Relatives.** Borrowing from a friend or relative is generally the most readily available source, especially when the capital requirements are smaller. This is frequently the least costly in terms of dollars, but may become the most costly in terms of personal relations if your repayment schedule is not timely or your venture does not work out. This avenue should be approached with great caution!

2. **Angel Programs.** For smaller business owners, women and minorities, there has been a growing trend toward the development of "Angel" programs through business organizations and companies specializing in small business. Individuals and small companies that want to invest smaller amounts in promising businesses are linked with those companies and the two decide whether or not the loan will be made. This avenue is still relatively new, but holds even more promise for the future.

Tech Tip

Search the Internet for Angel Investors

Several organizations exist that serve as an intermediary between Angel investors and business owners. Business owners can submit their business plans, which will then be matched and submitted to prospective investors with funding interests in specific plans.

For a list of intermediary networks and lists of Angel investors, use the following key words in the search box on the Internet: **Angel Investors**

3. **Traditional Lending Institutions.** Banks, savings and loans and commercial finance companies have long been the major sources of business financing, principally as short-term lenders offering demand loans, seasonal lines of credit and single-purpose loans for fixed assets.

   You should be aware of the fact that almost all lending institutions are strict about collateral requirements and may reasonably require established businesses to provide one-third of the equity injection and start-ups up to 50% or more. Again, as a borrower, you will be required to have a business plan with adequate documentation demonstrating a projected operating cash flow that will enable you to repay (on time) the loan with interest.

4. **SBA Guaranteed Loans.** The SBA guaranteed loan program is a secondary source of financing. This option comes into play after private lending options have been denied. The SBA offers a variety of loan programs to eligible small businesses that cannot borrow on reasonable terms from conventional lenders in the amount needed without governmental help. Most of the SBA's business loans are made by private lenders and then guaranteed by the Agency. Though it may not necessarily be easier to be approved for an SBA guaranteed loan, the guaranty will allow you to obtain a loan with a longer maturity at better repayment terms and interest rates, thereby reducing your monthly payments and the initial loan burden.

   a. **7(a) Guaranteed Loan Program.** This is the SBA's primary loan program. You can use a 7(a) loan to: expand or renovate facilities; purchase machinery, equipment, fixtures and leasehold improvements; finance receivables and augment working capital; refinance existing debt (with compelling reason); finance seasonal lines of credit; construct commercial buildings; and/or purchase land or buildings.

      Loan amounts of $150,000 or less receive an SBA guaranty as high as 85%. All other loans receive a 75% SBA guaranty. Currently, the maximum amount for a loan guaranty is $3,750,000 (75% of $5 million). The average size loan is $337,730 with a maximum loan amount of $5 million. The 7(a) loan program is available to businesses that operate for profit and qualify as small under SBA size standard criteria.

      You submit a loan application to a lender for initial review. If the lender approves the loan subject to an SBA guaranty, a copy of the application and a credit analysis are forwarded by the lender to the nearest SBA office.

      The SBA looks for good character, management expertise, financial resources to operate the business, a feasible business plan, adequate equity or investment in the business, sufficient collateral, and the ability to repay the loan on time from the projected operating cash flow.

      After SBA approval, the lending institution closes the loan and disburses the funds; you make monthly loan payments directly to the lender. As with any loan, you are responsible for repaying the full amount of the loan.

Generally, liens will be taken on assets financed by SBA proceeds, and the personal guarantee of the principal owners and/or the CEO are required. The borrower must pledge sufficient assets, to the extent that they are reasonably available, to adequately secure the loan. However, in most cases, a loan will not be declined by SBA where insufficient collateral is the only unfavorable factor. The lender sets the rate of interest: loans under 7 years, maximum prime +2.25%; 7 years or more, maximum 2.75% over prime; under $50,000, rates may be slightly higher. The length of time for repayment depends on the use of proceeds and the ability of the business to repay: usually up to seven years for working capital and up to 25 years for real estate.

b. **CAPLines.** Eligibility and interest rate rules are the same as for 7(a) guaranteed loans. It is for the financing of assets. The primary collateral will be the short-term assets financed by the loan. SBA will guarantee up to 75% of loans above $150,000 (85% on loans of $150,000 or less). There are four short-term working-capital loan programs for small businesses under CAPLines: (1) The Contract Loan Program, (2) The Seasonal Line of Credit Program, (3) The Builders Line Program, and (4) The Working Capital Line of Credit Program. In addition to financing assets, loan proceeds from the programs can be used for working capital, construction costs, service and supply contracts or purchase orders, or working capital lines of credit.

c. **International Trade Loan Program.** Applicants must establish either that the loan proceeds will significantly expand existing export markets or develop new ones, or that the applicant is adversely affected by import competition. SBA can guarantee 90% of an amount up to $2,000,000 in combined working-capital and fixed-asset loans. The lender must take a first-lien position on items financed. Only collateral located in the United States and its territories and possessions is acceptable as collateral under this program. Additional collateral may be required including personal guaranties, subordinate liens or items that are not financed by the loan proceeds. The proceeds of the loan may not be used for debt repayment. Fees and interest rates are the same as for 7(a).

d. **Export Working Capital Program (EWCP).** This program is for exporters seeking short-term working capital. The SBA will guarantee 90 percent of the principal and interest, up to $1,500,000. When an EWCP loan is combined with an International Trade Loan, the SBA's exposure can go up to $1.75 million. The EWCP uses a one-page application form and streamlined documentation, and turnaround is generally within ten days. You may also apply for a letter of prequalification from the SBA. Businesses must have operated for the past 12 months, not necessarily in exporting, prior to filing an application. Interest rates are not regulated by the SBA and the lender is not limited to the rates specified for regular 7(a) loans.

 ### *Streamlined Applications and Approvals (SBA Loan Guaranty)*

There are several options available to lenders that help streamline delivery of the SBA's loan guaranty.

1. **SBA Express.** This program makes capital available to businesses seeking loans of up to $350,000 without requiring the lender to use the SBA process. Lenders use their existing documentation and procedures to make and service loans. The SBA guarantees up to 50 percent of an SBA Express loan. Your local SBA office can provide you with a list of SBA Express lenders.

2. **Patriot Express Pilot Loan Program.** The Patriot Express Pilot Loan Program is for business start-up or expansion and it adopts many of the SBA Express Loan guidelines including streamlined documentation. To be eligible, the business must be owned and controlled (51% or more) by an eligible veteran and member of the military community. Offered by a wide network of nationwide lenders, the Patriot Express Pilot Program features one of the fastest turnaround times for loan approval. The maximum loan amount is $500,000 with the SBA providing a maximum guarantee of 85% for loans of $150,000 or less and 75% for loans above $150,000. Funds can be used for start-up, expansion, equipment purchases, working capital, and inventory.

3. **SBA Export Express.** This is the simplest export loan program available, with an approval time of 36 hours or less. The program, which offers financing up to $500,000, allows lenders to use their own forms and procedures. Loan proceeds are used for business purposes that enhance export development. Export Express can be a term loan or revolving line of credit.

4. **Preferred Lenders Program (PLP).** The most active and expert SBA lenders qualify for the SBA's Certified and Preferred Lenders Program. Participants are delegated partial or full authority to approve loans, which results in faster service. Certified lenders are those that have been heavily involved in regular SBA loan-guaranty processing and have met certain other criteria. Preferred lenders are chosen from among the SBA's best lenders and enjoy full delegation of lending authority. A list of participants in the Certified and Preferred Lenders Program may be obtained from your local SBA office.

5. **7(M) Microloan Program.** The Microloan Program provides small loans up to $50,000. Under this program, the SBA makes funds available to

nonprofit intermediaries; these, in turn, make the loans. The lending and credit requirements are determined by each individual intermediary. The average loan size is $13,000. Completed applications usually are processed by an intermediary in less than one week.

Micro loans may be used to finance machinery, equipment, fixtures and leasehold improvements. They may also be used to finance receivables and for working capital. They may not be used to pay existing debt or to purchase real estate. Depending on the earnings of your business, you may take up to six years to repay a microloan. Rates will generally be between 8% and 13%. There is no guaranty fee. Each nonprofit lending organization will have its own collateral requirements, but must take as collateral any assets purchased with the microloan. Generally the personal guaranties of the business owners are also required.

6. **Small/Rural Lender Advantage (S/RLA).** The Small/Rural Lender Advantage initiative is designed to help lenders in small/rural communities by providing a simpler and streamlined application process as well as procedures. This is all in an effort to help with economic development in local communities that are experiencing population loss, economic dislocation, and high unemployment. The Small/Rural Lender Advantage program allows for loans of up to $350,000 with the SBA providing a guarantee of 85% for loans of $150,000 or less and 75% for loans greater than 150,000. Routine loans are typically processed within a 3 to 5 day window. A one page application (two sided) is used with limited additional information required for loans above $50,000.

7. **504 Certified Development Company.** CDCs are nonprofit corporations set up to contribute to the economic development of their communities or regions. They work with the SBA and private-sector lenders to provide financing to small businesses. The program is designed to enable small businesses to create and retain jobs; the CDC's portfolio must create or retain one job for every $65,000 of debenture proceeds provided by the SBA. They provide small businesses with 10 or 20-year financing for the acquisition of land and buildings, machinery and equipment or for constructing, modernizing, renovating or converting existing facilities. To be eligible, the business must operate for profit. Tangible net worth must not exceed $7 million and average net income must not exceed $2.5 million for the past two years.

The maximum loan amount is generally $5,000,000. The amount may go up to $5.5 million if the project meets public policy goals (i.e., business district revitalization, expansion of export, expansion of minority business). Collateral may include a mortgage on the land and the building being financed. Personal guarantees of principals are required. SBA will take business assets as collateral. Interest rates are pegged to an increment above the current market rate for 5- and 10-year U.S. Treasury Bonds and are generally below market rate.

Tech Tip

Interest Rates Applicable to SBA Guaranteed Loans

Interest rates are negotiated between the borrower and the lender but are subject to SBA maximums, which are pegged to the Prime Rate. Interest rates may be fixed or variable. Fixed rate loans of $50,000 or more must not exceed Prime Plus 2.25 percent if the maturity is less than 7 years, and Prime Plus 2.75 percent if the maturity is 7 years or more.

Loans between $25,000 and $50.000: Maximum rates must not exceed Prime Plus 3.25 percent if the maturity is less than 7 years, and Prime Plus 3.75 percent if the maturity is 7 years or more.

Loans of $25,000 or less: Maximum interest rate must not exceed Prime Plus 4.25 percent if the maturity is less than 7 years, and Prime Plus 4.75 percent, if the maturity is 7 years or more.

- For current Prime rates, visit *www.bankrate.com*
- For more information on SBA programs, visit *www.sba.gov/financing*

Equity Financing

If your company has a high percentage of debt to equity (what you owe compared to what you own), you will find it difficult to get debt financing and you will probably need to seek equity investment for additional funds. What this means simply is that you will trade a certain percentage of your company for a specific amount of money to be injected into the company.

Where does equity financing come from?

As with debt capital, this type of capital can come from friends and relatives, from SBA licensed investment companies, or from professional investors known as a "*venture capitalists*."

1. **Friends and Relatives.** Again, be reminded that mixing your friends or relatives and your business may not be a good idea.

2. **SBA licensed investment companies.** The SBA also licenses Small Business Investment Companies (SBICs). They make venture/risk investments by supplying equity capital and extending unsecured loans to small enterprises that meet their criteria. The SBIC Program provides an alternative to bank financing, filling the gap between the availability of venture capital and the needs of small businesses that are either starting or growing. They use their own funds plus funds obtained at favorable rates with SBA guaranties and/or by selling their preferred stock to the SBA. SBICs are for-profit firms whose incentive is to share in the success of a small business. The Program provides funding to all types of manufacturing and service industries.

> ## *Tech Tip*
>
> ### Internet Info on SBICs
>
> For more information on Small Business Investment Companies, visit the following web site: www.sba.gov/category/lender-navigation/sba-loan-programs/sbic-program-0

3. **Professional Investors/Venture Capitalists.** The venture capitalist is a risk taker, usually specializing in related industries and preferring three to five year old companies that have shown high growth potential and will offer higher-than-average profits to their shareholders. These investments are often arranged through venture capital firms that act as "matchmakers".

   As risk takers, venture capitalists focus on and have a right to participate in the management of the business. If the company does not perform, they may become active in the decision making process. The most frequent question we get asked is, "*What is the standard amount of equity you have to trade for financing?*" The trade of equity for capital is based on supply and demand. In other words, the deal is made according to who has the best bargaining power.

   Venture capitalists also require the inclusion of an exit strategy in the company's business plan. The exit strategy lays out the future goals for the company and minimizes risk to the investor by providing a way out if there is a strong indicator that the business will fail to reach its profitability goals.

Which Type of Financing Costs the Most?

The cost of financing is usually related to the degree of risk involved. If the risk is high, so is the cost.

1. **The least expensive money to use is your own.** The cost to you is whatever you would have made on your money by investing it in other sources (savings, money market accounts, bonds, retirement plans, real estate, etc.).

    Note. At this point, we should mention credit cards. Many new business owners borrow heavily on their credit cards only to find themselves up to their ears in debt. Credit cards can be one of the most expensive sources of cash and have paved the road to bankruptcy court more than once. Don't get caught in this trap!

2. **Friends and relatives.** The next lowest in cost generally comes from friends and relatives who may charge you a lower interest rate. But don't forget that it may cost you in other ways.

3. **Banks & other traditional lenders.** The third on the cost ladder is probably the traditional lender (banks, SBA, etc.) This lender will want to know what the capital will be used for and will require that it be used for those specific needs. If the risk is too high, most conventional lenders cannot approve your loan because it would be a poor financial decision for the bank's investors. One default out of ten will undermine their whole program.

4. **Outside lenders and venture capitalists.** Traditionally, the most expensive is the outside lender who charges a high interest rate because of the risk involved and the venture capitalist who requires a percentage of your business.

Calculating the Cost

Before you get a loan, take time to understand the terms under which the loan will be made. What is the interest rate? How long do you have to repay the loan? When will payments begin and how much will they be? What are you putting up as collateral? If you have venture capital injected into the business, what will be the overall price to you of the equity and control that you will forfeit?

Any source of financing can and should be calculated as to cost before the financing is finalized. Again back to your business plan. Determine when the financing is needed, plug cash injection, repayment figures, and resulting income projections into your cash flow statement and checkout the result. Will the financing make you more profitable and enable you to repay the lender or distribute profits to the venture capitalist?

Summary

Securing financing for your company must be planned well in advance. The more immediate your need, the less likely you are to get the best terms. Don't ask your banker to give you a loan yesterday…and don't expect a venture capitalist to jump on the bandwagon because you suddenly need their money. Planning ahead for cash flow is one of the best means for determining if and when you will need a lender or investor. It will also help you to determine how much you need.

When you plan for financing, remember that you will not only have to show that your industry has good potential for profit. You will also have to present a strong case for the ability to manage your company through the period of debt. Getting financing is serious business for both you and for the lender/investor.

Take time to plan carefully for your financial needs and your company will prosper and grow accordingly.

Set Up Your Bookkeeping

It is not the purpose of this chapter to give you a course in small business accounting. However, we will attempt in the next few pages to acquaint you with the basic records that you will need to keep. For a more comprehensive guide, we have a book entitled "Keeping the Books: Basic Recordkeeping and Accounting for the Small Business" (www.business-plan.com). You can also take classes through universities and colleges and the IRS gives small business tax classes at various locations on a regular basis. We also urge you to form an alliance with a reputable tax professional to help you work with your accounting.

The Importance of Accurate Recordkeeping

Recordkeeping has two main functions:

1. **To provide you with tax information that can be easily retrieved and verified.**
   Poor recordkeeping can cause you a multitude of problems and may result in audits, penalties, and even in the termination of your business.

2. **To provide you with information that you can use to analyze your business.**
   Accurate financial statements will help you to see trends and implement changes during the life of your business.

The keeping of accurate accounting records is imperative if your business is to succeed. To be the most effective, you should set up a system that is as simple as possible and yet complete enough to give you any information that will be helpful in your business. If you have an accurate set of records, it will be possible for you to tell at a glance what is happening with your business—which areas are productive and cost-effective and which will require change.

Tech Tip

Use Accounting Software

If you use a computer, as is now the case with most people, it can be effectively utilized to do your small business accounting.

However, the use of accounting software is only beneficial if: (1) you first have a good working knowledge of accounting principles and (2) you have developed reasonable skills when it comes to the operation of your computer. Even the most simple accounting software will require that you can make decisions and adapt the setup to your own particular accounting needs.

QuickBooks Pro (not Quicken), by Intuit, is one of the accounting software packages that does a good job of tracking business finances. PeachTree and AccountEdge are two other popular accounting applications. Most are very reasonably-priced—many for around $300 depending on how many modules are attached. You can also subscribe to online accounting for a monthly price based on your individual needs.

Once you set it up for your business and develop a chart of accounts, you can use it for all of your bookkeeping. The program will allow you to do as much or as little as you wish. For instance, you can choose whether or not to generate invoices and/or write checks from within the software. At any time, you can generate reports (P&L, Balance Sheet, Customer accounts, etc.) for the time period of your choosing. This will enable you to look at your business at any time and to utilize the reports as analysis tools upon which you can make decisions and implement changes. At the end of the year, if you have kept your bookkeeping up-to-date, it will also enable you to generate, at a click of your mouse, an annual profit and loss statement and balance sheet to take to your tax accountant.

Note: It would be wise to have the accounting professional that will handle your annual income tax returns help you to do the initial setup of your software. The professional can recommend the software he or she believes will work best for you and get you started by helping you set up your business, develop a chart of accounts, and learn how to handle issues (such as sales tax) that may require more advanced understanding of the software.

Should You Hire an Accounting Professional?

If you will involve yourself in your bookkeeping as much as possible, you will be doubly aware of what is going on in your business. If you are a very small business, you can set up a hands-on system and maintain most of your own general records throughout the year. If you are a computer user, it is best to get one of the accounting software packages such as those mentioned previously.

Because there are very few business owners who are knowledgeable about all the fine points and changes in tax laws, it is best to delegate some jobs to an accounting professional. He or she can help you to initially develop a chart of accounts and set up your books using coordinating software for easy transfer of information. Your tax professional can also maintain difficult records such as payroll and depreciation. You will also want that same specialist to maximize your tax benefits by preparing your tax return at the end of the year.

Even if you feel more comfortable hiring an accounting professional to do your bookkeeping, you would still be wise to educate yourself about the basics. Ask your accountant to prepare a balance sheet and a profit and loss statement (P&L) at the close of every month and be sure that you will be able to read and understand them. The information on these two financial statements is essential to the effective running of your business.

When Do You Begin?

If you are reading this book, you are thinking about going into business or you have already begun your business. So now is the time to begin keeping records. All of the expenses that you incur in startup will be valid costs of doing business. Conversely, any income that you generate must also be accounted for.

You can start by keeping a journal of your daily activities: where you go, who you see, what you spend. Keep track of business classes, mileage, supplies purchased, telephone calls, professional materials purchased—everything that might relate to your business.

What Records do You Need to Keep?

Your bookkeeping must be tailored to your individual needs. Because no two businesses have exactly the same concerns, it is best that you do not buy a generic set of books. Familiarize yourself with the information that you will need and set up your records accordingly. As a business owner, you will be required to keep track of all of your income and expenses.

Again, simplicity is the key to small business accounting. There are many different types of general accounting records. Their purpose is to record each transaction that takes place in your business. The general records are then used to develop monthly and yearly financial statements to be used for tax reporting and financial analysis. You should set up only those general records that you will need to document the information for your particular business. For instance, a car wash that does only cash business would not need "accounts receivable" records. Fewer records are easier to read and they will require less bookkeeping time.

General Records

Every business will require certain records to keep track of its daily transactions. These records are used to generate your monthly profit and loss statements and balance sheets. You should set up a bookkeeping schedule and keep your records current.

 Note: *To acquaint you with the most common general records, we will define each one, provide you with a filled-in example at the back of the chapter, and give you a blank form in Appendix II for you to copy and use for your own business.*

If you use accounting software, most of these records will be handled from within the application. However, you still need to learn about them so you will understand what you are inputting!

1. **Income & Expense Journal.** This is the main general record used by a business. It is used to record individual transactions for which income is received and checks written by your business. The transactions are recorded as income (monies for sales and interest earned) and expenses (checks written to pay for products and services received by you). At the end of the month, the columns in the income & expense journal are totaled. The totals are then transferred to that month's profit & loss statement. The new month begins with all income and expense categories at zero. See page 119 for an example of an Income and Expense Journal.

2. **Petty Cash Record.** Petty cash refers to all of the purchases made with cash or personal checks when it is not convenient to pay with a business check. These transactions are recorded in a separate journal and paid by periodically writing a business check (made out to "Petty Cash") that is recorded as an expense in the Income & Expense journal and as a deposit in the Petty Cash Record. Petty cash transactions require careful recording. See page 120 for an example of a Petty Cash Record.

3. **Inventory Records.** These are records that keep track of all products purchased or manufactured for resale. The IRS requires a beginning and ending inventory for each taxable year. Inventory control is a major factor contributing toward business success – or business failure. Internal use of these records will greatly enhance your profits. See pages 121 and 122.

4. **Fixed Assets Log.** This is a list of all assets (tangible and intangible) that will have to be capitalized (or depreciated over a specified number of years). They are items purchased for use in your business (not resale), usually at a cost of $100 or more and not debited to an expense account. They are depreciated over a period determined by tax regulations. Examples might be as follows: buildings, vehicles, office equipment, production equipment, office furniture. Land does not depreciate. Depreciation can be difficult to calculate because of the many IRS regulations that must be applied. It is best to let your tax preparer figure out your depreciation at the end of the year. See page 123 for an example.

5. **Accounts Payable.** This is a record of debts owed by your company for goods purchased or services rendered to you in the pursuit of your business. You will need an efficient system for keeping track of what you owe and when it should be paid to get the best terms. If you are going to have a good credit record, the payment of these invoices must be timely. If you do not accumulate unpaid invoices, you may be able to dispense with this record. See page 124 for an Account Payable Record example.

6. **Accounts Receivable.** This record is used to keep track of debts owed to you by your customers as a result of the sale of products or the rendering of services. Each client with an open account should have a separate page with account information. Statements of balances due are sent to your account holders at the close of each month. If you do not have open accounts, you will also be able to dispense with this record. See page 125.

7. **Mileage, Entertainment and Travel Records.** These are the records used to keep track of auto and transportation expenses, meals and entertainment of clients, and travel out of your local area. Due to past abuse in these areas, the IRS requires careful documentation as proof that deductions claimed are in fact business-related expenses. We strongly suggest that you organize a travel log, trip records, and entertainment records so they can

be carried with you. It is much easier to keep track of them at the time they occur than to try to remember them and find receipts after the fact. In addition, keep all of your receipts. You can read more about "Travel and Entertainment" in IRS Publication #334, *Tax Guide for Small Business*. There are also separate IRS publications containing more detailed information. See pages 126 to 128 for examples of these three records.

8. **Payroll Records.** The IRS has strict regulations regarding withholding and payroll taxes and their reporting. Payroll records are not easy to keep, even with a payroll software program. Leave these records to a trained tax expert. You will be informed what checks to write and these will be recorded in the Income & Expense Journal. The accounting professional will do all the tax reporting for you.

9. **Business Checkbook.** Your checkbook is not only the means to pay your bills. It also serves as a record of who was paid, how much was paid, and what was purchased. Deposits are recorded and a balance of cash available is always at your fingertips. It is best to use a desk-size checkbook with plenty of space for recording information. Always reconcile your checkbook with your monthly bank statement and record any service charges, check purchases and interest earned. Your checkbook information will be transferred to your Income & Expense Journal when you do your bookkeeping.

10. **Customer Records (or Databases).** These records are kept as a means of helping a business deal more effectively with its customers. The type you keep is purely subjective. The basic idea is that you keep the information that will enable you to sell more of your products or services to the customer, give the customer better service, and have the information you need regarding your transactions with them at your disposal. The database can be as simple or as complicated as you choose. A simple example of hand-generated customer files is a set of 3 x 5 cards, one for each customer, with specialized information such as name, address, telephone number, services rendered, products sold, and any other information that will help you to better serve the customer. Customer records are especially effective in service industries or in small businesses dealing in specialty retail sales.

Tech Tip

Use Database Software:
Generate Customized Information and Lists

It is a common practice to set up database files using software such as *Microsoft Access*, or any of a variety of applications offered today. Database software will allow you to customize fields of information that can be accessed at the click of a mouse, generating targeted mailing lists, sales information, demographics, etc. You can also print mailing labels and customized letters.

With the search functions, you can narrow any list down to only those customers who meet the requirements of your current focus. It is important again to remember as you set up your database files and customize your fields, that the output will only be as good as the input.

Financial Statements

Financial statements are developed from the general records discussed on the preceding two pages. They are used to provide information for preparing tax returns. Even more importantly, the use of these financial statements can help you see the financial condition of your business and identify its relative strengths and weaknesses. Business owners who take the time to understand and evaluate their operations through financial statements will be far ahead of entrepreneurs who are concerned only with their products or services.

We will now introduce you to the two principal financial statements of any business: the Balance Sheet and the Profit & Loss Statement.

1. Balance Sheet

The balance sheet is a financial statement that shows the condition of your business as of a fixed date. It is most effectively done at the end of every accounting period. The closing balances from your general records will supply you with the information. ***Note:*** *If you are using accounting software, a balance sheet can be easily generated at the close of the accounting period.*

The balance sheet can be likened to a still photograph. It is the picture of your company's financial condition at a given moment and will show whether your financial position is strong or weak. Examination of this statement will allow you to analyze your business and implement timely modifications.

A balance sheet lists a business's assets, liabilities and net worth (or capital). The assets are everything your business owns that has monetary value (cash, inventory, fixed assets, etc.). Liabilities are the debts owed by the business to any of its creditors. The net worth (or owner's equity) represents the cumulative profits and losses of the company plus or minus any equity deposits or withdrawals. The relationship between assets, liabilities and net worth can be seen in the following well-known accounting formula:

Assets – Liabilities = Net Worth

If a business possesses more assets than it owes to its creditors (liabilities), then its net worth will be positive. If the business owes more than it possesses, its net worth will be a negative.

 Example. See filled-in example balance sheet on page 129.

2. Profit and Loss Statement (P&L or Income Statement)

This financial statement shows your business financial activity over a specific period of time. Unlike the balance sheet, a profit and loss statement can be likened to a moving picture. It shows where your money came from and where it was spent over a specific period of time. You will be able to pick out weaknesses in your operation and plan ways to run your business more effectively, thereby increasing your profits.

A profit and loss statement should be prepared at the close of each month. The totals from your income and expense journal are transferred to the corresponding columns of the profit and loss statement. At the end of December (or your tax year) you will have a clear picture of your income and expenses for the 12-month period. ***Note:*** *Accounting software is set up to automatically generate monthly and annual profit & loss statements for your business.*

Comparison of the profit and loss statements from several years will reveal such trends in your business as high revenue periods, effective advertising times, increases or decreases in profit margins, and a host of other valuable information. Do not underestimate the value of this important tool. Just as the balance sheet has an accepted format, a profit and loss statement must contain certain categories in a particular order.

 Example: A filled-in example of a profit and loss statement can be found at the end of the chapter on page 130.

Keeping the Books on Schedule

There is a specific order for keeping your books. It should be done in a timely manner if the records are to be effective. Since the two goals of accounting are the retrieval of tax information and the analysis of information for internal planning, your schedule will have to provide for these goals. The tasks (on the next page) are listed according to frequency: daily, weekly, monthly, and end of the year. Schedules for filing tax information are not included. They can be found in IRS Publication #334, *Tax Guide for Small Business* or in our small business accounting book, *Keeping the Books.*

Free IRS Publications

The Internal Revenue Service provides many free publications that will be helpful to you as a small business owner. Information on ordering all publications may be obtained by calling the IRS toll free at 1-800-TAX-FORM (1-800-829-3276). It is a good idea to start your tax publication file by asking for Publication #334, *Tax Guide for Small Business.* This publication provides a comprehensive overview on most tax topics. Other publications deal in more specific information relating to individual topics such as: business use of your car, legal structure, depreciation, etc. If you subscribe to an online service, the IRS offers the ability to download electronic print files of current tax forms, instructions, and taxpayer information publications by going to the IRS Web site at: www.ustreas.gov or www.irs.gov

---

Tech Tip

Access IRS Information on the Internet

The IRS has provided us with several ways to access and print out publications, forms, and tax information – Internet, phone, walk-in, mail, and DVD.

By Internet, you can access the IRS website 24 hours a day, 7days a week, at www.irs.gov to:

- Download forms, instructions, and publications.
- Order IRS products online.
- Research your tax questions online.
- Search publications online by topic or keyword.
- Send comments or request help by email.
- Sign up to receive local and national tax news by email.

General Recordkeeping Schedule
(Post for your convenience)

This Recordkeeping Schedule will help you to organize your bookkeeping chores. Copy it and keep it with your records. It will serve as a basic guide for a person who has no bookkeeping experience.

Daily

- Go through mail and sort according to action needed.
- Pay any invoices necessary to meet discount deadlines.
- Record current day's invoices in Accounts Receivable.*
- Unpack and shelve incoming inventory (product business).
- Record inventory information (product business).

   ***Accounting software users.** Invoices generated from within your accounting software will be automatically posted to the proper accounts.*

Weekly

- Prepare income deposit and make deposit in bank.
- Enter deposit in checkbook and Income & Expense Journal.*
- Enter sales information in Inventory Record (product business).
- Enter week's checking transactions in Income & Expense Journal.*
- Record petty cash purchases in Petty Cash Record. File receipts.*
- Pay invoices due. Be aware of discount dates. File invoices.
- Record purchase of any depreciable purchases in your Fixed Assets Log.*

   ***Accounting software users.** Enter deposits, checks written, and petty cash expenditures for the week.*

Monthly

- Balance checkbook and reconcile with bank statement.*
- Enter interest earned and bank charges in Income & Expense Journal and checkbook.
- Total and balance all Income & Expense Journal columns.*
- Check Accounts Receivable and send out statements to open accounts.
- Prepare monthly Profit & Loss Statement and Balance Sheet.*

   ***Accounting software users.** Perform bank reconciliation. P&L and Balance Sheets can be generated automatically using your software.*

End of the Year

- Pay all invoices, sales taxes and other expenses that you wish to use as deductions for the current year.
- Transfer 12th month totals from the Income & Expense Journal to the Profit & Loss.*
- Prepare annual P&L. Total horizontal columns to get yearly totals for each category.*
- Prepare an end-of-the-year Balance Sheet.*
- Prepare a Cash Flow Statement (budget) for the coming year using the P&L as an aid.
- Set up new records for the coming year.

***Accounting software users.** Annual P&L and Balance Sheet can be generated by the software. User selects date parameters for all reports (i.e., This Fiscal Year, This Month, Last Fiscal Year, etc.). Accounting is continuous and does not need to be set up annually.*

Ace Sporting Goods
Income & Expense Journal

July 2014, page 2

CHECK NO.	DATE	TRANSACTION	REVENUE	EXPENSE	SALES	SALES TAX	SERV-ICES	INV. PURCH	ADVERT	FREIGHT	OFF SUPP	MISC
		Balance forward——	1,826|00	835|00	1,218|00	98|00	510|00	295|00	245|00	150|00	83|50	61|50
234	7/13	J. J. Advertising		450|00					450|00			
235	7/13	BP & N Products		380|00				380|00				
236	7/16	Regal Stationers		92|50							92|50	
***	7/17	Deposit:	1,232|00									
		1. Sales (taxable)			400|00	32|00						
		2. Sales (out of state)			165|00	O.S.						
		3. Sales (resale)			370|00	Resale						
		4. Services					265|00					
O.K. BANK	7/19	Bank charges		23|40								(bank chg) 23|40
237	7/19	Petty Cash deposit		100|00								(p/cash) 100|00
		TOTALS	3,058|00	1,880|90	2,153|00	130|00	775|00	675|00	695|00	150|00	176|00	184|90

Ace Sporting Goods
Petty Cash Record

PETTY CASH - 2014					Page 6	
DATE	**PAID TO WHOM**	**EXPENSE ACCOUNT DEBITED**	**DEPOSIT**	**AMOUNT OF EXPENSE**	**BALANCE**	
	BALANCE FORWARD —				10	00
July 19	✳✳ Deposit (Ck. 237)		100 00		110	00
20	ACE Hardware	Maintenance		12 36	97	64
23	Regal Stationers	Office Supplies		20 00	77	64
23	U.S. Postmaster	Postage		19 80	57	84
31	The Steak House	Meals		63 75	(5	91)
Aug 1	✳✳ Deposit (Ck. 267)		100 00		94	09

Toward the end of the year, you can let the Petty Cash account run a minus balance. On December 31st, a check is written for the balance and the account is zeroed out.

The amount of cash spent during the year will be exactly equal to the amount deposited into the Petty Cash Account from your checking account.

NOTE: 1. Save all receipts for cash purchases.
2. Exchange receipt for cash from petty cash drawer.
3. Use receipts to record expenses on petty cash form.
4. File receipts. You may need them for verification.
5. Be sure to record petty cash deposits.

Ace Sporting Goods Inventory Record
Non-Identifiable Stock

DEPARTMENT/CATEGORY: *Ski Hats / Headwear*

PRODUCTION OR PURCHASE DATE	INVENTORY PURCHASED OR MANUFACTURED		NUMBER OF UNITS	UNIT COST		VALUE ON DATE OF INVENTORY (Unit Cost X Units on Hand)	
	Stock #	Description				Value	Date
2/05/12	07-43	Knitted Headbands	5,000	2	50	0	1/14
3/25/12	19-12	Face Masks	3,000	5	12	450.80	1/14
9/14/12	19-10	Hat/Mask Combo	1,200	7	00	3,514.00	1/14
4/18/13	19-09	Hats, Multi-Colored	10,500	4	00	5,440.00	1/14
8/31/13	19-07	Gortex (w/bill)	10,000	8	41	50,460.00	1/14
BEGIN 2014							
2/01/14	19-12	Face Masks	2,500	4	80		
2/28/14	19-09	Hats, Multi-Colored	10,300	4	00		

NOTE:

1. This record is used for inventory of like items that are manufactured or purchased in bulk. It is a good idea to divide your records by department, category, or by manufacturer.

2. Inventory of these items is done by a physical count or by computer records. A physical inventory is required at the close of your tax year.

3. Inventory is valued according to rules that apply for **FIFO** or **LIFO** (*first in first out* or *last in first out*). The selected method must be used consistently. In order to understand and apply rules for inventory evaluation, refer to IRS Publication 334, *Tax Guide for Small Business*.

Ace Sporting Goods Inventory Record
Identifiable Stock

WHOLESALER: *Anderson Custom Designs*						Page 1
PURCH DATE	**INVENTORY PURCHASED** Stock #	Description	**PURCH. PRICE**	**DATE SOLD**	**SALE PRICE**	**NAME OF BUYER** (Optional)
1/16/14	Blue M	Golf Design	16 00	2/24/14	32 00	J. Pearce
1/23/14	Red S	Tennis T-Shirts	12 00			
	Red M	Baseball T-Shirt	12 00			
	Blue L	Soccer T-Shirt	12 00	2/07/14	24 00	S. Wong
2/16/14	Wt. L	Golf T-Shirt	14 00	3/01/14	26 00	K. Lee
3/16/14	Wt. M	Soccer T-Shirt	14 00			
3/16/14	Gr. L	Tennis T-Shirt	14 00			
	Gr. M	Basketball T-Shirt	14 00			

NOTE:
1. Use this record for keeping track of identifiable goods purchased for resale. If your inventory is very large, it may be necessary to use some sort of **Point-of-Sale** inventory system.

2. Each page should deal with either: (1) purchases in one category, or (2) goods purchased from one wholesaler.

3. Use the name of the wholesaler or the category of the purchase as the heading.

Ace Sporting Goods
Fixed Assets Log

COMPANY NAME: _____ *Ace Sporting Goods* _____

ASSET PURCHASED	DATE PLACED IN SERVICE	COST OF ASSET	% USED FOR BUSINESS	RECOVERY PERIOD	METHOD OF DEPRECIATION	DEPRECIATION PREVIOUSLY ALLOWED	DATE SOLD	SALE PRICE
2007 Dodge Van	1/08/09	18,700 00	80%	5 yr.	MACRS	15,469 00	9/12/13	8,500 00
IBM Computer	7/15/10	3,450 00	100%	5 yr.	MACRS	1,820 00		
Xerox Copier	12/29/10	3,000 00	100%	5 yr.	MACRS	1,469 00		
Climbing Simulator	6/17/13	6,500 00	100%	15 yr.	MACRS	—		
2014 Toyota Truck	8/05/13	43,500 00	80%	5 yr.	MACRS	—		
Tennis ProString	3/15/14	1,840 00	100%	7 yr.	MACRS	—		

NOTE: See IRS Publication 334, *Tax Guide for Small Business,* for more detailed information on depreciation. Also see Publications 534, 544, and 551.

Ace Sporting Goods

Accounts Payable

Account Record

CREDITOR::   *Johnson Mills*

ADDRESS: *7222 Main Street*

           Johnson, NV 26401

TEL. NO: *(800) 555-7201*   ACCOUNT NO.   *2012*

INVOICE DATE	INVOICE NO.	INVOICE AMOUNT		TERMS	DATE PAID	AMOUNT PAID		INVOICE BALANCE	
2/16/14	264	600	00	Net 30	3/07/14	600	00	0	00
3/16/14	326	300	00	Net 30	4/15/14	300	00	0	00
6/20/14	417	1,200	00	N30/2%10	6/26/14	1,176	00	0	00
8/26/14	816	2,000	00	N30/2%10	9/01/14	500	00	1,500	00

Ace Sporting Goods

Accounts Receivable
Account Record

CUSTOMER: *Martin's Team Shoppe*

ADDRESS: *222 Stevens Road*

Winnemucca, NV 89502

TEL. NO: *(702) 555-2222*   ACCOUNT NO. *1024*

INVOICE DATE	INVOICE NO.	INVOICE AMOUNT		TERMS	DATE PAID	AMOUNT PAID		INVOICE BALANCE	
3/16/14	3621	240	00	Net 30	4/12/14	240	00	0	00
4/19/14	5400	316	00	Net 30	4/30/14	316	00	0	00
5/20/14	6172	525	00	N30/2%10	5/26/14	514	50	0	00
6/16/14	7511	800	00	N30/2%10	7/14/14	250	00	550	00
7/12/14	7633	386	00	N30/2%10				386	00

Ace Sporting Goods
Mileage Log

NAME: _Ace Sporting Goods (John Kelley)_

DATED: From _July 1_ **To** _July 31, 2014_

DATE	CITY OF DESTINATION	NAME OR OTHER DESIGNATION	BUSINESS PURPOSE	NO. OF MILES
7-01	San Diego, CA	Convention Center	California Sports Expo	187 mi.
7-03	Cypress, CA	The Print Co.	p/u brochures	13 mi.
7-04	Long Beach, CA	Wm. Long High	Deliver Uniforms	53 mi.
7-07	Fullerton, CA	Bank of America	Loan Meeting	17 mi.
7-17	Los Angeles, CA	Moore Corp.	Negotiate inventory purchase	96 mi.
7-23	Los Angeles, CA	IDT	Consultation	113 mi.
			TOTAL MILES THIS SHEET	479

NOTE: 1. A mileage record is required by the IRS to claim a mileage deduction. It is also used to determine the percentage of business use of a car.

2. Keep your mileage log in your vehicle and record your mileage as it Occurs. It is very difficult to recall after the fact.

Ace Sporting Goods
Entertainment Expense Record

NAME: _____John Kelley_____

DATED: From _____7-01-14_____ To _____7-31-14_____

DATE	PLACE OF ENTERTAINMENT	BUSINESS PURPOSE	NAME OF PERSON ENTERTAINED	AMOUNT SPENT	
7-01	The 410 Club	Sell Uniform Line	William Long	46	32
7-07	Seafood Chef	Consult w/attorney	Thomas Moore	23	50
7-18	The Cannon Club	Staff Dinner	Company Employees	384	00

NOTE: For more information on Meals and Entertainment, please refer to IRS Publication 463, *Travel, Entertainment and Gift Expenses.*

Ace Sporting Goods Travel Record

TRIP TO: _Dallas, Texas_

Dated From: _7-11-14_   To: _7-16-14_

Business Purpose: _Sports Technology Expo (show exhibitor)_

No. Days Spent on Business: _6_

DATE	LOCATION	EXPENSE PAID TO	MEALS				HOTEL	TAXIS, ETC.	AUTOMOBILE			MISC EXP
			Breakfast	Lunch	Dinner	Misc.			Gas	Parking	Tolls	
7-11	Phoenix, AZ	Mobil Gas				640			2100			
7-11	Phoenix, AZ	Greentree Inn		1250								
7-11	Chola, NM	Exxon							2350			
7-11	Las Cruces, NM	Holiday Inn			2700		4900					
7-12	Las Cruces, NM	Exxon							1900			
7-12	Taft, TX	Molly's Cafe		1625								
7-12	Dallas, TX	Holiday Inn			1875		5400					
7-13	Dallas, TX	Expo Center								800		
7-13	Dallas, TX	Harvey's Eatery		2100								
7-13	Dallas, TX	Holiday Inn			2450		5400					
7-14	Dallas, TX	Holiday Inn	950									(Fax) 900
7-14	Dallas, TX	Expo Center		1400						800		
7-14	Dallas, TX	Holiday Inn			1620		5400					
7-15	Pokie, TX	Texaco							2100			
7-15	Pokie, TX	Denny's		1850								
7-15	Chola, NM	Holiday Inn			2700		4800					
7-16	Chola, NM	Holiday Inn	1275									
7-16	Flagstaff, AZ	Texaco							2200			
		TOTALS ➝	2225	8225	11345	640	25900		10650	1600		900

Attach all receipts for Meals, Hotel, Fares, Auto, Entertainment, etc. Details of your expenses can be noted on the receipts. File your travel record and your receipts in the same envelope. Label the envelope as to trip made. File all travel records together. When expenses are allocated, be sure not to double expense anything. (Ex: Gas cannot be used if you elect to use mileage as the basis for deducting your car expenses.)

Ace Sporting Goods Balance Sheet

Business Name: *Ace Sporting Goods*   *Date: September 30, 2014*

ASSETS

Current Assets

Cash	$	8,742
Petty Cash	$	167
Accounts Receivable	$	5,400
Inventory	$	101,800
Short-Term Investments	$	0
Prepaid Expenses	$	1,967

Long-Term Investments $ 0

Fixed Assets

Land (valued at cost)		$	185,000
Buildings		$	143,000
1. Cost	171,600		
2. Less Acc. Depr.	28,600		
Improvements		$	0
1. Cost			
2. Less Acc. Depr.			
Equipment		$	5,760
1. Cost	7,200		
2. Less Acc. Depr.	1,440		
Furniture		$	2,150
1. Cost	2,150		
2. Less Acc. Depr.	0		
Autos/Vehicles		$	16,432
1. Cost	19,700		
2. Less Acc. Depr.	3,268		

Other Assets

1.	$	
2.	$	

LIABILITIES

Current Liabilities

Accounts Payable	$	2,893
Notes Payable	$	0
Interest Payable	$	1,842
Taxes Payable		
Federal Income Tax	$	5,200
Self-Employment Tax	$	1,025
State Income Tax	$	800
Sales Tax Accrual	$	2,130
Property Tax	$	0
Payroll Accrual	$	4,700

Long-Term Liabilities

Notes Payable	$	196,700

TOTAL LIABILITIES   **$ 215,290**

NET WORTH (EQUITY)

Proprietorship	$	
or		
Partnership		
John Smith, 60% Equity	$	153,077
Mary Blake, 40% Equity	$	102,051
or		
Corporation		
Capital Stock	$	
Surplus Paid In	$	
Retained Earnings	$	

TOTAL NET WORTH   **$ 255,128**

Assets - Liabilities = Net Worth
and
Liabilities + Equity = Total Assets

TOTAL ASSETS   **$ 470,418**

Ace Sporting Goods Profit & Loss Statement

Beginning: January 1, 2014   **Ending: December 31, 2014**

INCOME		
1. Sales Revenues		$ 500,000
2. Cost of Goods Sold (c-d)		312,000
a. Beginning Inventory (1/01)	147,000	
b. Purchases	320,000	
c. C.O.G. Avail. Sale (a+b)	467,000	
d. Less Ending Inventory (12/31)	155,000	
3. Gross Profit on Sales (1-2)		$ 188,000
EXPENSES		
1. Variable (Selling) (a thru h)		67,390
a. Advertising/Marketing	14,000	
b. Event Planning	9,000	
c. Freight	2,000	
d. Sales Salaries/Commissions	33,000	
e. Travels	3,000	
f. Vehicle	1,650	
g. Misc. Variable (Selling) Expense	390	
h. Depreciation (Prod/Serv Assets)	4,350	
2. Fixed (Administrative) (a thru h)		51,610
a. Financial Administration	1,000	
b. Insurance	3,800	
c. Licenses & Permits	2,710	
d. Office Salaries	14,000	
e. Rent Expense	22,500	
f. Utilities	3,000	
g. Misc. Fixed (Administrative) Expense	0	
h. Depreciation (Office Equipment)	4,600	
Total Operating Expenses (1+2)		119,000
Net Income from Operations (GP-Exp)		$ 69,000
Other Income (Interest Income)		5,000
Other Expense (Interest Expense)		7,000
Net Profit (Loss) Before Taxes		$ 67,000
Taxes		
a. Federal	21,000	
b. Statel	4,500	26,000
c. Local	500	
NET PROFIT (LOSS) AFTER TAXES		$ 41,000

CHAPTER 16

Control Your Cash Flow

It is a fact that a third or more of today's businesses fail due to a lack of cash flow. What is cash flow? How do you plan ahead to ensure your chances of success? The purpose of this chapter will be to introduce you to the concept of "cash flow" and to show you how careful planning can help you avoid business disaster.

What is a Cash Flow Statement?

The Pro Forma Cash Flow Statement is the financial document that **projects** what your Business Plan means in terms of dollars. A cash flow statement is the same as a budget. It is a pro forma (or projected) statement used for internal planning and estimates when and how much money will flow into and out of a business during a designated period of time, usually the coming tax year. Your profit at the end of the year will depend on the proper balance between cash inflow and outflow.

The Cash Flow Statement identifies when cash is expected to be received and when it must be spent to pay bills and debts. It also allows the manager to identify where the necessary cash will come from.

This statement deals only with **actual cash transactions** and not with depreciation and amortization of goodwill or other non-cash expense items. Expenses are paid from cash on hand, sale of assets, revenues from sales and services, interest earned on investments, money borrowed from a lender, and influx of capital in exchange for equity in the company. If your business will require $100,000 to pay its expenses and $50,000 to support the owners, you will need at least an equal amount of money flowing into the business just to maintain the status quo. Anything less will eventually lead to an inability to pay your creditors or yourself.

Webster's New World Dictionary defines cash flow as "the pattern of receipts and expenditures of a company, government, etc., resulting in the availability or non-availability of cash." The availability or non-availability of cash when it is needed for expenditures gets to the very heart of the matter. By careful planning, you must try to project not only **how much** cash will have to flow into and out of your business, but also **when** it will need to flow in and out. A business may be able to plan for gross receipts that will cover its needs. However, if those sales do not take place in time to pay the expenses, your venture soon will be history unless you plan ahead for other sources of cash to tide the business over until the revenues are realized. The publishing industry is a good example of a business that has heavy cash demands as many as six to nine months before it realizes any revenues as a result of those expenditures. If a publisher cannot pay the printer, there will be no books for sale. The printer will not produce the finished product on a promise that he or she will be paid nine months later at the completion of sales and receipt of invoice payments. To keep the business going, the publisher must plan ahead for sources of cash to tide the business over until the revenues are received.

Pre-Planning Worksheets

Because the cash flow statement deals with cash inflow and cash outflow, the first step in planning can be best accomplished by preparing two worksheets.

1. **Cash to be Paid Out.** Cash flowing out of your business (see pages 134-135).

   This worksheet documents the cash flowing out of your business. It identifies categories of expenses and obligations and the projected amount of cash needed in each category. You may wish to approach this task by compiling several individual budgets, such as start-up costs, inventory purchases, variable (selling) expenses, fixed (administrative) expenses, owner draws, etc.)

   These expenditures are not always easy to estimate. If yours is a new business, it will be necessary for you to do lots of market research. If you are an existing business, you will combine information from past financial statements with trends in your particular industry.

2. **Sources of Cash.** Cash flowing into your business (see pages 136-137).

   Use this worksheet to document the cash flowing into your business. It will help you to estimate how much cash will be available from what sources. To complete this worksheet, you will have to look at cash on hand, projected revenues, assets that can be liquidated, possible lenders or investors and owner equity to be contributed. This worksheet will force you to take a look at any existing possibilities for increasing available cash.

Example Worksheets

On pages 134 through 137, you will see examples of the two worksheets along with accompanying information explaining each of the categories used. The worksheets are filled in for our fictitious company, *Ace Sporting Goods*, to help you understand the process.

 Please note: *The Cash to be Paid Out Worksheet shows a need for $131,000. It was necessary in projecting Sources of Cash to account for $131,000 without the projected sales because payment is not expected to be received until November and December (too late for cash needs January through October). Next year, those revenues will be reflected in cash on hand or other salable assets.*

When you do your own worksheets:

- Try to be as realistic as possible. ***Do not understate revenues and/or overstate expenses—a*** deadly error frequently made during the planning process.

- Be sure to figure all of your estimates on both worksheets for the same time period (i.e., annually, quarterly, or monthly).

Cash to be Paid Out Worksheet
Explanation of Categories

1. Start-up Costs

These are the costs incurred by you to get your business underway. They are generally one-time expenses and are capitalized for tax purposes.

2. Inventory Purchases

Cash to be spent during the period on items intended for resale. If you purchase manufactured products, this includes the cash outlay for those purchases. If you are the manufacturer, include labor and materials on units to be produced.

3. Variable Expenses (Selling or Direct Expenses)

These are the costs of all expenses that will relate directly to your product or service (other than manufacturing costs or purchase price of inventory).

4. Fixed Expenses (Administrative or Indirect Expenses)

Include all expected costs of office overhead. If certain bills must be paid ahead, include total cash outlay even if covered period extends into the next year.

5. Assets (Long-Term Purchases)

These are the capital assets that will be depreciated over a period of years (land, buildings, vehicles, equipment). Determine how you intend to pay for them and include all cash to be paid out in the current period.   **Note:** Land is the only asset that does not depreciate and will be listed at cost.

6. Liabilities

What are the payments you expect to have to make to retire any debts or loans? Do you have any Accounts Payable as you begin the new year? You need to determine the amount of cash outlay that needs to be paid in the current year. If you have a car loan for $20,000 and you pay $500 per month for 12 months, you will have a cash outlay of $6,000 for the coming year.

7. Owner Equity

This item is frequently overlooked in planning cash flow. If you, as the business owner, will need a draw of $2,000 per month to live on, you must plan for $24,000 cash flowing out of your business. Failure to plan for it will result in a cash flow shortage and may cause your business to fail.

Note: Be sure to use the same time period throughout your worksheet.

---

* Variable & Fixed Expense Categories Must Be Determined By You *

Every business has expenses that are specific to its industry. You will have to customize your variable and fixed expense categories to match your business. We have suggested some in our examples to get you started. You will type in your own headings in the working spreadsheets. As you begin to operate your business, you will be better able to determine what your true expenditures are. You can change later if you find that your current categories do not meet your needs.

Ace Sporting Goods
Cash to be Paid Out Worksheet
(Cash Flowing Out of the Business)
Time Period Covered: January 1 thru December 31, 2014

1. START-UP COSTS:		**$ 1,450**
Business License	30	
Corporation Filing	500	
Legal Fees	920	
Other start-up costs:		
a.		
b.		
c.		
2. INVENTORY PURCHASES		32,000
Cash out for goods intended for resale		
3. SELLING EXPENSES (VARIABLE/DIRECT)		
Advertising/Marketing	6,000	
Event Planning	2,500	
Freight	0	
Sales Salaries/Commissions	14,000	
Travel	2,000	
Vehicle	1,550	
Miscellaneous Variable Expense	300	
TOTAL SELLING EXPENSES		27,150
4. FIXED EXPENSES (ADMINISTRATIVE/INDIRECT)		
Financial Administration	1,800	
Insurance	900	
Licenses/Permits	100	
Office Salaries	16,300	
Rent Expenses	8,600	
Utilities	2,400	
Miscellaneous Fixed Expense	400	
TOTAL OPERATING EXPENSES		30,500
5. ASSETS (LONG-TERM PURCHASES)		6,000
Cash to be paid out in current period		
6. LIABILITIES		9,900
Cash outlay for retiring debts, loans, and/or accounts payable		
7. OWNER EQUITY		24,000
Cash to be withdrawn by owner		
TOTAL CASH TO BE PAID OUT		**$ 131,000**

Sources of Cash Worksheet
Explanation of Categories

1. Cash on Hand

This is money that you have on hand (readily available). Be sure to include cash in the bank, petty cash and moneys not yet deposited.

2. Sales (Revenues)

This includes projected revenues from the sale of your products and/or services. If payment is not expected during the time period covered by this worksheet, do not include that portion of your sales. Think about the projected timing of sales. If receipts will be delayed beyond the time when a large amount of cash is needed, make a notation to that effect and take it into consideration when determining the need for temporary financing. Include deposits you require on expected sales or services. To figure collections on Accounts Receivable, you will have to project the percentage of invoices that will be lost to bad debts and subtract it from your Accounts Receivable total.

3. Miscellaneous Income

Do you, or will you have, any moneys out on loan or deposited in accounts that will yield interest income during the period in question?

4. Sale of Long-Term Assets

If you are expecting to sell any of your fixed assets such as land, buildings, vehicles, machinery, equipment, etc., be sure to include only the cash you will receive during the current period.

Important: At this point in your worksheet, add up all sources of cash. If you do not have an amount equal to your projected needs, you will have to plan sources of cash covered under numbers 5 and 6.

5. Liabilities

This figure represents the amount you will be able to borrow from lending institutions such as banks, finance companies, the SBA, etc. Be reasonable about what you think you can borrow. If you do not have collateral, do not have a business, or if you have a poor financial history, you will find it difficult, if not impossible, to find a lender. This source of cash requires **preplanning.**

6. Equity

Sources of equity come from owner investments, contributed capital, sale of stock, or venture capital. Do you anticipate the availability of personal funds? Does your business have the potential for growth that might interest a venture capitalist? Be sure to be realistic in this area. You cannot sell stock (or equity) to a nonexistent investor.

Ace Sporting Goods
Sources of Cash Worksheet
(Cash Flowing Into the Business)

Time Period Covered: January 1, 2014 to December 31, 2014

---

1. CASH ON HAND $ 20,000

2. SALES (REVENUES)

Product Sales Income*   90,000
* Most of the sales revenue will not be received until Nov. or Dec.

Service Income   22,000

Deposits on Sales or Services   0

Collections on Accounts Receivable   3,000

3. MISCELLANEOUS INCOME

Interest Income   1,000

Payments to be Received on Loans   0

4. SALE OF LONG-TERM ASSETS   0

5. LIABILITIES

Loan Funds (Banks, Lending Inst., SBA, etc.)   40,000

6. EQUITY

Owner Investments (Sole Prop. or Partnership)   10,000

Contributed Capital (Corporation)

Sale of Stock (Corporation)

Venture Capital   35,000

         A. Without product sales =   **$ 131,000**

TOTAL CASH AVAILABLE

         B. With product sales =   **$ 221,000**

Using the Worksheets to Build the Cash Flow Statement

Now that you have completed the two worksheets, you are ready to use that information. You have estimated **how much** cash will be needed for the year and you now know what sources are available.

In the next phase of cash flow planning you will break the time period of one year into monthly segments and predict **when** the cash will be needed to make the financial year flow smoothly. To make the job easier, you can follow these steps:

1. Figure the cost of goods and the variable and fixed expenses in monthly increments. Most will vary. When do you plan to purchase the most inventory? What months will require the most advertising? Are you expecting a rent or insurance premium increase? When will commissions be due on expected sales?

2. Project sales on a monthly basis based on payment of invoices, demand for your particular product or service and on how readily you can fill that demand. There will be no cash flowing in for orders that have not been filled and invoices that are not paid. If you are in a service business and you have no employees other than yourself, remember that income ceases when you are on vacation.

3. Determine your depreciable assets needs. When will you need them? How much will the payments be and when will they begin?

4. Fill in as much of the cash flow statement as you can by using these projections and any others that you can comfortably determine. Then proceed according to the directions and complete the rest.

How to Fill In the Forms

To clarify the process of filling in a cash flow statement, pages 140 and 141 have been devoted to walking you through January and part of February for Ace Sporting Goods.

 Pages 142 and 143 contain the directions for completing a Pro Forma Cash Flow Statement and an example of a filled-in form. There is also a blank form located in the Appendix for you to use to make your own projection

Remember

The Pro Forma Cash Flow Statement is one of the most useful financial tools available to the small business owner. It is also the first financial projection to be examined by a lender or investor. It shows the lender how you plan to make it through the year, repaying your loan plus interest and at the same time maintaining the necessary cash flow to operate the business for maximum profitability. Is convinces the investor that your business has the potential for fast and sustained growth that will return a desirable profit on the invested funds.

Tech Tip

Save Your Valuable Time:
Use Pre-formatted and Pre-formulated Spreadsheets

Planning your cash flow takes time in two ways. First you will have to spend the time to research all of your information and form your organizational and marketing concepts. Once you have your ideas, you will then have to interpret everything you want to do into numbers so that you will be able to analyze the projected results.

Building your cash flow statement (budget) is a long and tedious process, especially if you are trying to do it with a pencil and a piece of paper. There are about 350+ numbers to fill in and calculate. The job becomes compounded if you make a change and have to recalculate your numbers.

Computer Spreadsheets will solve your problems
Spreadsheet applications (such as Excel) enable the user to build and formulate spreadsheets that will automatically perform complex calculations in an instant. Every computer user should learn to use one of these programs. Unless you are adept at using these applications, you will find yourself in over your head and bogged down in formatting and formulation.

Even more pertinent, in this instance, is the availability to access spreadsheets that have already been developed specifically for use in making cash flow projections.

> **Example:** Our **Automate Your Business Plan software** generates an integrated (linked) spreadsheet workbook. The spreadsheets are pre-formatted and pre-formulated. The Cash Flow Statement, as well as other financial statements, is set up to instantly perform calculations at any time that you input a number. All spreadsheets will be customized to your own chart of accounts.

What-if Scenarios
The best part about using pre-formatted and pre-formulated computer spreadsheets is that you can try out different scenarios for your business. Add a product or service, buy a piece of equipment, or cut back on an expense. Input the new numbers and you will instantly be able to see what the probable financial effect will be on your business.

Ace Sporting Goods
Cash Flow for January and February 2015

January Projections

1. Ace Sporting Goods projects a beginning cash balance of $20,000.
2. Cash Receipts: The store has not opened, so there will be no sales. However, income of $4,000 is projected on receivables from a previous location.
3. Interest on the $20,000 will amount to about $100 at current rate.
4. There are no long-term assets to sell. Enter a zero.
5. Adding 1,2,3 and 4, the Total Cash Available will be $24,100.
6. Cash Payments: Inventory payment will not be due until February. However, there will be graphic design costs of $5,000 for local team uniforms.
7. Variable (Selling) Expenses: Estimated at $1,140
8. Fixed (Administrative): Estimated at $1215
9. Interest Expense: No outstanding debts or loans. Enter zero.
10. Taxes: No profit for previous quarter. No estimated taxes would be due.
11. Payments on Long-Term Assets: Ace Sporting Goods plans to purchase office equipment to be paid in full at the time of purchase. Enter $1139
12. Loan Repayments: No loans have been received. Enter zero.
13. Owner Draws: Owner will need $2,000 for living expenses.
14. Total Cash Paid Out: Add 6 through 13. Total $10,494
15. Cash Balance: Subtract Cash Paid Out from Total Cash Available ($13,606)
16. Loans to be Received: Being aware of the $30,000 inventory costs payable in February, a loan of $40,000 is anticipated to increase Cash Available. (This requires advance planning!)
17. Equity Deposit: Owner plans to add $5,000 from personal account.
18. Ending Cash Balance: Adding 15, 16, and 17, the sum is $58,606.

February Projections

1. Beginning Cash Balance: January's Ending Cash Balance is transferred to February's Beginning Balance. Enter $58,606.
2. Cash Receipts: Coaching clinic income of $1,000 plus $1,000 to be collected from opening sales at the end of the month. $2,000.
3. Interest Income: Projected at about $120.
4. Sale of Long-Term Assets: None. Enter zero.
5. Total Cash Available: Add 1,2,3 and 4. The result is $60,726.
6. Cash Payments: $30,000 due for store inventory. $400 due for graphic design.
7. Continue as in January. Don't forget to include payments on the loan that was received in January.

Ace Sporting Goods
Partial Cash Flow Statement

	Jan	Feb
BEGINNING CASH BALANCE	20,000	58,606
CASH RECEIPTS		
A. Sales/Revenues	4,000	2,000
B. Receivables	0	0
C. Interest Income	100	120
D. Sale of Long-Term Assets	0	0
TOTAL CASH AVAILABLE	24,100	60,726
CASH PAYMENTS		
A. Cost of goods to be sold		
1. Purchases	0	30,000
2. Material	0	0
3. Labor	5,000	400
Total Cost of Goods	5,000	30,400
B. Variable Expenses (Selling)		
1. Advertising/Marketing	470	
2. Event Planning	320	
3. Freight	0	
4. Sales Salaries/Commissions	0	
5. Travel	0	
6. Vehicle	285	
7. Miscellaneous Selling Expense	65	
Total Variable Expenses	1,140	
C. Fixed Expenses (Administrative)		CONTINUE
1. Financial Admin	80	as in
2. Insurance	125	JANUARY
3. License/Permits	200	
4. Office Salaries	500	
5. Rent Expenses	110	
6. Utilities	200	
7. Miscellaneous Administrative Expense	0	
Total Fixed Expenses	1,215	
D. Interest Expense	0	
E. Federal Income Tax	0	
F. Other uses	0	
G. Long-term asset payments	1,139	
H. Loan payments	0	
I. Owner draws	2,000	
TOTAL CASH PAID OUT	10,494	
CASH BALANCE/DEFICIENCY	13,606	
LOANS TO BE RECEIVED	40,000	
EQUITY DEPOSITS	5,000	
ENDING CASH BALANCE	58,606	

Directions for Completing a Cash Flow Statement

This page contains instructions for completing the cash flow statement on the next page.
A blank form for your own projections can be found in the Appendix.

VERTICAL COLUMNS are divided into twelve months and preceded by a "Total Column".

HORIZONTAL POSITIONS on the statement contain all sources of cash and cash to be paid out. The figures are retrieved from the two previous worksheets and from individual budgets.

Figures are projected for each month, reflecting the flow of cash in and out of your business for a one-year period. Begin with the first month of your business cycle and proceed as follows:

1. Project the Beginning Cash Balance. Enter under "January."

2. Project the Cash Receipts for January. Apportion your total year's revenues throughout the 12 months. Try to weight revenues as closely as you can to a realistic selling cycle for your industry.

3. Add Beginning Cash Balance and Cash Receipts to determine Total Cash Available.

4. Project cash payments to be made for cost of goods to be sold (inventory that you will purchase or manufacture). Apportion your total inventory budget throughout the year, being sure you are providing for levels of inventory that will fulfill your needs for projected sales.

5. Customize your Variable and Fixed Expense categories to match your business.

6. Project Variable, Fixed, and Interest Expenses for January. Fill out any that you can for all 12 months.

7. Project cash to be paid out on Taxes, Long-Term Assets, Loan Repayments and Owner Draws.

8. Calculate Total Cash Paid Out (Total of Cost of Goods to Be Sold, Variable, Fixed, Interest, Taxes, Long-Term Asset payments, Loan Repayments, and Owner Draws).

9. Subtract Total Cash Paid Out from Total Cash Available. The result is entered under "Cash Balance/Deficiency". Be sure to bracket this figure if the result is a negative to avoid errors.

10. Look at Ending Cash Balance in each of the months and project Loans to be Received and Equity Deposits to be made. Add to Cash Balance/Deficiency to arrive at Ending Cash Balance for each month.

11. Ending Cash Balance for January is carried forward and becomes February's Beginning Cash Balance. (Throughout the spreadsheet, each month's ending balance is the next month's beginning balance.)

12. Go to February and input any numbers that are still needed to complete that month. The process is repeated until December is completed.

To Complete the "Total" Column:

1. The Beginning Cash Balance for January is entered in the first space of the "Total" column.

2. The monthly figures for each category (except Beginning Cash Balance, Total Cash Available, Cash Balance/Deficiency, and Ending Cash Balance) are added horizontally and the result entered in the corresponding Total category.

3. The Total column is then computed in the same manner as each of the individual months. If you have been accurate, your computations, the December Ending Cash Balance will be exactly the same as the Total Ending Cash Balance.

 Note: *If your business is new, you will have to base your projections solely on market research and industry trends. If you have an established business, you will also use your financial statements from previous years. This process may seem complicated, but as you work with, I think that it will begin to make perfect sense and will be a straightforward and reasonable task to accomplish.*

Pro Forma Cash Flow Statement

Year: 2015

	Jan	Feb	Mar	Apr	May	Jun	6-MONTH TOTALS	Jul	Aug	Sep	Oct	Nov	Dec	12-MONTH TOTALS
BEGINNING CASH BALANCE	10,360	72,840	54,488	60,346	65,125	79,253	10,360	81,341	71,401	68,974	55,974	54,718	59,032	10,360
CASH RECEIPTS														
A. Sales/Revenues	14,000	9,500	9,500	15,000	18,000	12,000	78,000	9,000	8,000	9,500	16,000	28,000	43,000	191,500
B. Receivables	400	400	300	500	450	425	2,475	500	750	650	600	1,250	8,000	14,225
C. Interest Income	234	240	260	158	172	195	1,259	213	303	300	417	406	413	3,311
D. Sale of Long-Term Assets	2,000	0	4,000	0	0	0	6,000	0	0	0	0	0	0	6,000
TOTAL CASH AVAILABLE	26,994	82,980	68,548	76,004	83,747	91,873	98,094	91,054	80,454	79,424	72,991	84,374	110,445	225,396
CASH PAYMENTS														
A. Cost of Goods to be Sold														
1. Purchases	800	16,500	3,700	200	200	300	21,700	9,000	430	540	6,700	14,000	12,000	64,370
2. Material	2,000	1,430	200	300	250	200	4,380	359	750	5,000	400	300	350	11,539
3. Labor	4,000	2,800	400	600	500	450	8,750	600	1,500	8,000	750	500	540	20,640
Total Cost of Goods	6,800	20,730	4,300	1,100	950	950	34,830	9,959	2,680	13,540	7,850	14,800	12,890	96,549
B. Variable (Selling) Expenses														
1. Advertising	900	300	900	250	300	700	3,350	350	300	640	1,300	1,200	1,400	8,540
2. Freight	75	75	75	75	180	70	550	75	75	90	180	300	560	1,830
3. Fulfillment of Orders	300	300	300	400	350	300	1,950	300	280	325	450	600	975	4,880
4. Packaging Costs	2,100	0	0	0	600	0	2,700	0	200	230	0	0	0	3,130
5. Sales/Salaries	1,400	900	1,300	1,400	1,100	900	7,000	1,400	1,400	1,400	1,400	1,400	1,400	15,400
6. Travel	0	500	700	0	0	400	1,600	0	540	25	80	0	0	2,245
7. Misc. Variable Expense	100	100	100	100	100	100	600	100	100	100	100	100	100	1,200
Total Variable Expenses	4,875	2,175	3,375	2,225	2,630	2,470	17,750	2,225	2,895	2,810	3,510	3,600	4,435	37,225
C. Fixed Expenses														
1. Financial Admin	75	75	75	475	75	75	850	75	75	75	75	75	75	1,300
2. Insurance	1,564	0	0	0	0	0	1,564	1,563	0	0	0	0	0	3,127
3. License/Permits	240	0	0	0	0	0	240	0	0	0	0	0	125	365
4. Office Salaries	1,400	1,400	1,400	1,400	1,400	1,400	8,400	1,400	1,400	1,400	1,400	1,400	1,400	16,800
5. Rent Expenses	700	700	700	700	700	700	4,200	700	700	700	700	700	700	8,400
6. Utilities	200	200	140	120	80	80	820	75	75	75	90	120	155	1,410
7. Misc. Fixed Expense	100	100	100	100	100	100	600	100	100	100	100	100	100	1,200
Total Fixed Expenses	4,279	2,475	2,415	2,795	2,355	2,355	16,674	3,913	2,350	2,350	2,365	2,395	2,555	32,602
D. Interest Expense	0	0	0	234	233	232	699	231	230	225	223	222	220	2,050
E. Federal Income Tax	1,200	1	1	1,200	1	1,200	3,603	0	0	1,200	0	0	0	4,803
F. Other Uses	0	0	0	0	0	0	0	0	0	0	0	0	0	0
G. Long-Term Asset Payments	0	0	0	214	214	214	642	214	214	214	214	214	214	1,926
H. Loan Payments	0	1,111	1,111	1,111	1,111	1,111	5,555	1,111	1,111	1,111	1,111	1,111	1,111	12,221
I. Owner Draws	2,000	2,000	2,000	2,000	2,000	2,000	12,000	2,000	2,000	2,000	3,000	3,000	3,000	27,000
TOTAL CASH PAID OUT	19,154	28,492	13,202	10,879	9,494	10,532	91,753	19,653	11,480	23,450	18,273	25,342	24,425	214,376
CASH BALANCE/DEFICIENCY	7,840	54,488	55,346	65,125	74,253	81,341	6,341	71,401	68,974	55,974	54,718	59,032	86,020	11,020
LOANS TO BE RECEIVED	65,000	0	0	0	0	0	65,000	0	0	0	0	0	0	65,000
EQUITY DEPOSITS	0	0	5,000	0	5,000	0	10,000	0	0	0	0	0	0	10,000
ENDING CASH BALANCE	72,840	54,488	60,346	65,125	79,253	81,341	81,341	71,401	68,974	55,974	54,718	59,032	86,020	86,020

Market Your Business

Now it is time to think about how you will market your products and/or services to your customers. Many companies with wonderful products and services have failed because they were unable to reach and sell to their target markets.

In this chapter, you will learn how to set the goals and objectives for your marketing strategy. You will then learn how to develop a marketing plan for your start-up company that will help you reach those goals. Your marketing plan should have all of the following components:

✓ *Overview and Goals of Your Marketing Strategy*

✓ *Market Analysis (Target Market, Competition, Industry Trends, Research)*

✓ *Sales Strategy (Online and Offline)*

✓ *Advertising (Traditional and Web)*

✓ *Public Relations*

✓ *Customer Service*

 Note: If your business is larger and more complex, you may need a marketing plan with additional elements. You can use the headings and subheadings in the Marketing Plan Outline at the end of the chapter as a guide to follow in laying out your own marketing plan, omitting those topics that do not apply to your business.

Overview and Goals of a Marketing Strategy

Your marketing strategy is the comprehensive approach your business will take to achieve your business objectives.

Definition of a Marketing Strategy

Your marketing strategy integrates the activities involved in marketing, sales, advertising, public relations, and networking. Each of these components of your overall marketing strategy serves a unique purpose, offers specific benefits, and complements every other component. All components must work together to enhance your company image, reinforce your brand strength, and ensure that your company is distinct from your competitors. A list of the major components of a successful multi-media (online and offline) marketing strategy is shown in Figure 17.1, pages 158-160.

The traditional (offline) and new media (online) components of your marketing strategy should all fit together precisely. These components include promotion of your range of services and products; determination of your prices or rate structure; creation of an advertising plan, public relations endeavors, promotional campaigns; and a long list of multi-media considerations. It is important to think through your strategy and gather information about your market and your competition before you set your fee structure or book ad space. Trial-and-error marketing plans are too expensive.

Note: U.S. Small Business Administration (SBA) District Offices and local Small Business Development Centers (SBDCs) offer workshops on marketing, publications and reference materials at little or no cost to you. Both have consultants that are readily available to help you. Self-help business books are also available in abundance on every aspect of your marketing plan.

Goals of Your Marketing Strategy

What do you hope to accomplish through your marketing strategy? Your market research, advertising campaigns, sales incentives, public relations efforts, and networking plans should all move your business in the direction of achieving your marketing goals. Many companies hope to expand their customer base, increase sales, achieve profitability, promote new products and services, and other similar idealistic objectives. Not every business owner, however, can articulate precisely what these goals mean for his/her own company.

The best marketing plans are results-oriented; they define specific, realistic, measurable goals within time parameters. All sales, advertising, and public relations efforts are then designed to work together to achieve these goals. If the goals are not accomplished within a planned schedule, individual components of the marketing plan should be reassessed and redesigned.

Goals of your marketing strategy, for example, could include creating a strong brand, building a strong customer base, increasing product/service sales, and developing a social media presence. Each goal should be explained in specific terms, that is, what do these goals mean to your company? As an illustration, let's examine four examples of goals:

- **Create a strong brand.** What is the current level of brand awareness for your company/product/service? Are you starting from scratch or building on a familiar name? What are the characteristics of this brand that you want to reinforce in the minds of consumers? What level of brand awareness do you hope to achieve?

- **Build a strong customer base.** Who are your best customers? What customers are most likely to spend money, and return? What is the profile (demographics, psychographics) of your ideal customer? How can you reach this market, online and offline? What particular characteristics of your company/product/service are most likely to inspire loyalty in your ideal customers?

- **Increase product/service sales.** How can you predict the future demand for your product/service? What new level of sales growth can your business handle? What quantities of your product can you produce/distribute? What level of service can you support through existing or additional staff?

- **Develop a social media presence.** How will you integrate social media into your marketing strategy? Which social media channels, technologies, and tools do you plan to use? How do you plan to utilize them?

   Note: Detailed information on social media is provided on pages 161-164. Be sure to read it!

Basic Marketing Questions

Five fundamental questions should be answered in order to identify your marketing goals—who, what, where, when, and how? Specifically:

- **Who** are your customers? Who are your competitors?
- **What** are you selling? What quantities and prices of your products will you sell?
- **Where** is your target market located? Where can you reach your target market?
- **When** are your customers most likely to buy? When are your busy seasons?
- **How** will you reach your customers (stores, offices, website, catalogs)?

Marketing Musts

Four activities will help you organize your marketing efforts in the most effective direction to achieve your goals.

1. **Sell selectively.** This will help you define your market niche. What will *you* offer that is distinctly different (better, less expensive, faster, higher quality, etc.) from *your competitors*? Why should anyone buy from you? What market share can you seek?

2. **Know your niche.** What type of individuals and/or businesses do you plan to serve? Start by answering in general terms (professionals, women, service companies, retailers, etc.). Then try to be very specific. Spell out the demographics first—age, sex, income, etc. Then you can move on to psychographics, or lifestyle considerations. When you clearly define the population you hope to sell to, you'll have a better view of what services they require. Where do they spend their free time? What activities are they involved in? How do they spend their disposable income?

3. **Create your pitch.** Define precisely what "your product/service attributes" mean so that your product or service comes *alive* for your prospective clients. Make it so important that they will no longer want to live or work without it. Appeal to their individual needs.

4. **Price for profits.** The goal of your business is to make a profit. Many start-up businesses fail to make a profit as early as projected because they didn't price properly. Know what your competition charges, and determine if you should be less

than, equal to or higher priced. Be sure for product pricing that you have covered your materials, labor and overhead costs. Services, like consulting, can be difficult to pinpoint. Some products and services will fall into an *hourly rate* structure; others are better-suited to a *service fee*. Pricing decisions will have to take into account what your market will bear.

 Note: Worksheets are available in Appendix II on pages 185-188 for each of the four *"Marketing Musts"*.

Market Analysis

The Market Analysis section of your Marketing Plan contains information about your target market, competitors, and marketing trends. Market research methods and results are also delineated in this section. Details about each of these components follow.

Identify Target Markets

Who are you selling to? Who are your ideal customers? Your target market should be defined in terms of demographics, psychographics, and special characteristics of niche markets, if applicable. For research information about your target market, we developed a special web page at www.business-plan.com/research/aybp.html. You will be guided through a full listing of marketing research sites with hot links to each of the resources.

- **Demographics** refer to the statistical data of a population, including average age, income, and education. Government census data is a common source of demographic information.

- **Psychographics** use demographics to determine the attitudes and tastes of a particular segment of a population. Psychographics examines lifestyles: where people spend their vacations, where they shop, how they spend their disposable income, what sports they participate in or watch, which clubs/organizations they join, and more. Social media has proved to be of great value in helping businesses to research customer behavior and preferences.

- **Niche markets** are small segments of the population that share common characteristics, interests, spending habits, etc. Successful niche marketing focuses on a small segment of a total market. Examples of niche markets include SOHOs (small office/home office), Generation X or Y, cultural niches, hip hop, to name a few.

Research Your Competition

Who is competing with you? After you have identified your target market, it is important to discern what other companies are after the same market. What are their strengths and weaknesses relative to your business?

If you are not certain who your competitors are, use several search engines to see what company names are presented when you seek your own products and services online. Check trade associations, manufacturing company listings, and other directories available in your library reference section if you want to do an offline search.

In researching your competitors, check out the general health of the business, their approach to marketing, and their financial information. In addition, specifically investigate the following:

- **Check out their websites**
- **Determine their level of activity on social media**
- **Investigate the prices of their products and services**

Note: You will find a ***Competition Evaluation Worksheet*** in Appendix II on page 184. You can fill out a worksheet for each of your major competitors.

Assess Market Trends

Your marketing plan should reflect your observations and insight about trends in your industry and in your target market. Information about the general direction of the marketplace can help you target what people want. Futurist Faith Popcorn identified sixteen market trends in her book, *Clicking* (HarperCollins, 1996) that are still accurate today. She coined the phrase "cocooning" to describe the phenomenon of staying-at-home to relax and unwind. Dramatic increases in the sales of home theatre equipment, rentals of VHS/DVD movies, and take-out food are a testimonial to the longevity of this trend. What market trends will have an impact on your business, influencing the demand for your products and services? Are you on-trend?

- **Industry trends** influence almost every business within its segment. These are major trends such as the increase in service businesses in the U.S., the decline of manufacturing, the precarious position of Internet pure-plays, to name a few.

- **Target market trends**, like the events categorized by Faith Popcorn and other marketing gurus, have an impact on the direction of a smaller segment of the population or business community. Trends can be influenced by demographics, such as the aging of our population and the huge number of baby-boomers reaching age 50 every minute, or by cultural and social influences outside the realm of demographics. Examples of market trends that evolve from demographic shifts include the increase in the number of assisted-living facilities, and the growth of innovative products and services designed for a more "youthful" retired population.

Conduct Market Research

Market research can prevent your company from making erroneous decisions that result in expensive design mistakes in new products, marketing campaigns, and more. Market research has traditionally been conducted through techniques such as questionnaires, polls, surveys, and focus groups. Today your business can take advantage of both online and offline market research techniques.

Methods of Research

- **Questionnaires** can be administered by paper or by online surveys. In either case, questionnaires are more likely to be answered if there is an incentive (reward) for the consumer to respond.

- **Focus Groups** offer more insight regarding customer preferences and thought processes than questionnaires. In focus groups, small groups of consumers are brought together under the direction of a moderator while researchers record their observations (usually behind one-way mirrors or on videotape), responses, reactions, and comments. Focus groups can also be conducted online using an Internet chat room.

- **Surveys** — telephone surveys are the terror of many quiet dinners and have become increasingly unpopular (and unreliable). Online surveys, on the other hand, meet with surprising success if presented positively. Websites can include several questions (un-intrusive, simple, quick to answer) in their format to elicit comments and suggestions from website visitors, particularly shoppers.

Database Analysis

In this part of your marketing plan, the contents shift to more detailed planning. You will describe your sales strategy, for example, and also elaborate on the materials you will produce and the campaigns you will organize. When you define your advertising strategy, you will need to identify how you will spend your money on each medium and in what markets.

Marketing Strategy

In this section of your marketing plan, the contents shift from descriptive to extremely detailed. For example, when you describe your sales strategy, you will also elaborate on the materials you will produce and the campaigns you will organize. When you define your advertising strategy, you will need to identify how you will spend your money on each medium and in what markets. Web advertising campaigns will be described in terms of specific portals, size of banner ads, frequency of e-mail marketing, and more.

Method of Sales and Distribution

How will your company reach your customers? Are your sales primarily handled by bricks (physical stores), clicks (website), catalogs (direct mail), or hybrid (multiple channels)? Do you have plans to expand your methods of sales/distribution as sales increase?

Packaging

If you provide a product, your *packaging* will be a crucial early consideration. If you are not a trained or talented designer, seek assistance for this. Packaging has a huge impact on the consumer's decision to buy.

If you provide a service, the "package" is you. Your company *image* should be defined before you begin any other marketing efforts. The image of a professional such as a lawyer or accountant, for example, involves building a private practice that will be distinctly different from an advertising agency seeking clients in the fashion industry. Your message should come across loud and clear. Are you conservative? Trendy? Cost-conscious? Flashy? Keep your message consistent and simple for your market. All your online and offline marketing efforts, your sales pitch, public relations activities, advertising, and promotional campaigns should be supportive of one another and of your image.

Pricing

How much flexibility is there in your pricing strategy? What is your price floor (the lowest price you can charge and still cover your costs) and what is your price ceiling (the highest price the market will bear)? Your marketing plan must address your pricing policy and how prices can be adjusted if necessary to increase demand or cover unanticipated revenue shortfalls.

- **Price strategy.** You may find the range between your price floor and price ceiling offers considerable leeway. Somewhere in this range is the right price point for your product or service. How do you find out what that point is? Your pricing strategy can be tested through focus groups and surveys. What price is the average customer willing to pay?

- **Competitive position.** Should your prices be greater than, less than, or equal to your competitors? Do you need to adjust your prices when your competitors make a change? If you are claiming to offer the highest quality and most personalized service, you may be able to justify charging more than your competitors. If you are appealing to a more "elite" clientele than your competitors, you will also be able to establish your pricing independently. If you hope to beat your competitors on price by going lower, you'll have to be sensitive to your price floor—what you can truly afford to discount and still be a profitable business? If you want to remain equal to your competitors you'll have to be extremely sensitive to any "value-added" offerings and special promotions they are offering.

Sales Strategies

This section outlines your use of online and offline sales materials to reach your target market. Traditional sales involve the creation of printed materials to accompany your sales efforts. Online sales involve refinement of your web strategy in order to present your products and services in the best possible manner.

Direct Sales

If you are a start-up company, you may find yourself working as both CEO and chief salesperson (not to mention, head of office maintenance…). Your marketing plan should identify how you plan to contact prospects, what materials you will send out or deliver, and what follow-up will occur. Your direct sales approach should combine offline (personal) contact with prospective customers and online sales through your website.

- **Offline sales** require materials that can be sent to prospective customers and brought with a salesperson (or you) to presentations. Do you have to design new sales materials? What is required? Will you have to create a new logo and graphics for your material? Consider the traditional list of printed materials: brochures, pamphlets, flyers, stationery, business cards, catalog, promotional flyers, etc. Identify the specific materials that you will need to design and print for use in your sales campaign.

- **Online sales** require a website and social media that double as marketing tools. In addition to the technological considerations of site design, special attention must be directed to engaging the site visitor and providing incentives to buy. Websites and social media sites that contain creative features that attract new visitors and encourage them to return to the site are called "sticky," which refers to the ability of a site to bring visitors back for additional shopping. Your online "pitch" must be just as engaging and irresistible as your in-person sales appeal.

Two important early steps of your online sales strategy are search engine registration and website and social media optimization. Search engines direct traffic to your website. They rank sites by such things as frequent updating, popularity, etc. Businesses optimize (SEO) their websites and their social media sites so they will be found by the search engines. Frequent updating of your website, Facebook, blogs, tweets, etc. – plus "likes" and "follows" – improve chances to achieve higher placement.

Direct Mail

The cost of direct mail campaigns has been estimated to be about $1 to $2 per item. As postage and paper costs escalate, direct mail becomes a less attractive sales option. If your business decides to conduct a direct mail campaign, you may find it preferable to create your own mailing list rather than purchase a list, unless you deal with a reputable list supplier that guarantees their list is current and highly accurate. But even with the best mailing list, be prepared for a low rate of return. Direct mail coupled with incentive offerings can be slightly more effective.

E-Mail Marketing

Compared to direct mail, e-mail marketing is a bargain at $.01 to $.25 per item. E-mail marketing has now outpaced direct mail, according to experts. E-mail correspondence is more likely to be read than direct mail. It offers opportunities to send personalized offers, based on understanding of your customers' preferences. However, your company must avoid spamming, or sending unwanted e-mail (like junk mail) to large lists of recipients. To avoid any perception of spamming, your e-mail marketing strategy should allow for "opt-in" and "opt-out"—the method by which your customers and website visitors elect or decline to receive future e-mail correspondence from you.

Affiliate Marketing

Affiliate marketing engages the services of a virtually limitless sales force through some type of commission structure for sales, leads, or website visits. Affiliates are only paid for the actual sales, and their commission is a small percentage of the total sale. One of the most popular affiliate programs is run by Amazon.com (www.amazon.com). Affiliate programs can offer a creative strategy for service-based businesses to sell related products on their website without having to develop the products themselves.

Reciprocal Marketing

Arrangements in which one company offers customers a discount for another company's goods, either in their store or on their website, are examples of reciprocal marketing. Creative opportunities within local communities or online communities can make this a beneficial and inexpensive alternative to promote your company. Chambers of Commerce often extend these offers within their own circle of member businesses. Online opportunities can cross these geographic boundaries to offer virtually limitless possibilities among complementary companies.

Viral Marketing

Viral marketing occurs when a company offers something that people find so intriguing that they spread the word on their own. In order to be effective, your company offering must be simple, entertaining, or engaging in some way. It also must include your company's insignia or the whole point is missed. Viral marketing by word-of-mouth has been highly effective, but viral marketing by the web has even greater impact. Word can spread more quickly, and to greater numbers of people, by e-mail and forwarded web links than by telephone calls. And when people see an e-mail from someone they know, they are most likely to read it.

Advertising Strategies

Advertising is the most potentially expensive investment of your marketing strategy. Because of the high costs involved, the efforts should be researched thoroughly before you begin. This is not an area for amateurs. If you hire no other consultants, and you know you need to advertise your business, hire someone with advertising expertise. The standards today are very high, even in the smallest local papers. Online advertising is a relatively new field and uses different guidelines than print. Graphics, photos, layouts, text, and design have to be completely professional for a positive impact in both the online and offline advertising options.

If you can pinpoint your target market in the finest detail, you can specify precisely where your ad campaign should be located. Size, timing, duration, frequency all come into play. Don't try this by trial and error. Get guidance from an expert.

Traditional Advertising

How will you invest your advertising dollars in traditional media? Traditional media includes television, radio, print, and extreme advertising. Your investment in market research truly pays off when you begin to determine how to allocate your advertising budget. Only the venues that have an impact on your target market are worth your investment. What television shows do they watch? What radio programs do they listen to? What do they read for business and for entertainment? Where are they traveling and by what method of transportation? With accurate market research to guide you, you can avoid costly advertising mistakes.

- **Television (network and cable).** Network television advertising remains the most costly advertising investment. Within this top tier, the highest price for commercial time is still the Super Bowl. Network prime time follows in rank-order, followed by non-prime time network buys. In spite of the recent growth of national cable television, network television advertising still has the power to create brands in a way that few other advertising alternatives can.

  Cable advertising, which is predicted to assume an increasing share of the total television advertising dollars, works at several levels. National cable advertising can be as costly as network television programming, but local cable television offers rates that may be affordable for even very small businesses.

- **Radio.** Radio advertising offers small businesses an opportunity to reach a national or local audience with a rate schedule far below television advertising. Radio advertisements can reach your target market during business hours as well as personal time, during commute time, and mid-day programming.

- **Print.** Your marketing research should provide you with information about the newspapers, magazines, periodicals, and professional or trade journals that are of interest to your target market. Print ads are most effective when they have a single focal point, a distinctive picture, and an explicit headline message of nine words or less.

- **Extreme advertising.** Extreme advertising includes billboards, bus wraps, blimp, and any other form of oversize outdoor ads. Extreme advertising is most effective when the message is straightforward and simple, without complex graphics and extended narratives.

Web Advertising/New Media

Your online advertising dollars should be invested with the same care and precision as your investment in traditional media. Web advertising options include banner ads, pay per click advertising, mobile device advertising, advertising on portals, and interactive television. Market research again serves as the foundation from which to build your campaign, directing your strategy to include the online options that are most visible to your target market. What websites do they visit? Where do they shop online? What portals do they use?

- **Banner ads.** Banner ads have been widely criticized, but they are still a popular form of online advertising. New standards for online ads, which include a more advertiser-friendly format that closely resembles a traditional print ad and a new form of sidebar, have breathed new life into banner ads. Even critics agree that banner ads offer a method of headlining a brand name over and over again, building brand awareness, even if the "click through" rate is lower than five percent.

- **Pay per click.** Pay per click is a form of web advertising where you pay a certain amount when a visitor clicks on the link to your website. It allows you to control your advertising budget by giving you the ability to specify the maximum amount you are willing to pay for each click through. This click amount also determines how high your ad will place in search results. This service is available through various search engine websites such as Google ("AdWords"), Yahoo, and Bing.

- **Mobile device advertising.** Mobile device advertising meets the unique space and size requirements of specific mobile devices. Advertising is most effective when it is specifically designed for these devices rather than personal computers. Web marketing campaigns need to be restructured to meet restrictions of smaller screen space, lack of color and font choices, graphic restrictions, and slow content delivery due to narrow bandwidth—restrictions that will eventually be eliminated. The best use of this form of advertising is to reach consumers on-the-go for things like travel arrangements, comparison pricing, auction bidding, hotel and entertainment plans, and stock activities.

- **Portals.** Portals guarantee a tremendous number of viewers at an extremely high cost. Advertising on a portal is beyond the scope of most small businesses, but placement in a marketplace on a portal may be a way to build online traffic. Amazon.com's zShops, Shopping@Yahoo.com, iMall, and other similar locations offer the opportunity for broader exposure without the high price tag of a portal ad. Advertising on portals requires an understanding of consumer behavior in your target market to achieve the best results.

- **Interactive television.** Interactive advertising, or advertising on "smart television," has evolved from the need to engage consumers in new and different ways to make an impact. Interactive television units are expected to increase worldwide in the next five years to over 81 million units, accompanied by an increase in interactive advertising. Interactive advertising is most effective when they are completely innovative, entertaining, and provide interesting content in a creative way.

Long-term Sponsorships

Sponsorships can be designed to meet the marketing goals of any company. Long-term sponsorships offer the benefit of helping to strengthen brand awareness in niche markets. In both the online and offline areas, long-term sponsorships help to build strong relationships with a business or organization and it's direct market, offering opportunities to co-brand multiple events, functions, advertisements, and more, providing high visibility for the advertiser. Co-branding can be set up as an exclusive arrangement or as a joint sponsorship among several complementary companies.

Public Relations

The primary difference between advertising and public relations is that you always pay for advertising space, while press coverage from your public relations efforts is "free" (aside from the fact that you may have paid to orchestrate the event that subsequently became newsworthy). Activities that demonstrate your strengths and the terrific qualities of your business in a newsworthy way can be of more value in the long run than the most expensive advertising campaign. Public relations campaigns strive to build credibility in the marketplace through routes that are more discreet than direct advertising.

Building an Online Presence

Your website and social media websites offer vehicles for public relations a company without an online presence can't imitate. Increasingly, customers and potential strategic partners check out a business online, and wonder whether a business that doesn't have a website and email address really exists. Research shows that almost two-thirds of people looking for a product or service in their community are more likely to use a business that displays information on a social media site. Different people may have broader or narrower definitions, but most will agree that social media are online platforms to provide interactive communication using web-based and mobile technologies. They are online content in the form of text, photographs, audio, video or graphics that invite comment, collaboration and exchange among participants.

Events (Online and Offline)

Can you create an event that will attract people to your website or to your physical store or office location? Grand openings, anniversary celebrations, celebrity visits, and other creative events serve a dual purpose. If they are done well, they will reinforce your relationship with existing customers and attract new business. If they are significant and newsworthy events, you may be fortunate enough to receive press coverage.

Publicizing Your Efforts

Seek opportunities for press coverage of your work and your accomplishments whenever you can. Use your social media page to post events, announcements, news, or other company updates. The impact of public relations is cumulative. You may not see immediate results, so consistency is critical.

Press Releases

A simple press release, preferably one-page, accompanied by a photo, can gain more visibility for you than an advertisement if the newspapers pick it up. *Press releases* should be interesting, *newsworthy*, concise, and sent to the right person. Watch the newspapers carefully to determine who the correct contact for your press release is. The Business Editor generally receives huge numbers of releases. If a specific reporter tends to cover stories about your industry or interests, try addressing the release to that individual instead. The media brings you into the broader public view than your advertising can. It is your way to reach larger numbers in less time. Use it wisely.

Send your press releases to:

- **Weekly newspapers** – reporters are always looking for great new stories.
- **Daily newspapers** – usually want only a local twist, so stay close to home, unless it's a national story.

- **Wire services** – seek up-to-the-second news items, so move quickly if you have a hot item to report.

- **Magazines** – offer a chance to look like an expert, but you will need longer lead time. Plan ahead.

- **Radio** – attracts the attention of the mobile and the sedentary. A guest spot can boost you into a whole new spectrum.

- **Television** – the most important medium to be prepared for. Take the time to learn how to present yourself on television to make effective use of the incredible power of this medium. With television, you need to be concise and controlled, speaking in sound bites, to be sure your point gets across the way you want it to and isn't edited out.

Press kits can also be helpful. You can prepare your own press kit or hire a marketing consultant to help you out. Your press kit should build your credibility as an expert in your field or profession. It should include:

- **Biography** (short and directed to events that are significant today)

- **Photo** (headshot, 8x10 or 5x7 black and white)

- **Brochure**

- **Copies of articles** that have quoted or featured you

Networking

Networking can mean the difference between isolation and involvement for any business owner. For home-based businesses networking takes on a particularly significant role. It replaces the water-cooler and coffee-pot contact that occurs daily in every corporate office. Networking is by definition a supportive system of sharing information and services among individuals and groups having a common interest. Networking will keep you in contact with the outside world, help you avoid isolation and stagnation, and build your business contacts for current and future plans.

Networking is a two-way street, an exchange of information. Real networking requires that you do more than reach out to give and receive business cards. Give a little information, and get a sincere grasp of what one another's skills are. Then you've really reached out. You will need to become involved in several levels of networks to provide contacts for you within:

- The business community at large

- Your peer group of professionals

- Your local community

- The world at large

Involvement in some organization at each of these levels of networks will provide public relations opportunities that will not develop from within your own home. Your degree of involvement in any organization should reflect the importance of this organization or association to your business success—unless, of course, you are joining for purely social reasons. The best use of your time, however, will be to find and focus on a few organizations that offer both business and personal satisfaction. Why waste your time? In a position of leadership in any type of organization you will give the most time but will also gain the best contacts. You will get to know the most people. You will have the most opportunity for media exposure.

Customer Service

Consumer expectations of high quality service must be met if you want to keep your customers. Consumers expect to be able to contact a customer representative with questions, concerns, problems, complaints, and returns. Business customers expect the same. Your business will need to identify your plans to meet these needs.

Description of Customer Service Activities

Will you offer 24/7 access to customer service representatives? Can your customers reach you by phone, fax, or e-mail at any time? As your business grows, you will probably need to consider the addition of the services of a call center, which offers uninterrupted service for your customers. How will you deal with customer contact in the meantime?

Expected Outcomes of Achieving Excellence

It's an old marketing maxim that it is far less expensive to retain existing customers than to add new ones, so your business gains an immediate benefit from building a loyal customer base.

Assessment of Marketing Effectiveness

Once your marketing plan is implemented, you will need to assess your results. You will need to continuously monitor the effectiveness of each online and offline campaign.

- Are your website promotions reaching your target market?

- What online advertising methods are the most effective in driving traffic to your website?

- What is the cross-over from online promotions to offline sales – and from offline promotions to online sales?

- Should certain radio, print, or television advertisements be strengthened? Should any be abbreviated or eliminated?

Assessment of the effectiveness of your marketing plan provides the management information you need to direct your future efforts and to make the wisest investment of your marketing dollars.

To Help You

The remaining pages in this chapter are as follows:

- **Multi-Media Marketing Strategy tables** will make it easier to for you to plan your offline and online marketing strategies (pages 158-160).

- ***"Using Social Media to Build Your Business"*** is a 4-page article contributed by Jan Norman, 25-year "It's Your Business" columnist for *The Orange County Register.* Learn what social media means, how their use has grown, how they supplement your marketing plan, what the different types are, and how to use them for your business (pages 161-164).

- **Marketing Plan Outline** will provide you with an outline overview of the marketing plan components and will help you with the formatting and development of your own marketing plan (pages 165-166).

Customer Service

Consumer expectations of high quality service must be met if you want to keep your customers. Consumers expect to be able to contact a customer representative with questions, concerns, problems, complaints, and returns. Business customers expect the same. Your business will need to identify your plans to meet these needs.

Description of Customer Service Activities

Will you offer 24/7 access to customer service representatives? Can your customers reach you by phone, fax, or e-mail at any time? As your business grows, you will probably need to consider the addition of the services of a call center, which offers uninterrupted service for your customers. How will you deal with customer contact in the meantime?

Expected Outcomes of Achieving Excellence

It's an old marketing maxim that it is far less expensive to retain existing customers than to add new ones, so your business gains an immediate benefit from building a loyal customer base.

Assessment of Marketing Effectiveness

Once your marketing plan is implemented, you will need to assess your results. You will need to continuously monitor the effectiveness of each online and offline campaign.
- Are your website promotions reaching your target market?

- What online advertising methods are the most effective in driving traffic to your website?

- What is the cross-over from online promotions to offline sales – and from offline promotions to online sales?

- Should certain radio, print, or television advertisements be strengthened? Should any be abbreviated or eliminated?

Assessment of the effectiveness of your marketing plan provides the management information you need to direct your future efforts and to make the wisest investment of your marketing dollars.

To Help You

The remaining pages in this chapter are as follows:

- **Multi-Media Marketing Strategy tables** will make it easier to for you to plan your offline and online marketing strategies (pages 158-160).

- ***"Using Social Media to Build Your Business"*** is a 4-page article contributed by Jan Norman, 25-year "It's Your Business" columnist for *The Orange County Register*. Learn what social media means, how their use has grown, how they supplement your marketing plan, what the different types are, and how to use them for your business (pages 161-164).

- **Marketing Plan Outline** will provide you with an outline overview of the marketing plan components and will help you with the formatting and development of your own marketing plan (pages 165-166).

Components of a Successful
Multi-Media Marketing Strategy

Marketing - Traditional (Offline) + New Media (Online)	
Identify target market(s). - Demographics - Psychographics - Niche market specifics Research/assess competition. Assess industry trends. Conduct market research. - questionnaires - focus groups - surveys Create packaging/image. Determine pricing strategy. Create branding/image strategy. - logo - slogan - pitch Develop customer database assessment. Identify co-marketing opportunities. Design reciprocal marketing strategies. Evaluate effectiveness of all components of the marketing plan.	Identify online target market(s). - Online demographics - Online psychographics - Online niche market specifics Research /assess competitors' websites. Assess online industry trends. Conduct market research. - e-mail questionnaires - online focus groups (structured chats) - online (website/social media) surveys Mirror branding/image online. Design online customer database assessment. Merge online/offline database analysis. Identify online co-marketing opportunities. Identify links to/from other websites. Evaluate effectiveness of online marketing.

Sales – Traditional (Offline) + New Media (Online)	
Refine the sales pitch. Design and print all sales materials. - Brochures - Pamphlets, folders - Stationery, business cards, etc. - Catalog - Promotional flyers, other Create direct mail campaign. Instigate viral marketing.	Determine the online sales pitch. Design/implement the website. - Introduce the company - Define products/services - Identify additional content needs Register with search engines. Optimize to improve rankings (SEO) Create an e-mail marketing campaign. Create affiliate programs. Create viral marketing opportunities online.

Figure 17.1 – page 1

Sales Incentive/Promotions (Offline) +	New Media (Online)
Create in-store campaigns and mailers: - cash back coupons - discounts/coupons - special introductory offers - free samples Design sweepstakes and contests. Identify give-aways. Identify trade show opportunities. - determine level of involvement (exhibitor vs. attendee)	Create campaigns on the website, social media sites, and via e-mail for: - cash back coupons - discounts/coupons - special offers (ex: free shipping) Design online sweepstakes or points programs - example: points for frequent web shoppers) Identify giveaways (e.g., as a thank you for completing a website survey).

Advertising – Traditional (Offline) +	New Media (Online)
Determine if an advertising agency should be hired. Determine placement, frequency, and prices for each of the following options. - Television (network, cable) - Radio (national, local) - Print (newspapers, magazines, trade journals, bulletins, yellow pages, newsletters, etc.) - Extreme advertising (billboards, buses, blimps, etc.) - Other (event signage, t-shirts, point-of-purchase signs, etc.) Identify opportunities for sponsorship (of events, programs, materials, etc.).	Determine if an advertising network should be hired. Determine placement, frequency, and prices for each of the following options. - Banner ads (vertical, rectangle, click thru) - Pay per click advertising - Mobile device advertising - Portal advertising - Online newsletters, newspapers - Interactive television - Direct TV - Links to/from - Advertorials on other websites Identify opportunities for online sponsorships (of Web events, of portions of a website, of online newsletters).

Figure 17.1 – page 2

Components of a Successful Multi-Media Marketing Strategy

Public Relations – Traditional (Offline)   +   New Media (Online)

Determine if a public relations agency should be hired. Conduct scheduled events for public/niche: - workshops - open house - seminars - celebrations Arrange for: - participation in other events (special lectures, speeches, workshops) - guest appearances (radio, television, guest columnist) - interviews (print) Identify community and charitable events for personal and financial contributions.	Determine if the public relations function should be outsourced. Arrange for online events: - special guest expert chats - regularly scheduled chat groups - community-building activities - message boards - website simulcast of offline events Arrange for guest appearances on other websites: - webinars - webcasts - podcasts - interviews (in online newsletters, magazines)

Networking – Traditional (Offline)   +   New Media (Online)

Identify groups, associations, organizations and conferences: - your local community - trade associations - business organizations - professional groups Determine level of involvement in each: - join - seek a leadership position - attend meetings/events only	Identify online networking opportunities to actively participate in: - social media threads relevant to your business - tweet and re-tweet Twitter comments - participation in free webcasts - professional association websites - other Establish regular e-mail contact with: - current clients - prospective clients - business and professional associates

Figure 17.1 – page 3

Components of a Successful Multi-Media Marketing Strategy

Using Social Media
to Build Your Business

by Jan Norman

"It's Your Business" Columnist, Orange Co. Register, 1988-2013

The rise of the Internet and explosion of the sales of personal computers, laptops, tablets and smartphones have opened huge marketing opportunities for businesses that must not be ignored. The buzz phrase is "social media," which encompasses everything from social networking sites such as Facebook to web logs or blogs including Twitter, to photo-sharing websites such as Pinterest.

These media are more than marketing devices to supplement newspaper advertisements or direct mail flyers. Social media fundamentally change how people get and give information, and therefore change marketing from merely pushing information about your business out to potential customers to engaging them in interactive conversations.

In fact, the use of technology to enable online conversations and collaborations among users is a defining hallmark of the second generation of Internet activity, dubbed Web 2.0, going back to 1999. In many cases, your customers and strategic partners will start those conversations themselves, will keep them going and draw in others who might not otherwise be aware of your company's existence.

Social media are for businesses of every size, in every location, and in every industry. The number of online resources for social media interaction grows daily. The challenge for marketers is choosing the right ones for their type of business and marketing goals.

What Does 'Social Media' Mean?

Different people may have broader or narrower definitions, but most will agree that social media are online platforms to provide interactive communication using web-based and mobile technologies. They are online content in the form of text, photographs, audio, video or graphics that invite comment, collaboration and exchange among participants.

Business owners cannot choose for their firms not to use social media. If they try, their customers, critics and competitors still will express their views and experiences online – positive and negative – about the company and its products or services for everyone to see. So, business owners need to monitor and respond to all of those online conversations, even if they think they can avoid setting up web sites, blogs, Facebook pages, Twitter accounts and YouTube channels. Why would entrepreneurs who intend to succeed avoid social media, given its prevalence and continual growth? It would be like not getting a business telephone or a mailing address. It would be like failing to greet customers when they walk into the office or store.

Increasingly, customers and potential strategic partners check out a business online, and wonder whether a business that doesn't have a web site and email address really exists. Research shows that almost two-thirds of people looking for a product or service in their community are more likely to use a business that displays information on a social media site.

Social Media Use Grows

A major reason for businesses to engage in social media is that their potential, ideal customers are probably on social platforms already. Approximately 2.5 billion people worldwide have access to the Internet and the number is growing rapidly. Approximately 1.1 billion use Facebook; 1 billion use YouTube; and 500 million use Twitter. In the United States alone, people spend a cumulative 121 billion minutes annually on social media on their computers and mobile devices, according to audience measurement company Nielsen Co. That usage has been growing by double-digit percentages each year as individuals and businesses find more ways to incorporate social media in their online presence.

Similarly, research shows that three-fourths of businesses use some form of social media; seven out of ten use Facebook and almost half use Twitter. They report that they do so because social media channels are easy to use and inexpensive, and don't require a lot of time, although the assessment of time usage can be deceiving. Entrepreneurs must budget time as well as money to spend on social media, or find themselves with too little of either left for other necessary tasks. Budgeting time to participate in social media will make these efforts habitual, which is important because continual updating is essential to social media success.

Business owners are finding that social media help them with other parts of their marketing plan. Social media can help businesses research customer behavior and preferences, build their brands, develop relationships, manage customer loyalty programs, correct mistakes quickly and deliver sales promotions and discount coupons.

Most important, businesses use social media because they bring in business: One survey of business owners found that six out of ten respondents had won new customers through LinkedIn; half had brought in new customers through Twitter; and four out of ten had attracted customers using Facebook.

Social Media Supplement (not Replace) Your Marketing Plan

Entrepreneurs who want to succeed in business over the long term don't merely buy an ad here or pass out some business cards. They develop their marketing plans to identify their ideal (and most profitable) customers, establish goals, plan strategies and organize marketing efforts into a comprehensive whole. Similarly, they build social media into those plans; they don't merely set up a Facebook page that never changes, tweet once or twice or fill out a profile on LinkedIn.

Planning is vital to successful marketing. The use of social media is an integral part of your marketing plan. It is not a replacement.

- **Define goals and branding**. First, business owners should define their general business goals and what the company's brand will be. That clarity will help understand how they can integrate social media to achieve those goals and they can avoid having their use of social media work at cross purposes or being ineffective in building the company.

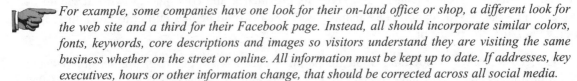 *For example, some companies have one look for their on-land office or shop, a different look for the web site and a third for their Facebook page. Instead, all should incorporate similar colors, fonts, keywords, core descriptions and images so visitors understand they are visiting the same business whether on the street or online. All information must be kept up to date. If addresses, key executives, hours or other information change, that should be corrected across all social media.*

- **Implementation has to come from the top.** Support for social media's role as part of a company's marketing strategy must come from the owner and top managers.

Implementation must not be left to a low-level intern who does not have adequate knowledge of the industry, the company or the owners' vision. People who represent the business online should understand and buy into that vision so that the message is consistent.

- **The foundation is the same.** Success in social media is built upon the same foundation as a company's success in general: Everyone involved knows who the company is, how it fits into the marketplace and how to keep its message consistent, whether online or in an office or shop. Generally, even with companies that sell online, there isn't a direct correlation between revenue growth and the number of tweets or Facebook updates. Just because a company attracts a lot of Facebook "likes" or Twitter followers doesn't necessarily show up on next month's balance sheet.

- **Return on investment is difficult to measure.** Still, setting goals for social media participation is important. One goal might be to increase traffic to the company web site a specific amount through social media posts. Another might be an increased number of customer interactions such as web site inquiries. Top social media platforms influence search engine rankings, so another goal might be an improvement in online search results.

Types of Social Media

Social media channels, technologies and tools are multiplying so rapidly that any list of the most popular or most effective is quickly obsolete. Even the platforms themselves evolve and expand to retain their users. As social media sites' capabilities expand, they overlap with others. What Facebook or YouTube do today may bear little resemblance to their functions in the future. MySpace, for example, started as an online data storage site, evolved into a social network and then started specializing in music sharing as Facebook eclipsed its general social networking popularity.

An understanding of the variety of social media available will contribute to your marketing plans to grow your business.

- **Facebook** (for years) has been the most visited social media networking platform.

- **LinkedIn** has been growing in popularity among business people looking for career advancement, customers and other work-related uses.

- **Google**, the most-used Internet search engine, created Google+ as a social networking site to encourage use of Google properties, such as Gmail.

- **Twitter** combines social networking and blogging in 140-character bites and has exploded far beyond that basic explanation.

- **YouTube** established itself as the go-to video sharing site.

- **Pinterest** shares images, and within two years of its launch, retailers were getting more referrals from Pinterest than from Facebook, Twitter or Google Plus+.

- **Instagram**, bought in 2012 by Facebook, shares photos and videos.

- **Yelp** is a customer-written review site that has become essential for many types of retail and services.

- **Wikipedia** is a user-written encyclopedia criticized for its inaccuracies and often abused, but nevertheless widely used.

A novice to social media should start with the better known platforms. Set up a Facebook page, Twitter and Pinterest accounts and a LinkedIn profile. Many business web sites include links to their Facebook, Twitter, LinkedIn and YouTube presence. Conversations online and in person with customers may suggest specialty social media presences that are unique to your industry or geographic location. Ask your best customers and partners where they participate in social media online, what content they respond to and where they get information. Those answers are a good place to start in the search for more customers like them. However, it could be a waste of money and effort to try to be on all social media platforms. Decisions about which sites to use – and how much time and effort to spend on them – should be made based on what the business is trying to achieve.

Different Ways to Use Social Media

Business use of social media should contribute to the overall goals of the company. An executive's tweets should reflect company values and marketing goals, not merely personal preferences. Pinterest photos should relate to products and services the company is ready and willing to sell.

One of the most basic ways businesses can use social media is to answer customer questions or to respond to complaints. This activity requires company representatives to monitor frequently what is being said about the company online and respond quickly. A complaint that goes unanswered can enable a critic with a worldwide megaphone.

Entrepreneurs use social media in many different ways. A business can determine the time when and location where a user comments about its products, store appearance, and more. It can use that information for market research, such as when customers are most likely to shop or their reaction to a specific product or in-store display. To encourage that type of feedback, one restaurant chain gave away $5 gift cards randomly to people who checked in at one of the restaurants. A retail clothing store offered 10 percent to 20 percent discounts to social media commenters based on how often they checked in to the company's Facebook page. Social media users love to be asked their opinion, so a bakery created polls to select new flavors of cupcakes to sell.

Some companies build online-only ad campaigns. Utah-based manufacturer Blendtec attracted millions of viewers to its series of "Will It Blend?" YouTube videos that featured founder Tom Dickson putting iPods, marbles, golf balls and remote controls into the company's product and blending them to bits. An environmental clean-up company posted videos of its work following the 2011 Japanese earthquake and tsunami. A California restaurant conducted its initial staff hiring on Facebook. Applicants had to "like" the company to apply and to find out when in-person interviews were scheduled. The restaurant posted photos of would-be servers and cooks lined up outside the restaurant for interviews and used those users to build its online community.

Businesses that sell their professional expertise (example: attorneys, real estate advisers, etc.) share tips and testimonials through Twitter, electronic newsletters and blogs. Such postings should always include a "call to action" that encourages readers to sign up for the newsletter, send questions or call for an appointment.

Use of social media to build a business
is limited only by the entrepreneur's imagination

Marketing Plan Outline

I. Overview and Goals of Marketing Strategy

A. Overview of Marketing Strategy

B. Goals of Marketing Strategy

1. Creating a Strong Brand
2. Building a Strong Customer Base
3. Increasing Product/Service Sales

II. Market Analysis

A. Target Market(s)

1. Demographics
2. Psychographics
3. Niche market specifics

B. Competition

1. Description of Major Competitors
2. Assessment of Their Strengths/Weaknesses

C. Market Trends

1. Industry Trends
2. Target Market Trends

D. Market Research

1. Methods of Research
2. Database Analysis
3. Summary of Results

III. Marketing Strategy

A. General Description

1. Allocation of marketing efforts (% of budget dedicated to online v. offline)
2. Expected return on investment from most significant components

B. Method of Sales and Distribution

1. Stores, offices, kiosks
2. Catalogs, direct mail
3. Website

C. Packaging

1. Quality Considerations
2. Packaging

D. Pricing

1. Price strategy
2. Competitive position

E. Branding

F. Database Marketing (Personalization)

G. Sales Strategies

1. Direct Sales
2. Direct Mail
3. Email Marketing
4. Affiliate Marketing
5. Reciprocal Marketing
6. Viral Marketing

H. Sales Incentives/Promotions

1. Free Samples
2. Cash Back Coupons
3. Sweepstakes
4. Online Promotions
5. Add-ons
6. Rebates
7. Other

I. Advertising Strategies

1. Traditional Advertising (TV, Radio, Print, Extreme)

2. Web Advertising/New Media (banner ads, pay per click advertising, mobile device advertising, portals, interactive television)

3. Long-term Sponsorships

J. Public Relations

1. Building an Online Presence (social media)

2. Events (online and offline)

3. Press releases (print, radio, television, online)

4. Interviews (online newsletters and websites, print, radio, television, online events)

K. Networking (memberships and leadership positions)

IV. Customer Service

A. Description of Customer Service Activities

B. Expected Outcomes of Achieving Excellence

V. Implementation of Marketing Strategy

A. In-House Responsibilities

B. Out-Sourced Functions

1. Advertising, Public Relations, Marketing Firms
2. Advertising Networks
3. Other

VI. Assessment of Marketing Effectiveness *

*Note. *The assessment is for existing businesses and is added after periodic evaluations.*

Write a Business Plan:
The Key to Your Success

The purpose of this chapter is to convince you that you need to write a business plan and to give you some basic information about business planning. We will also provide you with an overview listing the components of a well-written plan. If you decide to go ahead with the project—*and I hope you will*—we have a very comprehensive, step-by-step book that will guide you through the entire process. It is entitled *Anatomy of a Business Plan, 8th edition.* If you are computer-oriented, we have also developed a PC compatible standalone software version of the book, complete with word processing and pre-formatted and pre-formulated spreadsheets. It is entitled AUTOMATE YOUR BUSINESS PLAN *for Windows*®. You can also take classes through most colleges, small business development centers or from the U.S. Small Business Administration (SBA).

Lack of adequate planning is one of the principal reasons that most businesses fail. When the concept of business planning is considered, three critical facts always seem to emerge:

1. All lenders and investors require a business plan.

2. All businesses would operate more profitably with a business plan.

3. Most business owners do not know how to write a winning business plan.

We have been teaching business classes to entrepreneurs for more than twenty-five years and have found that no task seems to cause more consternation and dread than that of facing the ominous task of preparing a business plan. In fact, most new business owners will forge ahead without one—being sure that good ideas, enthusiasm, and the desire to achieve their goals will be enough to ensure business success.

Unfortunately, there is a major flaw in this type of thinking. Many business owners are not proficient in all phases of their particular industries and, therefore, don't have enough knowledge to make the best decisions and see what changes will have to be implemented in the future. Business planning is the most effective way to overcome this deficiency and enable you to organize the making of business decisions into a logical process. Most business owners would love it if they could spend all of their time practicing their skills and, at the same time, avoid anything that resembles paperwork.

You will soon learn that about 20% of your time as a business owner will be spent directly working with your product or service. The other 80% of the time you will be kept busy doing all of the managerial and miscellaneous chores that need to be done to keep your business functioning well.

Why You Should Write a Business Plan

There are two main purposes for writing a business plan. What are they and why are they important enough to make you decide to write one?

1. **To serve as a guide during the lifetime of your business.** This is the most important reason for writing a business plan. Writing a business plan will force you to consider everything that will come into play to make a success out of your business. It will also provide you with a means to periodically analyze what is happening in your business and give you a solid basis upon which to make decisions and implement changes. In short, it is the blueprint of your business and will serve to keep you on the right track. If you will spend the time to plan ahead, many pitfalls will be avoided and needless frustrations will be eliminated.

2. **To fulfill the requirement for securing lenders and investors.** If you are planning to seek loan funds or venture capital, you will be required to submit solid documentation in the form of a business plan.

   The days are gone when your local banker would extend a loan because you are a good trustworthy person with an entrepreneurial idea that sounds great. The world is more complex, the economy is tight and the banker has to have complete documentation that will justify your loan. Remember, a banker is the caretaker of his clients' money. If your business plan is realistic and has complete financial documentation that indicates that you will be able to repay your loan plus interest, there is a basis on which to lend you the funds you need to operate or expand your business. This also applies to venture capitalists who invest in your business in return for a share of the business.

Your business plan will provide potential lenders and investors with detailed information on all aspects of the company's past and current operations and future projections. It will detail how the desired investment or loan will further the company's goals. Every lender and investor wants to know how the loan will improve the worth of your company. Your business plan will detail how the money will be used and how it will enhance the company's profitability.

Revising Your Business Plan

Writing a business plan does not mean that you can never vary from that plan. In fact, if your plan is going to be effective either to the business or to a potential lender or investor, it will be necessary for you to update it on a regular basis.

Changes are constantly taking place in your industry, in technology and with your customers. You, as the owner, must be aware of everything that is happening in relation to your business in particular and your industry in general. You must be prepared to take the necessary steps to stay ahead of your competition. Every quarter, you will want to look at what has happened in your business, make decisions about what you can do better and revise your plan to reflect the changes you want to implement.

A Winning Business Plan Format

One of the things that I also noticed regarding business planning was that most business planning workshops focused heavily on why you should hire a professional planner (usually their company). Since getting into the software business, we have also been confronted with a lot of hype claiming that you can install your business planning software and create a business plan in a few hours.

The fact is that writing a business plan requires many days and possibly months depending on the complexity of your business. But, you can write it yourself—and if you do, you will know your business better before you finish. There is a lot of research to be done. Even if you hire a professional planner, you will be required to supply the information and statistics that will go into your business plan. This phase will be about 80% of the job. The other 20% is a matter of knowing how to put the information together into a readable plan.

Much of the confusion seems to stem from the fact that most business owners do not know what elements to include or how to organize their information in a logical sequence.

> As one student so aptly put it, *"If God had boxes of arms, legs, heads and other parts, and no instructions for putting a human being together, we might be pretty funny looking and not very functional. I think a business plan is the same."*

He was right! In order to be effective, a business plan must not only have all of the necessary parts, but must be put together in a functional pattern. When you write your business plan, you will want to cover specific subjects in a particular order. You will also need to maintain 100% continuity between all sections of the plan. Whatever you document in the text sections must be reflected in the financial documents.

Anatomy of a Business Plan Overview

To help make your task easier, we have included an overview (based on the book, *Anatomy of a Business Plan*, and the software, AUTOMATE YOUR BUSINESS PLAN) for you to follow when you write your business plan. Your plan should include all of the elements listed on pages 171-172.

Tech Tip

Business Planning Software:
Using Technology to Streamline the Process

There is no quick fix when it comes to writing a business plan. However, utilizing the proper tools can make your job easier and save you valuable time. Combining the research capabilities of the Internet and the use of a good business planning software package can help you to create a credible and defensible business plan for your new company.

Unfortunately, in today's world full of over-hyped products, much of the software purchased does not live up to everything promised on the outside of the package. I have seen one popular package that indicates on its box front that you can just fill in the numbers and write a business plan in a few hours. This should be your clue to run—not walk—to the nearest exit.

What Should You Look For in Business Planning Software?

Remember that your business plan is only as good as the information that you are able to input into the program. It's the old *"Garbage In—Garbage Out"* adage. Keeping the desired result in mind, look for software that will enable you to completely customize your business plan to your particular business. This means staying away from templates that create canned plans.

Good software will guide you step-by-step through your business plan, giving you instructions and examples for each piece of your plan, but it will not generate the text for you by having you fill in the blanks. Especially important is your financial plan. Be sure that all of your spreadsheets can be completely customized to your chart of accounts. Generic financial statements will not help you run your business.

We Have a Preference — *of course!*

AUTOMATE YOUR BUSINESS PLAN *for Windows* is the companion software to our award-winning book, *Anatomy of a Business Plan*. It will walk you through the entire business planning process with instructions, examples, and working templates. The Chart of Accounts Wizard will quickly customize all of your spreadsheets to your specific chart of accounts. You will then work in the Integrated (Linked) Spreadsheet Workbook where all of the spreadsheets are pre-formatted and pre-formulated. Information and numbers that you input (or change) will automatically be reflected on all related spreadsheets. As a bonus to users, there is an International Research Web Page (available only to our users) that will guide you through your research and *hot link* you via the Internet directly to the marketing and financial information you will need to write your business plan. The software also includes an Amortizing program that will calculate principal and interest payments on your loans. For more information: *www.business-plan.com*

Business Plan Overview

adapted from: *Anatomy of a Business Plan,* 8th Edition
and
Automate Your Business Plan
Out of Your Mind...and Into the Marketplace, Tustin, CA

THE COVER SHEET

(The title page of your plan)

The cover sheet should contain the name, address, telephone number, and website address of the business and the names, addresses and telephone numbers of all owners or corporate officers. It should also tell who prepared the business plan and when the plan was prepared or revised. To help you keep track of copies out to lenders, mark each cover sheet with a copy number. You may also opt to include a confidentiality statement.

THE EXECUTIVE SUMMARY

(The summary of your plan)

The Executive Summary summarizes your plan and states your objectives. If you are seeking loan funds or investment capital, it will list your capital needs, how you intend to use the money, benefit of the loan or investment funds to the business and how you intend to repay the loan plus interest to the lender—or generate profits to the investor. Investors will be specifically interested in your exit strategy.

While you are writing your plan, many previous ideas will change and new ideas will develop. Therefore, the Executive Summary is most effectively formulated after writing your plan. This statement should be concise, but should effectively address the key points of interest to the reader.

TABLE OF CONTENTS

(Listing of contents of your plan with page numbers)

Having a table of contents will help the reader to move smoothly from one section of the plan to another when verifying information.

For example: If a lender is reading financial information regarding advertising on a pro forma cash flow statement, he can use the table of contents to locate the advertising section for specifics on where you will be advertising and how the advertising dollars will be spent. The table of contents will also refer to the page in the supporting documents section that will contain advertising rate sheets backing up the advertising plan.

PART I: THE ORGANIZATIONAL PLAN

(The first main section of your business plan)

The organizational plan contains information on how your business is put together. The first section is devoted to a summary of the business with mission, business model, strategy, strategic relationships, and a SWOT analysis, and an overview of your products and services. This is followed by an administrative plan that includes such things as location, legal structure, management and personnel, accounting and legal, Insurance, and security.

PART II: THE MARKETING PLAN

(The second main section of your business plan)

Your marketing plan is based on the overview and goals you establish for your business. The plan addresses market analysis, identifying target markets, competition research, market trends, and market research. The marketing plan defines all of the components of your marketing strategy (sales and distribution, packaging, pricing, branding, database marketing, sales strategies, advertising strategies, public relations, and networking. The marketing plan should integrate traditional (offline) programs with new media (online) strategies. The marketing plan is completed by addressing customer service, the implementation of your marketing strategy, and plans for assessing marketing effectiveness.

PART III: FINANCIAL DOCUMENTS

(The third major section of your business plan)

Your financial documents translate the information in the first two sections of your plan into financial figures that can be used to analyze your business and make decisions for higher profitability.

You will have pro forma (projected) financial statements, actual (historical) statements, and a financial statement analysis. Include a pro forma cash flow statement, three-year income projection, break-even analysis, quarterly budget analysis, profit & loss statement, balance sheet, and a financial statement analysis ratio summary. If you are going to a lender or investor, you will also need a summary of financial needs and loan fund dispersal statement (sources and uses of funds) and business financial history.

PART IV: SUPPORTING DOCUMENTS

(Documents referred to and used to back up statements made in the three main sections of your business plan)

This section will include: owner/manager resumes, personal financial statements, articles of incorporation, partnership agreements, legal contracts, lease agreements, proprietary papers (such as copyrights, trademarks, and patents), letters of reference, demographics, and any other documents which are pertinent to the support of the plan.

U.S. and International
Resources for Business Research

How Can You Find the Information You Need?

One of the main questions asked by small business owners is, *"How do I find the information I need to make marketing and financial projections?"*

In this chapter, you will be provided with both online and offline resources that will assist you with your marketing and financial research efforts.

Resources in this chapter have been organized in the following sections:

✓ *Internet Research Links*

✓ *Library Resources*

✓ *Publications and Periodicals*

✓ *Books*

✓ *U.S. Government Departments*

✓ *U.S. Small Business Administration*

Internet Resources

Consumer Information

U.S. Demographic Information
www.census.gov

Consumer Market Research Information
www.npd.com

Values and Lifestyles (VALS)
www.strategicbusinessinsights.com/vals/

Company Information

Industrial Classifications
www.census.gov/

International Company Listing
www.trade.gov/

U.S. Small Business Administration
www.sbaonline.sba.gov/

Yahoo Industry List of Businesses
dir.yahoo.com/Business_and_Economy/Directories/Companies/

Industry Standard Ratios
www.bizstats.com

Competitive Analysis

Fortune Magazine
money.cnn.com/magazines/fortune/

Hoover's Online
www.hoovers.com

International Competitive Analysis
www.trade.gov/

U.S. Securities and Exchange Commission
www.sec.gov

Country Information

Foreign Government Information
dir.yahoo.com/Government/countries

Import and Export
www.census.gov/foreign-trade/www/

Middle East
arabia.com

Asia
www.asia-inc.com

World Trade Search
world-trade-search.com

Economic Environment

Economic Indicators from the U.S. Census Bureau
www.census.gov/econ/www/

Economic Growth Research
econ.worldbank.org/programs/macroeconomics/

Entrepreneur Resources

EntreWorld
www.entreworld.org/

The Entrepreneurial Edge
peerspectives.org

U.S. Small Business Administration
www.sbaonline.sba.gov/

Wall Street Journal
online.wsj.com/public/us

Foreign Markets

European Demographics Statistics
epp.eurostat.ec.europa.eu/portal/page/portal/population/introduction

Foreign Government Data Sources
www.lib.umich.edu/browse/International%20Government%20Information

Legal Environment

International Law Dictionary & Directory
august1.com/pubs/dict/index.shtml

International Legal Resources
www.wcl.american.edu

www.lawschool.cornell.edu

www.law.indiana.edu

Intellectual Property Law
www.patents.com

Law Library of Congress
lcweb.loc.gov

Meta-Index for U.S. Legal Research
gsulaw.gsu.edu/metaindex

North American Free Trade Agreement
www.ustr.gov/trade-agreements/free-trade-agreements/north-american-free-trade-agreement-nafta

United States Patent and Trademark Office
www.uspto.gov

Legislative and Regulatory Environments

Food and Drug Administration
www.fda.gov

Federal Trade Commission
www.ftc.gov

Federal Communications Commission
www.fcc.gov

Thomas Legislative Information on the Internet
thomas.loc.gov

Nonprofits

The Society for Nonprofit Organizations
www.snpo.org

Establishing a Nonprofit Organization
foundationcenter.org/getstarted/tutorials/establish/index.html

Information and Services for Nonprofits
www.usa.gov/Business/Nonprofit.shtml

Library Resources

The resources listed below can be found in the business section of your local library. The librarian in the business section of your library can help you with locating the materials you need. For your convenience, the resources below have been arranged in alphabetical order.

American Manufacturers Directory (American Business Information). Lists American manufacturers with 25 or more employees.

City and County Data Book (U.S. Dept. of Commerce). This book (updated every three years) contains statistical information on population, education, employment, income, housing, and retail sales.

Directory of Directories (Gale Research Inc.). Describes over 9,000 buyer's guides and directories.

Dun and Bradstreet Directories (Dun and Bradstreet). Lists companies alphabetically, geographically, and by product classification.

Encyclopedia of Associations (Gale Research Inc.). Lists trade and professional associations throughout the United States. Many publish newsletters and provide marketing information. These associations can help business owners keep up with the latest industry developments.

Incubators for Small Business (U.S. Small Business Administration). Lists over 170 state government offices and incubators that offer financial and technical aid to new small businesses.

Industry Norms & Key Business Ratios (Dun & Bradstreet). Provides balance sheet figures for companies in over 800 different lines of business as defined by SIC number.

Lifestyle Market Analyst (Standard Rate & Data Service). Breaks down population geographically and demographically. Includes extensive lifestyle information on the interests, hobbies, and activities popular in each geographic and demographic market.

National Trade and Professional Associations of the U.S. (Columbia Books, Inc.). Trade and Professional Associations are indexed by association, geographic region, subject, and budget.

Reference Book for World Traders (Alfred Croner). This three volume set lists banks, chambers of commerce, customs, marketing organizations, invoicing procedures, and more for 185 foreign markets. Also included are sections on export planning, financing, shipping, laws, and tariffs, with a directory of helpful government agencies.

RMA Annual Statement Studies (Risk Management Association). Industry norms and ratios are compiled from income statements and balance sheets. For each SIC code three sets of statistics are given with each set representing a specific size range of companies based upon sales.

Sourcebook for Franchise Opportunities (Dow-Jones Irwin). Provides annual directory information for U.S. franchises, and data for investment requirements, royalty and advertising fees, services furnished by the franchiser, projected growth rates, and locations where franchises are licensed to operate.

Standard and Poor's Industry Review. Provides updated information on all industries including current trends, merges and acquisitions, and industry projections.

Statistical Abstract of the U.S. (U.S. Dept. of Commerce). Updated annually, provides demographic, economic, and social information.

Publications and Periodicals

Business Week, McGraw-Hill, Inc., 1221 Avenue of the Americas, New York, NY 10020.

Entrepreneur Magazine, 2392 Morse Avenue, Irvine, CA 92714.

Fast Company, P.O. Box 52760, Boulder, CO 80328.

Inc., 38 Commercial Wharf, Boston, MA 02110.

Books

Bray, Ilona. *Effective Fundraising for Nonprofits: Real-World Strategies That Work.* Berkeley, CA: Nolo Press, 2013.

Clifford, Denis and Ralph Warner. *Form a Partnership.* Berkeley, CA: Nolo Press, 2012.

Cohen, Brian and Kador, John. *What Every Angel Investor Wants You to Know: An Insider Reveals How to Get Smart Funding for Your Billion Dollar Idea.* New York, NY: McGraw-Hill, 2013.

Elias, Stephen R. *Trademark: Legal Care for Your Business & Product Name.* Berkeley, CA: Nolo Press 2013.

McKaskill, Tom. *Raising Angel Finance: Securing private equity funding for early stage firms.* Breakthrough Publications, 2011.

Metrick, Andres, *Venture Capital and the Finance of Innovation.* Hoboken, NJ: Wiley, 2010.

Pakroo, Peri. *Starting & Building a Nonprofit: A Practical Guide.* Berkeley, CA: Nolo Press, 2013.

Pinson, Linda. *18 Pasos para Desarrollar tu Negocio.* Tustin, CA: Out of Your Mind…and Into the Marketplace, 2008.

Pinson, Linda. *Anatomía de un Plan de Negocio.* Tustin, CA: Out of Your Mind…and Into the Marketplace, 2011.

Pinson, Linda. *Anatomy of a Business Plan (*8th ed*).* Tustin, CA: Out of Your Mind…and Into the Marketplace, 2014.

Pinson, Linda. *Keeping the Books (*8th ed*).*Tustin, CA: Out of Your Mind…and Into the Marketplace, 2014.

Pinson, Linda. *Steps to Small Business Start-up (*8th ed*).*Tustin, CA: Out of Your Mind…and Into the Marketplace, 2014.

Pressman, David. *Patent It Yourself: Your Step-by-Step Guide to Filing at the U.S. Patent Office.* Berkeley, CA: Nolo Press 2013.

Priestly, Daniel. *Entrepreneur Revolution: How to develop your entrepreneurial mindset and start a business that works.* Mankato, MN: Capstone, 2013.

Safco, Lon. *The Fusion Marketing Bible: Fuse Traditional Media, Social Media, & Digital Media to Maximize Marketing.* New York, NY: McGraw-Hill. 2012.

Schaffer, Neal. *Maximize Your Social: A One-Stop Guide to Building a Social Media Strategy for Marketing and Business Success.* Hoboken, NJ: Wiley, 2013.

Scott, David Meerman. *The New Rules of Marketing and PR: How to Use Social Media, Online Video, Mobile Applications, Blogs, News Releases, and Viral Marketing to Reach Buyers Directly.* Hoboken, NJ: Wiley, 2013.

Steingold, Fred. *The Complete Guide to Buying a Business.* Berkeley, CA: Nolo Press, 2011.

Wheeler, Alina. *Designing Brand Identity.* Hoboken, NJ: Wiley, 2012.

U.S. Government Departments

Federal agencies are an excellent resource for researching your industry. In addition to the federal agencies provided below, it is recommended that you also gather information from governmental agencies on your state and local level. Please be aware that the phone numbers given for some agencies are for a central office. Upon calling, you can be directed to the department, which can meet your specific needs. To receive appropriate materials and a catalog, be sure to ask to be put on a mailing list.

Consumer Products Safety Commission
www.cpsc.gov

Department of Commerce
www.commerce.gov

Department of Education
www.ed.gov

Department of Labor
www.dol.gov

Department of State
www.state.gov

Department of Transportation
www.dot.gov

Department of the Treasury
www.treasury.gov

Environmental Protection Agency
www.epa.gov

Federal Communications Commission
www.fcc.gov

Federal Trade Commission
www.ftc.gov

Food and Drug Administration
www.fda.gov

Internal Revenue Service
www.irs.gov

Library of Congress
www.loc.gov

Patent and Trademark Office
www.uspto.gov

U.S. International Trade Commission
www.usitc.gov

U.S. Small Business Administration

The Small Business Administration is a federal agency, but it is singled out because of its importance to small businesses in America. The SBA offers an extensive selection of information on most business management topics from how to start a business to exporting your products. The SBA has offices throughout the country. Consult the U.S. Government section in your telephone directory for the office nearest you. The SBA offers a number of programs and services, including training and educational programs, counseling services, financial programs and contact assistance. These organizations are available to you through the SBA:

Service Corp of Retired Executives (SCORE). Sponsored by the SBA, SCORE is a national organization of volunteer business executives who provide free counseling, workshops and seminars to prospective and existing small business people.

Small Business Development Centers (SBDCs). Sponsored by the SBA in partnership with state and local governments, the educational community and the private sector, SBDCs provide assistance, counseling and training to prospective and existing business people.

Small Business Institutes (SBIs). Organized through SBA on more than 500 college campuses around the nation, Small Business Institutes provide counseling by students and faculty to small business clients.

For more information about SBA business development programs and services:

1. Call the SBA Small Business Answer Desk at 1 (800) 827-5722.

2. SBA has a website that provides an interactive guide to SBA programs. www.sba.gov

3. The SBA address is as follows:

> **U.S. Small Business Administration**
> 1441 L Street NW
> Washington, DC 20005

Blank Forms
and Worksheets

The forms and worksheets on the following pages have been provided for you to copy and use for your new business venture.

Insurance, Location, and Marketing Worksheets

The first seven pages (182-188) in this appendix are forms and worksheets that were referred to in the insurance, location, and marketing chapters. Included are: Insurance Update Form, Location Analysis Worksheet, Competition Evaluation Worksheet, and four Marketing Musts Worksheets.

Financial Worksheets

The remaining pages in this Appendix (pages 189-202) are financial forms that you can fill in for your own use. The financial forms that contain "Variable Expenses" and "Fixed Expenses" have spaces for you to fill in your own categories. They should be customized to your particular business. This will require you to decide on categories (accounts) that will fit your business and to follow through using the same categories throughout all of your financial statements.

The categories you use on your financial statements are those that you determine to be the major types of expenses your business will have. Those that are frequent and sizable will have a heading of their own (i.e., advertising, rent, salaries, etc.). Those expenses that are very small and infrequent will be included under the heading "miscellaneous" in either the variable or fixed expenses sections of each of your financial statements.

If you have a difficult time developing categories/accounts for your business, you can ask for help from an accounting professional.

Note: If you decide to write a business plan and would like to use our **Automate Your Business Plan** software, the insurance, location, and marketing worksheets in this Appendix (plus more) are built into the application. We will guide you through information input—and your financial spreadsheet workbook will be automatically generated and customized to your business. All spreadsheets are pre-formatted, pre-formulated and integrated (linked). This means that numbers input in one spreadsheet automatically flow to all related spreadsheets, saving you countless hours of your valuable time (for information, see pages 219-220).

Insurance Update Form

Company	Contact Person	Coverage	Cost Per Year
			$
			$
			$
			$
			$
			$
1. TOTAL ANNUAL INSURANCE COST			$
2. AVERAGE MONTHLY INSURANCE COST			$

Notes:

1.

2.

Location Analysis Worksheet

Address: _____

Property Owner: _____

Name, address, phone number of realtor/contact person: _____

_____

Lease Terms – Years: _____ Square feet: _____ Price per square foot: _____

Additional costs (utilities, insurance improvements, etc.): _____

_____

Additional conditions of lease agreement: _____

_____

History of location: _____

Location in relation to your target market: _____

Traffic patterns for customers: _____

Availability of parking (include diagram): _____

Availability for vender deliveries: _____

Crime rate for the area: _____

Quality of public services (e.g., police, fire protection): _____

Notable features of area: _____

_____

Neighboring shops and local business climate: _____

_____

Competitive businesses nearby: _____

Zoning regulations: _____

Tax rates (state, county): _____

Special assessments: _____

Competition Comparison

Competitor Profile	
COMPETITOR	Name: Location:
PRODUCTS AND/OR SERVICES	Products/Services: Pricing Comparison:
BACKGROUND & OVERVIEW OF COMPANY	Background: Current Overview:
ESTIMATED MARKET SHARE	Target Market Served: Market Share: Demographics/Psychographics of customers:
GENERAL MARKETING STRATEGY	Advertising : Promotion: Community Involvement:
STRENGTHS & WEAKNESSES	Strengths: Weaknesses:
Additional Notes:	

Marketing Musts

1. Sell Selectively

Describe your products and/or services.

What trends today have an impact on your products and services?

How can you apply information about these trends to your own marketing strategy?

Marketing Musts

2. Know Your Niche

Describe your customers in detail. In addition to demographic data, consider psychographic issues:

- *hobbies*
- *disposable income*
- *leisure activities*
- *memberships*
- *vacations*
- *family status*
- *other lifestyle information*

What additional information should you obtain about your customers?

How does this information have an impact on your marketing strategy?

- *Marketing*
- *Sales*
- *Advertising*
- *Public Relations*
- *Networking*

Marketing Musts

3. Create Your Pitch

Define precisely the attributes of your products and services.

- Product/Service A:

- Product/Service B:

- Product/Service C:

How can you make your products and services come alive for your prospective customers/clients?

For one of your products or services, write a brief pitch that grabs attention. Focus on the <u>needs</u> of your customers and the product/service <u>benefits</u>.

Marketing Musts

4. Set Prices for Profits

How does your present pricing structure compare to your competitors? (Equal to, More than, or Less than)

Have you covered all of your expenses to produce this product or provide this service, considering:

- *Materials*
- *Labor*
- *Overhead expenses*
- *Shipping costs*
- *Handling costs*
- *Storage*

For services you provide, what are the advantages and disadvantages of the following pricing structures:

- *Hourly billing rates*
- *Project by project estimates*
- *Monthly retainer structure*

What is your price floor? Ceiling?

Income & Expense Journal

Month: _____   _____20___, page ___

— Customize headings to match the business —

CHECK NO.	DATE	TRANSACTION	REVENUE	EXPENSE									MISC
		Balance forward —											
TOTALS													

Petty Cash Record

PETTY CASH - 20___					Page ___
DATE	PAID TO WHOM	EXPENSE ACCOUNT DEBITED	DEPOSIT	AMOUNT OF EXPENSE	BALANCE
	BALANCE FORWARD				

Inventory Record
Non-Identifiable Stock

DEPARTMENT/CATEGORY: _____

PRODUCTION OR PURCHASE DATE	INVENTORY PURCHASED OR MANUFACTURED		NUMBER OF UNITS	UNIT COST	VALUE ON DATE OF INVENTORY (Unit Cost X Units on Hand)	
	Stock #	Description			Value	Date

Inventory Record
Identifiable Stock

WHOLESALER:						Page____

PURCH DATE	INVENTORY PURCHASED		PURCH. PRICE	DATE SOLD	SALE PRICE	NAME OF BUYER (Optional)
	Stock #	Description				

Accounts Payable
Account Record

CREDITOR: _____

ADDRESS: _____

_____

TEL. NO: _____   ACCOUNT NO. _____

INVOICE DATE	INVOICE NO.	INVOICE AMOUNT	TERMS	DATE PAID	AMOUNT PAID	INVOICE BALANCE

Accounts Receivable
Account Record

CUSTOMER: _____

ADDRESS: _____

_____

TEL. NO: _____   ACCOUNT NO. _____

INVOICE DATE	INVOICE NO.	INVOICE AMOUNT	TERMS	DATE PAID	AMOUNT PAID	INVOICE BALANCE

Mileage Log

NAME: _____

DATED: From_____To_____

DATE	CITY OF DESTINATION	NAME OR OTHER DESIGNATION	BUSINESS PURPOSE	NO. OF MILES

	TOTAL MILES THIS SHEET	

Entertainment Expense Record

NAME: _____

DATED: From_____ To_____

DATE	PLACE OF ENTERTAINMENT	BUSINESS PURPOSE	NAME OF PERSON ENTERTAINED	AMOUNT SPENT	

Travel Record

TRIP TO: _____

Dated From: _____ To: _____

Business Purpose: _____

No. Days Spent on Business _____

| DATE | LOCATION | EXPENSE PAID TO | MEALS | | | HOTEL TAXIS, ETC. | AUTOMOBILE | | | MISC EXP |
			Breakfast	Lunch	Dinner	Misc.		Gas	Parking	Tolls	
TOTALS →											

Balance Sheet

Business Name: Date: _____ ___, _____

ASSETS

Current Assets

Cash	$ _____
Petty Cash	$ _____
Accounts Receivable	$ _____
Inventory	$ _____
Short-Term Investments	$ _____
Prepaid Expenses	$ _____

Long-Term Investments $ _____

Fixed Assets

Land (valued at cost) $ _____

Buildings		$ _____
1. Cost	_____	
2. Less Acc. Depr.	_____	

Improvements		$ _____
1. Cost	_____	
2. Less Acc. Depr.	_____	

Equipment		$ _____
1. Cost	_____	
2. Less Acc. Depr.	_____	

Furniture		$ _____
1. Cost	_____	
2. Less Acc. Depr.	_____	

Autos/Vehicles		$ _____
1. Cost	_____	
2. Less Acc. Depr.	_____	

Other Assets

1.	$ _____
2.	$ _____

TOTAL ASSETS $ _____

LIABILITIES

Current Liabilities

Accounts Payable	$ _____
Notes Payable	$ _____
Interest Payable	$ _____

Taxes Payable

Federal Income Tax	$ _____
Self-Employment Tax	$ _____
State Income Tax	$ _____
Sales Tax Accrual	$ _____
Property Tax	$ _____

Payroll Accrual $ _____

Long-Term Liabilities

Notes Payable $ _____

TOTAL LIABILITIES $ _____

NET WORTH (EQUITY)

Proprietorship $ _____

or

Partnership

name_____, ___% Equity	$ _____
name_____, ___% Equity	$ _____

or

Corporation

Capital Stock	$ _____
Surplus Paid In	$ _____
Retained Earnings	$ _____

TOTAL NET WORTH $ _____

Assets - Liabilities = Net Worth
and
Liabilities + Equity = Total Assets

Profit & Loss (Income) Statement
Business Name: _____

Beginning: _____ ___, _____   Ending: _____ ___, _____

INCOME		$
1. Sales Revenues		$
2. Cost of Goods Sold (c-d)		
a. Beginning Inventory (1/01)		
b. Purchases		
c. C.O.G. Avail. Sale (a+b)		
d. Less Ending Inventory (12/31)		
3. Gross Profit on Sales (1-2)		$
EXPENSES		
1. Variable (Selling) (a thru h)		
a.		
b.		
c.		
d.		
e.		
f.		
g. Misc. Variable (Selling) Expense		
h. Depreciation (Prod/Serv Assets)		
2. Fixed (Administrative) (a thru h)		
a.		
b.		
c.		
d.		
e.		
f.		
g. Misc. Fixed (Administrative) Expense		
h. Depreciation (Office Equipment)		
Total Operating Expenses (1+2)		
Net Income from Operations (GP-Exp)		$
Other Income (Interest Income)		
Other Expense (Interest Expense)		
Net Profit (Loss) Before Taxes		$
Taxes		
a. Federal		
b. State		
c. Local		
NET PROFIT (LOSS) AFTER TAXES		$

Cash to Be Paid Out Worksheet

Business Name: _____   Time Period:_____ to _____

1. **Start-Up Costs:** $ _____
       Business License   _____
       Corporation Filing   _____
       Legal Fees   _____
       Other start-up costs:
          a.   _____
          b.   _____
          c.   _____
          d.   _____

2. **Inventory Purchases**   _____
       Cash out for goods intended for resale

2. **Variable Expenses (Selling)**
          a.   _____
          b.   _____
          c.   _____
          d.   _____
          e.   _____
       Miscellaneous Variable Expense   _____
    Total Selling Expenses   _____

4. **Fixed Expenses (Administrative**
          a.   _____
          b.   _____
          c.   _____
          d.   _____
          e.   _____
          f.   _____
       Miscellaneous Fixed Expense   _____
    Total Operating Expenses   _____

5. **Assets (Long-Term Purchases)**   _____
       Cash to be paid out in current period

6. **Liabilities**   _____
       Cash outlay for retiring debts, loans, and/or
       accounts payable

7. **Owner Equity**   _____
       Cash to be withdrawn by owner

Total Cash to Be Paid Out $_____

Sources of Cash Worksheet

Business Name: _____

Time Period Covered: _____ to _____

1. **Cash On Hand** $ _____

2. **Sales (Revenues)**

   Sales   _____

   Service Income   _____

   Deposits on Sales or Services   _____

   Collections on Accounts Receivable   _____

3. **Miscellaneous Income**

   Interest Income   _____

   Payments to be Received on Loans   _____

4. **Sale of Long-Term Assets**   _____

5. **Liabilities**

   Loan Funds (Banks, Lending Inst., SBA, etc.)   _____

6. **Equity**

   Owner Investments (Sole Prop. or Partnership)   _____

   Contributed Capital (Corporation)   _____

   Venture Capital   _____

                                    A. Without sales = $ _____

Total Cash Available

                                    B. With sales   = $ _____

Pro Forma Cash Flow Statement

Business Name _____

Year: _____

	Jan	Feb	Mar	Apr	May	Jun	6-MONTH TOTALS	Jul	Aug	Sep	Oct	Nov	Dec	12-MONTH TOTALS
BEGINNING CASH BALANCE														
CASH RECEIPTS														
A. Sales/Revenues														
B. Receivables														
C. Interest Income														
D. Sale of Long-Term Assets														
TOTAL CASH AVAILABLE														
CASH PAYMENTS														
A. Cost of goods to be sold														
1. Purchases														
2. Material														
3. Labor														
Total Cost of Goods														
B. Variable (Selling) Expenses														
1.														
2.														
3.														
4.														
5.														
6.														
7. Misc. Variable Expense														
Total Variable Expenses														
C. Fixed Expenses														
1.														
2.														
3.														
4.														
5.														
6.														
7. Misc. Fixed Expense														
Total Fixed Expenses														
D. Interest Expense														
E. Federal Income Tax														
F. Other Uses														
G. Long-Term Asset Paymts														
H. Loan Payments														
I. Owner Draws														
TOTAL CASH PAID OUT														
CASH BALANCE/DEFICIENCY														
LOANS TO BE RECEIVED														
EQUITY DEPOSITS														
ENDING CASH BALANCE														

Glossary

The following glossary will define business and financial terms with which you may not be familiar. Use of these terms will help you to communicate in language that will be understood by business associates with whom you may be dealing.

Account. A separate record showing the increases and decreases in each asset, liability, owner's equity, revenue and expense item. Also a contract, arrangement, written or unwritten, to purchase and take delivery with payment to be made later as arranged.

Account balance. The difference between the debit and the credit sides of an account.

Accounting professional. A person who is skilled at keeping business records. Generally, a highly trained professional rather than one who keeps books. An accountant can set up the books needed for a business to operate and help the owner understand them.

Accounts payable. A record of what you owe to your creditors for goods or services received.

Accounts receivable. A record of what is owed to your business as a result of extending credit to a customer who purchases your products or services. All of the credit accounts taken together are your "accounts receivable."

Accrual basis. A method of keeping accounts that shows expenses incurred and income earned for a given fiscal period, even though such expenses and income have not been actually paid or received in cash.

Actuary. A professional expert in pension and life insurance matters, particularly trained in mathematical, statistical, and accounting methods and procedures, and in insurance probabilities.

Administrative expense. Expenses chargeable to the managerial, general administrative, and policy phases of a business in contrast to sales, manufacturing, or cost of goods expense.

Advertising. The practice of bringing to the public's notice the good qualities of something in order to induce the public to buy or invest in it.

Agent. A person who is authorized to act for or represent another person in dealing with a third party.

Amortization. To liquidate on an installment basis; the process of gradually paying off a liability over a period of time.

Analysis. Breaking an idea or problem down into its parts; a thorough examination of the parts.

Appraisal. Evaluation of a specific piece of personal or real property. The value placed on the property evaluated.

Appreciation. The increase in the value of an asset in excess of its depreciable cost due to economic and other conditions.

Arrears. Amounts past due and unpaid.

Asset. Anything of worth (having cash value) that is owned by your business (i.e. cash on hand, inventory, land, buildings, vehicles and equipment). Accounts receivable, notes receivable and prepaid purchases are also assets.

Articles of Incorporation. A legal document filed with the state which sets forth the purposes and regulations for a corporation. Each state has different regulations.

Audit. An examination of accounting documents and supporting evidence for the purpose of reaching an informed opinion concerning their propriety.

Bad debts. Money owed to you, but that you cannot collect.

Balance. The amount of money remaining in an account.

Balance Sheet. An itemized statement which lists the total assets and the total liabilities of a given business to portray its net worth at a given moment in time.

Bank Statement. A monthly statement of account that a bank renders to each of its depositors.

Benchmarking. Rating of your company's products, services, and practices against those of the front-runners in the industry.

Bill of lading. A document issued by a railroad or other carrier. It acknowledges the receipt of specified goods for transportation to a certain place, sets forth the contract between the shipper and the carrier, and provides for proper delivery of the goods.

Bill of sale. Formal legal document that conveys title to or interest in specific property from the seller to the buyer.

Board of directors. Those individuals elected by the stockholders of a corporation to manage the business.

Bookkeeping. The process of recording business transactions into the accounting records.

Brand. A design, mark, symbol, or other device that distinguishes one line or type of goods from those of a competitor.

Brand name. A term, symbol, design, or combination thereof, that identifies and differentiates a seller's product or service.

Break-even analysis. A method used to determine the point at which the business will neither make a profit nor incur a loss. That point is expressed in either the total dollars of revenue exactly offset by total expenses or in total units of production, the cost of which exactly equals the income derived by their sale.

Bottom line. A business's net profit or loss after taxes for a specific accounting period.

Budget. A plan expressed in financial terms. The business is then evaluated by measuring its performance in terms of these goals. The budget contains projections for cash inflow and outflow.

Business venture. Taking financial risks in a commercial enterprise.

Capital. Money available to invest or the total of accumulated assets available for production. See "Owner's Equity."

Capital equipment. The equipment that you use to manufacture a product, provide a service, or use to sell, store, and deliver merchandise. Such equipment will not be sold in the normal course of business, but will be used and worn out or consumed in the course of business.

Capital expenditures. An expenditure for a purchase of an item of property, plant or equipment that has a useful life of more than one year. (Fixed assets)

Capital gains (and losses). The difference between purchase price and selling price in the sale of assets.

Cash. Money in hand or readily available.

Cash discount. A deduction that is given for prompt payment of a bill.

Cash flow. The actual movement of cash within a business; cash inflow and cash outflow.

Cash receipts. The money received by a business from customers.

Certified Public Accountant (CPA). An accountant who has met prescribed requirements designed to ensure competence on the part of the public practitioner in accounting as directed by the state.

Chamber of commerce. An organization of business people designed to advance the interests of its members. There are three levels: national, state, and local.

Collateral. Something of value given or held as a pledge that a debt or obligation will be fulfilled.

Contract. An agreement regarding mutual responsibilities between two or more parties.

Controllable expenses. Those expenses which can be controlled or restrained by the business person. Variable expenses.

Corporation. A voluntary organization of persons, either actual individuals or legal entities, legally bound together to form a business enterprise; an artificial legal entity created by government grant and treated by law as an individual.

Co-signers. Joint signers of a loan agreement, pledging to meet the obligations in case of default.

Cost of goods sold. The cost of inventory sold during an accounting period. It is equal to the beginning inventory for the period plus the cost of purchases made during the period minus the ending inventory for the period.

Credit. Another word for debt. Credit is given to customers when they are allowed to make a purchase with the promise to pay later. A bank gives credit when it lends money.

Creditor. A company or individual to whom a business owes money.

Credit line. The maximum amount of credit or money a financial institution or trade firm will extend to a customer.

Current assets. Cash plus any assets that will be converted into cash within one year plus any assets that you plan to use up within one year.

Current liabilities. Debts that must be paid within one year.

Current ratio. A dependable indication of liquidity computed by dividing current assets by current liabilities. A ratio of 2.0 is acceptable for most businesses.

Debt. That which is owed.

Debt capital. The part of the investment capital which must be borrowed.

Debt measures. The indication of the amount of other people's money that is being used to generate profits for a business. The more indebtedness, the greater the risk of failure.

Debt ratio. The key financial ratio used by creditors in determining how indebted a business is and how able it is to service the debts. The debt ratio is calculated by dividing total liabilities by total assets. The higher the ratio, the more risk of failure. The acceptable ratio is dependent upon the policies of your creditors and bankers.

Default. Failure to pay a debt or meet an obligation.

Deficit. The excess of a business' liabilities over its assets; a negative net worth.

Depreciable base of an asset. The cost of an asset used in the computation of yearly depreciation expense.

Depreciation. A decrease in value through age, wear or deterioration. Depreciation is a normal expense of doing business which must be taken into account. There are laws and regulations governing the manner and time periods that may be used for depreciation.

Desktop publishing. Commonly used term for computer-generated printed materials such as newsletters and brochures.

Differentiated marketing. Selecting and developing a number of offerings to meet the needs of a number of specific market segments.

Direct expenses. Those expenses that relate directly to your product or service.

Direct mail. Marketing goods or services directly to the consumer through the mail.

Direct selling. The process whereby the producer of a product or service sells to the user, ultimate consumer, or retailer without intervening middlemen.

Discount. A deduction from the stated or list price of a product or service.

Distribution channel. All of the individuals and organizations involved in the process of moving products from producer to consumer.

Distributor. Middleman. A wholesaler, agent, or company distributing goods to dealers or companies.

Downsize. Term currently used to indicate employee reassignment, layoffs, and restructuring in order to make a business more competitive, efficient, and/or cost-effective.

Entrepreneur. An innovator of business enterprise who recognizes opportunities to introduce a new product, a new process, or an improved organization, and who raises the necessary money, assembles the factors for production, and organizes an operation to exploit the opportunity.

Equipment. Physical property of a more or less permanent nature ordinarily useful in carrying on operations, other than land, buildings, or improvements to either of them. Examples are machinery, tools, vehicles, furniture, and furnishings.

Equity. The monetary value of a property or business which exceeds claims and/or liens against it by others. An equity investment in a business carries with it a share of ownership of the business, a stake in the profits, and a say in how it is managed.

Equity capital. Money furnished by owners of the business.

Exchange. The process where two or more parties give something of value to one another to satisfy needs and wants.

Expenses. The costs of producing revenue through the sale of goods or services.

Facsimile machine (fax). A machine capable of transmitting written input via telephone lines.

Financial statements. Periodic reports that summarize the financial affairs of a business.

Fixed assets. Items purchased for use in a business which are depreciable over a fixed period of time determined by the expected useful life of the purchase. Usually includes land, buildings, vehicles and equipment not intended for resale. Land is not depreciable, but is a fixed asset.

Fixed expenses. Costs that don't usually vary from one period to the next. Generally, these expenses are not affected by the volume of business.

Franchise. A business that requires three elements: franchise fee, common trade name, and continuous relationship with the parent company.

Fundraising. Events staged to raise revenue.

Gross. Overall total revenues before deductions.

Gross profit on sales. The difference between net sales and the cost of goods sold.

Gross profit margin. An indicator of the percentage of each sales dollar remaining after a business has paid for its goods. It is computed by dividing the gross profit by the sales.

Guarantee. A pledge by a third party to repay a loan in the event that the borrower cannot meet the loan obligation.

Home page. The "table of contents" to a Web site, detailing what pages are on a particular site. The first page one sees when accessing a Web site.

Horizontal analysis. A percentage analysis of the increases and decreases on the items on comparative financial statements. A horizontal financial statement analysis involves comparison of data for the current period with the same data of a company for previous periods. Percentage of increase or decrease is listed.

Income Statement. A financial document that shows how much money (revenue) came in and how much money (expense) was paid out.

Interest. Cost of borrowing money. The price charged or paid for the use of money or credit.

Internet. The vast collection of interconnected networks that provide electronic mail and access to the World Wide Web.

Inventory. Stock of goods that a business has on hand for sale to its customers.

Invest. To lay out money for any purpose from which a profit is expected.

Investment measures. Ratios used to measure an owner's earnings for his or her investment in the company. See "Return on investment (ROI)."

Invoice. A bill for the sale of goods or services sent by the seller to the purchaser.

Lead. The name and address of a possible customer.

Lease. A long term rental agreement.

Liabilities. The amounts owed by a business to its creditors. The debts of a business.

Liability insurance. Risk protection for actions for which a business is liable.

License. Formal permission to conduct business.

Lifestyle. A pattern of living that comprises an individual's activities, interests, and opinions.

Limited partnership. A legal partnership where some owners are allowed to assume responsibility only up to the amount invested.

Liquidate. To settle a debt or to convert to cash.

Liquidity. Ability of a company to meet its financial obligations. A liquidity analysis focuses on the balance sheet relationships for current assets and current liabilities.

Loan. Money or other assets let out temporarily, usually for a specified amount of interest.

Loan agreement. A document that states what a business can and cannot do as long as it owes money to the lender.

Long-term liabilities. Liabilities that will not be due for more than a year in the future.

Management. The art of conducting and supervising a business.

Market. A set of potential or real buyers or a place where there is a demand for products or services. Actual or potential buyers of a product or service.

Marketing. All the promotional activities involved in the buying and selling of a product or service.

Market demand. Total volume purchased in a specific geographic area by a specific customer group in a specified time period under a specified marketing program.

Market forecast. An anticipated demand that results from a planned marketing expenditure.

Market niche. A well-defined group of customers that are interested in what you have to offer.

Market positioning. Finding a market niche that emphasizes the strengths of a product or service in relation to the weaknesses of the competition.

Market share. A company's percentage share of total sales within a given market.

Market targeting. Choosing a marketing strategy in terms of competitive strengths and marketplace realities.

Market mix. The set of product, place, promotion, price, and packaging variables that a marketing manager controls and orchestrates to bring a product or service into the marketplace.

Market research. The systematic design, collection, analysis, and reporting of data regarding a specific marketing situation.

Mass marketing. Selecting and developing a single offering for an entire market.

Merchandise. Goods bought and sold in a business. "Merchandise" or stock is a part of inventory.

Micro business. An owner-operated business with few employees and less than $250,000 in annual sales.

Middleman. A person or company that performs functions or renders services involved in the purchase and/or sale of goods in their flow from producer to consumer.

Multilevel sales. Also known as network marketing. Rather than hiring sales staff, multilevel sales companies sell their products through thousands of independent distributors. Multilevel sales companies offer distributors commissions on both retail sales and the sales of their "down line" (the network of other distributors they sponsor).

Need. A state of perceived deprivation.

Net. What is left after deducting all expenses from the gross.

Net income. The amount by which revenue is greater than expenses. On an income statement this is usually expressed as both a pre-tax and after-tax figure.

Net loss. The amount by which expenses are greater than revenue. On an income statement this figure is usually listed as both a pre-tax and after-tax figure.

Net profit margin. The measure of a business's success with respect to earnings on sales. It is derived by dividing the net profit by sales. A higher margin means the firm is more profitable.

Net Worth. The owner's equity in a given business represented by the excess of the total assets over the total amounts owing to outside creditors (total liabilities) at a given moment in time. The net worth of an individual is determined by deducting the amount of all personal liabilities from the total of all personal assets.

Niche. A well-defined group of customers for whom what you have to offer is particularly suitable.

Nonrecurring. One time, not repeating. "Non-recurring" expenses are those involved in starting a business which only have to be paid once and will not occur again.

Note. A written promise with terms for payment of a debt.

Operating expenses. Normal expenses incurred in the running of a business.

Operating profit margin. The ratio representing the pure operations profits, ignoring interest and taxes. It is derived by dividing the income from operations by the sales. The higher the percentage of operating profit margin the better.

Organizational market. A marketplace made up of producers, trade industries, governments, and institutions.

Other expenses. Expenses that are not directly connected with the operation of a business. The most common is interest income.

Other income. Income that is earned from non-operating sources. The most common is interest income.

Outsourcing. Term used in business to identify the process of subcontracting work to outside vendors.

Overhead. A general term for costs of materials and services not directly adding to or readily identifiable with the product or service being sold.

Owners' equity. The financial interest of the owner of a business. The total of all owner equity is equal to the business's assets minus its liabilities. The owners' equity represents total investments in the business plus or minus profits or losses the business has accrued to date.

Partnership. A legal business relationship between two or more people who share responsibilities, resources, profits, and liabilities.

Payable. Ready to be paid. One of the standard accounts kept by a bookkeeper is "accounts payable." This is a list of those bills which are current and due to be paid.

Personal financial history. A summary of personal financial information about the owner of a business. The personal financial history is often required by a potential lender or investor.

Prepaid expenses. Expense items that are paid for prior to their use. Some examples are insurance, rent, prepaid inventory purchases, etc.

Price. The exchange value of a product or service from the perspective of both the buyer and seller.

Price ceiling. The highest amount a customer will pay for a product or service based on perceived value.

Price floor. The lowest amount a business owner can charge for a product or service and still meet all expenses plus acceptable profit.

Principal. The amount shown on the face of a note or a bond. Unpaid principal is the amount remaining at any given time.

Pro forma. A projection or estimate of what may result in the future from actions in the present. A pro forma financial statement is one that shows how the actual operations of the business will turn out if certain assumptions are achieved.

Product. Anything capable of satisfying needs, including tangible items, services, and ideas.

Product life cycle (PLC). The stages of development and decline through which a successful product typically moves.

Product line. A group of products related to each other by marketing, technical, or end-use considerations.

Product mix. All of the products in a seller's total product line.

Profit. Financial gain; returns over expenditures. The sum remaining after deducting costs.

Profit and Loss Statement. A list of the total amount of sales (revenues) and total costs (expenses). The difference between revenues and expenses is your profit or loss. Income statement.

Profit Margin. The difference between your selling price and all of your costs.

Promotion. The communication of information by a seller to influence the attitudes and behavior of potential buyers.

Promotional pricing. Temporarily pricing a product or service below list price or below cost in order to attract customers.

Psychographics. The system of explaining market behavior in terms of attitudes and lifestyles.

Publicity. Any nonpaid, news-oriented presentation of a product, service, or business entity in a mass media format.

Quarterly budget analysis. Method used to measure actual income and expenditures against projections for the current quarter of the financial year and for the total quarters completed. The difference is expressed as the amount and percentage over or under budget.

Questionnaire. A data-gathering form used to collect information by a personal interview, with a telephone survey, or through the mail.

Quick ratio. A test of liquidity subtracting inventory from current assets and dividing the result by current liabilities. A quick ratio of 1.0 or greater is usually recommended.

Ratio analysis.   An analysis involving the comparison of two individual items on financial statements. One item is divided by the other and the relationship is expressed as a ratio.

Receivable. Ready for payment. When you sell on credit, you keep an "accounts receivable" as a record of what is owed to you and who owes it. In accounting, a "receivable" is an asset.

Retail business. A business that sells goods and services directly to individual consumers.

Retained earnings. Earnings of a corporation that are kept in the business and not paid out in dividends. This amount represents the accumulated, undistributed profits of the corporation.

Return on investment (ROI). The rate of profit an investment will earn. The ROI is equal to the annual net income divided by total assets. The higher the ROI, the better.

Revenue. The income that results from the sale of products or services or from the use of investments or property.

Sales Representative. An independent salesperson who directs efforts to selling your products or services to others, but is not an employee of your company. Sales reps often represent more than one product line from more than one company and generally work on commission.

Sample.   A limited portion of the whole of a group.

Security.   Collateral that is promised to a lender as protection in case the borrower defaults on a loan.

Service Business. A business that provides services rather than products to its customers. A product business can also provide services.

Share. One of the equal parts into which ownership of a corporation is divided. A "share" represents a part ownership in a corporation.

Short-term notes. Loans that come due in one year or less.

Social media. Online platforms to provide interactive communication using web-based and mobile technologies. They are content in the form of text, photographs, audio, video or graphics that invite comment, collaboration, and exchange among participants.

Sole proprietorship. A legal structure of a business having one person as the owner.

Stock. An ownership share in a corporation. Another definition would be accumulated merchandise.

Stockholders' equity. The stockholders' shares of stock in a corporation plus any retained earnings.

Suppliers. Individuals or businesses that provide resources needed by a company in order to produce goods and services.

Survey. A research method in which people are asked questions.

SWOT Analysis. "SWOT" stands for Strengths, Weaknesses, Opportunities, and Threats. A SWOT analysis is an in-depth examination of key factors that are internal (strengths and weaknesses) and external (opportunities and threats) to a business.

Takeover. The acquisition of one company by another.

Tangible personal property. Machinery, equipment, furniture and fixtures not attached to the land.

Target Market. Specific individuals, distinguished by socio-economic, demographic, and/or interest characteristics, who are the most likely potential customers for the goods and services of a business.

Target marketing. Selecting and developing a number of offerings to meet the needs of a number of specific market segments.

Telemarketing. Marketing goods or services directly to the consumer via the telephone.

Terms of Sale. The conditions concerning payment for a purchase.

Three-year projection. A pro forma (projected) income statement showing anticipated revenues and expenses for a business.

Trade Credit. Permission to buy from suppliers on open account.

Undifferentiated marketing. Marketing by selecting and developing one offering for an entire market.

Unearned income. Revenue that has been received, but not yet earned.

Variable costs. Expenses that vary in relationship to the volume of activity of a business.

Venture capital. Money invested in enterprises that do not have access to traditional sources of capital.

Vertical analysis. A percentage analysis used to show the relationship of the components in a single financial statement. In vertical analysis of an income statement each item on the statement is expressed as a percentage of net sales.

Volume. An amount or quantity of business; the "volume" of a business is the total it sells over a period of time.

Wholesale. Selling for resale.

Wholesale business. A business that sells its products to other wholesalers, retailers, or volume customers at a discount.

Working capital. Current assets minus current liabilities. This is a basic measure of a company's ability to pay its current obligations.

Index

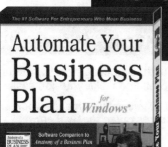

AUTOMATE YOUR BUSINESS PLAN *for Windows*

from Linda Pinson
Author of the SBA Publication, "How to Write a Business Plan"

WRITE YOUR BUSINESS PLAN WITH AN EXPERT AT YOUR SIDE

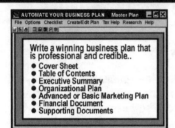

Write a winning business plan that is professional and credible..
- Cover Sheet
- Table of Contents
- Executive Summary
- Organizational Plan
- Advanced or Basic Marketing Plan
- Financial Document
- Supporting Documents

"Simply put, **Automate Your Business Plan** is the best step-by-step software for starting, building, and raising capital for your business. We have raised over $20 million for our clients by using AYBP. Use it - it works!"
Tom Wacker
Centaur Holdings Corporation

"Automate Your Business Plan" assumes you know nothing about writing a business plan. We walk you through the process and make your job easier.

Our step-by-step planning process will enable you to organize your industry expertise into a working business plan that will attract capital and ensure success.

- Complete instructions guide you through each part of your plan.
- **Bonus** *Special Web page "hot links"* you to marketing & financial research sites.
- Five complete real business plans (1 product, 2 services, a dot.com, and a nonprofit organization) will help you overcome writer's block.
- **Automate Your Business Plan** is a stand-alone software program. It is not a set of templates depending on someone else's software for compatibility and support. If you have questions, call us.

ATTRACT LENDERS & INVESTORS WITH A CUSTOMIZED BUSINESS PLAN

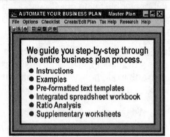

We guide you step-by-step through the entire business plan process.
- Instructions
- Examples
- Pre-formatted text templates
- Integrated spreadsheet workbook
- Ratio Analysis
- Supplementary worksheets

Investors are turned off by canned plans that look and sound like everyone else's. A customized working business plan is a plan to succeed.

Your plan will be tailored to your specific industry and to your situation.
- We help you research and write a winning executive summary and marketing plan.
- We help you develop <u>valid</u> financial assumptions and projections for your business.

These are some of the great features you will like about our software:
- Instructions, examples, formatted files for all parts of your plan; Word® & Excel® compatible
- All files set with headers, fonts, margins, and print commands (including Print Plan to PDF)
- Multiple plans; import/export projects between computers; create P-Point Presentations

SAVE 100+ HOURS WITH OUR INTEGRATED (LINKED) FINANCIAL SPREADSHEETS

Open/Edit Your Spreadsheet Workbook

"Automate Your Business Plan and *Anatomy of a Business Plan* are thorough, practical, and easy- to-understand."
Sandy Sutton, District Director (ret.)
Santa Ana District Office, U.S. Small Business Administration

We help you develop realistic financial projections so you can make the right decisions for a successful and profitable business future.

You will move with ease through your entire financial plan.
- We set up and formulate all of your financial spreadsheets.
- Our Chart of Accounts Wizard generates a customized spreadsheet workbook.
- Numbers input in one spreadsheet flow to all related spreadsheets.
- **Bonus** *Amortizing Software* calculates loan principal & interest payments.

Your lender will be happy to see the following financial information:
- Sources & Uses of Funds
- Pro-Forma Cash Flow Statement
- Three-Year Income Projection
- Break-Even Analysis
- Quarterly Budget Analysis
- P&L Statement & Balance Sheet
- Financial Ratio Analysis
- Charts & Graphs